The Letters of Barsanuphius and John

The spiritual letters of Barsanuphius and John, two sixth-century ascetics from the Gaza Strip, are extraordinary documents. They open a window into the heart of Early Christian monasticism. The exchange of question and answer touches on the hopes, fears, and temptations of all kinds (even the most banal), experienced by every kind of persons—monks and laity alike. Here are the rugged rocks in which the honey drops of Desert Wisdom were distilled. John Chryssavgis does full justice to these unique letters of advice. Two wise and loving Christians speak from his pages. And as they do, the icy modern image of the monk as an exalted authority figure melts away to reveal a tenderness and a skill in one-to-one spiritual counsel that lifts the heart, even at distance of fifteen hundred years.

Peter Brown
Emeritus Professor of History
Princeton University

John Chryssavgis has translated into English the vast correspondence of Barsanuphius and John, and so he writes in this book from an exact knowledge of their teaching. He is in deep sympathy with their spiritual outlook. While placing the two Old Men in their historical context, he shows also the timeless quality of their answers. As Chryssavgis rightly points out, their counsel is not "scripted or prescriptive," but consistently situational, involved, and full of loving tenderness. I am particularly moved by the way he associates solitary contemplation with social consciousness. The message of these elders, as the author presents it, is both simple and yet full of hope. It is the closest that the desert literature comes to a transliteration of notes from case studies of a personal therapist.

Metropolitan Kallistos of Diokleia
Emeritus Professor of Theology
University of Oxford

An insightful, encouraging, and challenging book! Dare one call a book these days "inspiring?" Indeed, yes. In this volume the Spirit is alive and well. Monasticism, early, medieval, modern, still has plenty to say to us today, but not only say—show rather than tell, live out in love rather than prescribe, teach embodied rather than lecture from a distant podium or pulpit. There is so much here! Barsanuphius and John guide us in the ways of true community, communion that offers transformation.

Tim Vivian
Emeritus Professor of Religious Studies
California State University (Bakersfield)

The Letters of Barsanuphius and John

Desert Wisdom for Everyday Life

John Chryssavgis

LONDON • NEW YORK • OXFORD • NEW DELHI • SYDNEY

T&T CLARK
Bloomsbury Publishing Plc
50 Bedford Square, London, WC1B 3DP, UK
1385 Broadway, New York, NY 10018, USA
29 Earlsfort Terrace, Dublin 2, Ireland

BLOOMSBURY, T&T CLARK and the T&T Clark logo are
trademarks of Bloomsbury Publishing Plc

First published in Great Britain 2022

Copyright © John Chryssavgis, 2022

John Chryssavgis has asserted his right under the Copyright, Designs and
Patents Act, 1988, to be identified as Author of this work.

For legal purposes the Acknowledgments on pp. 190–1 constitute an
extension of this copyright page.

Cover image: stock_colors / Getty Images Plus

All rights reserved. No part of this publication may be reproduced or transmitted
in any form or by any means, electronic or mechanical, including photocopying,
recording, or any information storage or retrieval system, without prior
permission in writing from the publishers.

Bloomsbury Publishing Plc does not have any control over, or responsibility for,
any third-party websites referred to or in this book. All internet addresses given
in this book were correct at the time of going to press. The author and publisher
regret any inconvenience caused if addresses have changed or sites have ceased
to exist, but can accept no responsibility for any such changes.

A catalogue record for this book is available from the British Library.

A catalog record for this book is available from the Library of Congress.

ISBN:	HB:	978-0-5677-0484-9
	PB:	978-0-5677-0485-6
	ePDF:	978-0-5677-0487-0
	eBook:	978-0-5677-0486-3

Typeset by Integra Software Services Pvt. Ltd.

To find out more about our authors and books visit www.bloomsbury.com
and sign up for our newsletters.

CONTENTS

List of Illustrations ix
Foreword x

Introduction 1

Part One: The Desert Blossoms: Setting the Scene 13

1. Monasticism in Egypt and Palestine: A Historical Framework 15
2. Luminaries of Gaza: Prominent Personalities and Identities 39
3. Fundamental Concepts and Principles: Looking through a Window Frame 58

Part Two: The Desert Beckons: Sitting by the Cell 85

4. Spiritual Direction: Two Extraordinary Models 87
5. Fasting and Feasting: Sustained by God in the Wilderness 113
6. Mourning and Tears: The Way of Brokenness and Imperfection 134
7. Discernment and Compassion: The Way of Awareness and Authenticity 147

8 Solitude, Silence, and Stillness: Subtle Variances of the Soul 166

Conclusion 185

Select Bibliography 189
Acknowledgments 190
Index 192

ILLUSTRATIONS

1 Hermit cells in Palestine 34
2 Icon of Sts Barsanuphius and John 61
3 First edition of Barsanuphius and John (Venice) 115
4 Vatopedi manuscript, *Letters* 241–243 148

FOREWORD

If we had been visiting Gaza in the early sixth century, we would have found, not far off in the desert, a remarkable monastic community. At its center were two elders living in strict seclusion, Barsanuphius and John, known respectively as "the Great Old Man" and "the Other Old Man." These two elders had come to be widely respected as charismatic counselors. Neither of them, however, spoke face to face with those who sought their guidance. Enquirers were required to submit their questions in writing, and in due course they received a written reply from one of the Old Men, or occasionally from both.

In an earlier work, John Chryssavgis has translated into English the entire correspondence of Barsanuphius and John. It is indeed fortunate that there survive in Greek some 850 of these questions and answers. No other document from the early Christian era shows us in such vivid detail how spiritual direction was understood and exercised in practice. With minimal editing, the Letters reveal the actual voices of the inquirers and their respondents with immediacy and intimacy, as well as with vividness and verve. It is the closest that the desert literature comes to a transliteration of notes from case studies of a personal therapist.

The enquirers came from all levels of society: not only from the members of the community where Barsanuphius and John dwelt, but also from those outside, bishops and monastics, clergy and laity. The topics are highly varied. As we would expect, many of the questions concern the life of prayer: for example, "Tell me, father, about unceasing prayer" (*Letter* 87). Another recurrent theme is physical illness: the elders, for instance, have to assure a novice who cries out that he cannot "bear the affliction of his illness" (*Letter* 613). Often the questions are specific and practical: "How much should I eat?" (*Letter* 154); "If one enters the church during the time of the Liturgy and leaves before the end, is this a sin?" (*Letter* 736); "The locusts ravage my fields. If I drive them away, my neighbors grow furious with me"—presumably because the locusts then move on to their fields—"but if I leave them, I suffer loss. What should I do?" (*Letter* 684).

As Chryssavgis notes, whereas contemporary lives of the saints are full of miracles, it is noteworthy that miracle stories are almost entirely absent from the correspondence of the two elders of Gaza. There is little on fear of the supernatural or reliance on the superstitious; the advice is realistic and down to earth. Often it is expressed in brief and somewhat riddling phrases. "Forget yourself and know yourself," they say (*Letter* 112); "Let us weep in order that we may laugh" (*Letter* 196); "Die completely, that you may live completely" (*Letter* 37). It is for the recipient to work out the riddle and apply it to himself.

There is also little on theoretical mysticism or speculative theology; the emphasis is on ascetic moderation. The objective is reaching inward; the inner is far more important than the outer (*Letter* 77). "Labor" and "violence" (*Letters* 239 and 340), along with "pain" (*Letters* 256 and 267) and "suffering" (*Letter* 703), are inseparable from "bearing the cross" (*Letters* 45, 191, 243, and 519) and "restraining the will" (*Letters* 16, 121, 232, and 243) in imitation of Christ Himself (*Letters* 20, 106, 150, 191, and 239).

In this regard, Barsanuphius and John write without evasion or compromise, but at that the same time with profound compassion. They are humane and generous. Avoiding extremes, they caution against excessive asceticism and austerity in eating and fasting, sleep and vigilance (*Letters* 146 and 570); instead, they insist, "Always keep the middle way" (*Letter* 314). While conscious of the authority that they have received from God, they display a sensitive respect for the freedom of others. "Do not force the will," they affirm in characteristic terms, "but only sow in hope. For our Lord did not force anyone, but only preached the Gospel; and whosoever wanted, listened" (*Letter* 35). They do not offer elaborate rules, but say: "Do not look for a command. I do not want you to be under the law but under grace" (*Letter* 23). "It is always beneficial to practice freedom," they state (*Letter* 378); "so the two go together: the free will of the human being and the power of God" (*Letter* 763).

Yet as Chryssavgis emphasizes throughout this book, this respect for the freedom of others did not signify that the two Old Men were in any way distant or indifferent. On the contrary, one of their favorite Scriptural texts is Galatians 6:2: "Bear one another's burdens." They see the spiritual father or mother, not as a legislator, but par excellence as a burden bearer, a companion, and a fellow-sufferer. "Hold my hand and walk," they write (*Letter* 31); "I have spread out my wings over you and bear your burdens" (*Letter* 239).

Again and again, in moving terms, they emphasize how closely they feel involved in the joys and sorrows of their disciples. "The Lord has bound your soul to mine," they affirm (*Letter* 164). "There is not a blink of the eye or a moment that I do not have you in my mind and in my prayer" (*Letter* 113). "I will never abandon you, even in the age to come" (*Letter* 239). As John Chryssavgis rightly points out, their counsel is not "scripted or prescriptive," but consistently situational, involved, and full of loving tenderness. What matters to them are not rules but persons. They understand the weakness and vulnerability of others, their secret pain and insecurity, yet at the same time they are acutely conscious of the greatness of human nature, of its boundless possibilities.

John Chryssavgis writes in this book from an exact knowledge of their teaching. He is in deep sympathy with their spiritual outlook. I am particularly moved by the way he associates solitary contemplation with social consciousness. While placing the two Old Men in their historical context, he shows also the timeless quality of their answers. Their message, as he presents it, is both simple and full of hope, both enriching and enduring. It is best summed up in two quotations that illustrate this simplicity and hopefulness: "Simply do your best, brother, and God will come to your assistance in everything" (*Letter* 343); "Rejoice in the Lord, rejoice in the Lord, rejoice in the Lord" (*Letter* 10). Whenever I read the correspondence of the two elders of Gaza, this threefold repetition comes at once into my mind and heart. This is an engaging contemporary book about a remarkable classic text.

Metropolitan Kallistos of Diokleia
Professor Emeritus, University of Oxford

Introduction

The Appeal of the Desert

The modern revival of interest in desert spirituality is doubtless associated with a search for purpose in—and arguably perhaps escape from—the daily grind or frenzied race of urban life. For many, pursuing contemplation in a competitive world invites the prospect of penetrating the surface of mere survival in order to perceive the meaning and mystery of life in abundance. Discerning the stirrings of the heart through inwardness and introspection invites a rediscovery and recovery of classical virtues for the sake of refining and redefining contemporary existence.[1]

The quest for an adequate vocabulary to describe and distinguish tested ways and virtues of ancient philosophy and spirituality comes in response to the gross caricature of self-exploration and self-examination that promotes the self and projects the selfie. Isolation and communication—or individualism and communion—are regarded as irreconcilable opposites. Sociability and not solitude is the disposition considered inherent to the human heart, while an aversion to or attrition of the world is considered abhorrent to the human mind.[2] Nonetheless the notion of living with sacrifice,

---

[1] See Elisabeth Lasch-Quinn, *Ars Vitae: The Fate of Inwardness and the Return of the Ancient Art of Living* (Notre Dame, IN: University of Notre Dame Press, 2020), who suggests that contemporary therapy "suggests a felt need that takes the bigger picture of a person's life into account. ... In the writings of the ancient philosophers, we find a completely different interpretation of what is wrong and what would help," through such principles as detachment, freedom, and compassion. [Here at 26].

[2] See David Vincent, *A History of Solitude* (Medford, MA: Polity Press, 2020), 1–30, where Vincent reviews the treatise by Johann Georg Zimmermann, *Solitude Considered with Respect to Its Dangerous Influence Upon the Mind and Heart* (1784–5).

simplicity, and service can present an appealing counterstatement, even contradiction to living without intention, motivation, or determination. The search for depth in a superficial urban world, or quiet in a noisy suburban society, or stability in a tumultuous global context, exposes something unpretentious, inconceivable, and invigorating in the early desert fathers and mothers, who explored the rough terrain and barren wilderness along their journey for knowledge of self and knowledge of God.

This renewed focus on the early desert experience is deeply indebted to a recent access to desert literature and an increasing familiarity with the desert dwellers themselves. Regardless of original source and historical influence—through some biography, chronicle, or collection of stories and sayings—every rise and reformation of monasticism through the centuries in East and West has been rooted in or shaped by the early desert tradition. Beyond the contrasting provenance of its miscellaneous and unconventional personalities—whether someone like Macarius of Egypt or Paula of Rome, Poemen of Scetis or Melania of Jerusalem—the remoteness of the early desert has been illuminated by contemporary scholarship, rendering its spiritual legacy a prolific resource of information and inspiration.

The fourth-century desert fathers and mothers of Egypt reflect and represent a way of inner transformation through external retreat and physical withdrawal that long predates any alternative spiritual or social lifestyles recently advocated by theologians and bloggers alike[3] as methods of separation or segregation ostensibly for the sake of sustaining political honor or preserving moral integrity. Such a mindset or worldview is not, however, the approach envisaged or endorsed by Barsanuphius and John as heirs apparent to the fourth-century desert dwellers in the East and historic peers of Benedict of Nursia (480–547) in the West. The desert provided the fundamental and essential conditions for shaping models of spirituality among those aspiring to seclusion or silence and fellowship or community in a diverse range of living conditions and circumstances. It is the aim of this book to reimagine the implications and intricacies of the

---

[3]See, for example, Alasdair MacIntyre, *After Virtue: A Study in Moral Theory* (Notre Dame, IN: University of Notre Dame Press, 1981), 163; and Rod Dreher, *The Benedict Option: A Strategy for Christians in a Post-Christian Nation* (New York, NY: Sentinel, 2017).

spirituality of the desert through the lens of Barsanuphius and John, and to do so in the modern context.

The Tradition of the Desert

During the late-fourth and through the mid-fifth centuries, some of the key personalities and representative communities of Egyptian monasticism began to disperse from the centers of Alexandria and Egypt, for various reasons traveling eastward to the neighboring regions of Palestine and Sinai. But of course they did not travel alone; they brought along with them an entire tradition of "stories" and collection of "sayings" that shaped their own understanding of the ascetic way and subsequently circulated among those who approached them in search of a "word of advice" for day-to-day existence or a "counsel of life" for ultimate salvation.

In the earliest years, of course, the teaching and training were transmitted by word of mouth—from elder to disciple, from cell to cell, and from generation to generation. Eventually, however, the stories and sayings came to be preserved in collections of *Sayings of the Desert Fathers* (*Apophthegmata Patrum*), recorded in many languages of the Christian tradition, including Greek and Latin, Coptic and Syriac, as well as Armenian and Arabic. What began as a verbal tradition, conveying all the charisma and charm of the wise elders—male (*abba*) and female (*amma*)—gradually found record in a written tradition conveying the virtues and ways, all the wit and wisdom of former generations, for the purpose of imitation by and instruction for the disciples and successors of the abbas and ammas.

The two figures at the center of this book certainly regard themselves as part of this broader tradition. The "great old man" Barsanuphius says: "I regard myself as a slave on a mission" (*Letter* 139), even describing the "other old man" John as "a fellow slave"— echoing the Pauline tradition in the New Testament (Col. 1:7). This self-deprecating self-designation belies any slavish attitude on the part of the two renowned Palestinian elders. Instead it defines an identity captured and captivated by inspiration and imagination. But it also describes the embodiment of a long tradition of spiritual direction inherited from the early desert of Egypt and imparted to countless people approaching for spiritual guidance and edification.

Such at least is the deeper conviction of these elders as they offer counsel in full assurance that their disciples are receiving no more and no less than "the healing medicine of the word of the Spirit" (*Letter* 570c).

The Two Elders: Barsanuphius and John

The following chapters explore the history and heritage, the context and contents of a vast collection of letters—a correspondence course in the way and life of the Spirit—as dictated by two humble monks, Barsanuphius and John, around the middle of the sixth century in Gaza of Palestine.[4] The two elders lived in absolute seclusion and strict reclusion for over half a century (in the case of Barsanuphius) and almost two decades (in the case of John), bringing consolation and counsel to numerous visitors and pilgrims. Their widespread reputation induced near-legendary holiness—reportedly raising the dead (*Letter* 90) and themselves allegedly ascending to heaven—which accounted for their spiritual prominence and social prestige across the region and through the centuries. Not only were they considered giants of profound empathy and personal edification, but their discernment and judgment could sway the highest civil authorities—an extraordinary legacy built on a deceptively ordinary lifestyle.

These unassuming and unostentatious hermits lived during the grandiose time of Emperor Justinian I (482–565) and died after the controversial period in the wake of the Fourth Ecumenical Council (451). This accounted for an aura of popularity and celebrity among their contemporaries, while also for a cloud of confusion and suspicion among their successors who frequently mistook Barsanuphius the Great with Barsanuphius the Monophysite condemned at the Sixth Ecumenical Council of 680-1.

Notwithstanding any mythical or heretical eclipse, the letters of Barsanuphius and John certainly offer an unparalleled glimpse into the

---

[4]References to the letters of Barsanuphius and John are in parentheses. For the English translation of the full correspondence, see John Chryssavgis, *Barsanuphius and John: Letters*, 2 volumes in *The Fathers of the Church Patristic Series* (Washington, DC: The Catholic University of America Press, 2006–7), 113–14.

sixth-century religious and secular worlds of Gaza and Palestine at a time increasingly marred by intense doctrinal debate and controversy as well as in a world inordinately shaped by early martyrdom and monasticism. Their correspondence includes questions and answers ranging from monastic partnership to municipal taxation. Some letters respond to inquiries about everyday life, including the veterinary treatment of a horse, the leprous infection of a servant, or the devastating vandalism of a vineyard. People inquire about a variety of predicaments and problems, from promotions at work to complaints about a stone falling on their foot! Questions address prayer and forgiveness, relations with bishops and relations with non-Christians, and even ethical aspects of purchasing property or taking a bath. People seek advice on the replacement of an unworthy bishop, the management of alms donated to the poor, and the quality of public entertainment in faraway Constantinople.

The religious diversity of the region surrounding Gaza at this time—a century prior to the rise of Islam—generates questions concerning Christians interacting with Jews, Manichaeans, and pagans. Above all, however, the letters abound in subtle insights about the human heart, offering timeless teachings on the inner warfare against resentment and temptation, vacillation and frustration, as well as depression and tension.[5] They explain why prayers may not be heard; they explore the nature of virtue and vice; and they expose the hypocrisy of false humility. In general, they examine human foibles arising from personal friendships to relationships between monks and abbots. Throughout, a serene clarity emanates from the charismatic experience of the elders and the introspective asceticism of the desert. Compassion and discernment (perpetual watchwords of the monastic life) combine with authenticity and perspicacity (persistent catchwords of the Christian life) to create a literary corpus that both illumines and informs the intricate and complicated relationship between the

---

[5]See Lorenzo Perrone, "Trembling at the Thought of Shipwreck: The Anxious Self in the Letters of Barsanuphius and John of Gaza," in *Between Personal and Institutional Religion: Self, Doctrine, and Practice in Late Antique Eastern Christianity*, ed. Brouria Bitton-Ashkelony and Lorenzo Perrone (Turnhout: Brepols, 2013), 9–36. See also Inbar Graiver, *Asceticism of the Mind: Forms of Attention and Self-Transformation in Late Antique Monasticism* (East Toronto: Pontifical Institute of Mediaeval Studies, 2018).

heart within and the world outside. The elders and their letters are an incarnation and extension of the golden precept of monastics called to be "apart-from all and yet a-part-of all."[6]

A Spirituality of Transparency

Arguably the most striking feature of this unique methodology is that it fosters an overt and transparent system of spiritual direction, allowing ample space for conversation as well as conflict in personal and spiritual relations, while at the same time smashing all fallacies of religious authority as rigidly unidirectional or unidimensional. The freedom to choose—ultimately, even the license to err—is, for Barsanuphius and John, part and parcel of "the perfect law, the law of liberty" (Jas 1:25). Thus, while the "great old man" advises an inquiring monk to "do as he was told by the Other Old Man," assuring him that "from now on, one response should be sufficient [for him], for the God of Barsanuphius and John is one" (*Letter* 224), Abba John elsewhere suggests that two recommendations are actually better than one!

> A certain Christ-loving layman once said to the Old Man, John: "Why are you mocking us, father John, by sending us to the holy and Great Old Man, father Barsanuphius, when you have the same power of the Spirit?"
> He responded as follows. I am nothing; and even if I was, I would not be mocking you. For if I had sent you to him and you had not obtained a response, then it would have been mockery. In fact, it is to your benefit that there are two people praying for you; for two people are better than one. It appears that even the Lord does the same; for ... not once but many times He would send His disciples to the Father, saying: "If you ask anything of my Father in my name, he will give it to you" (Jn 16:23); and again: "I do nothing on my own (Jn 14:16), but the Father who dwells in me does his works." (*Letter* 783)

And here is where Barsanuphius and John constitute a refreshing peculiarity in the early ascetic tradition but also in medieval and

---

[6] Evagrius of Pontus, *Chapters on Prayer*, 124.

contemporary spiritual practice. There are not too many spiritual directors and certainly far fewer church leaders—throughout the centuries and especially today—known for concluding their decision or judgment with the words from our correspondence: "Feel free to seek a second opinion" (*Letter* 504)! This is because, echoing the sensitivity and subtlety of the desert tradition,[7] Barsanuphius and John understand the end of spiritual direction as being forgiveness, compassion, and communion—not austerity, control, or exploitation:

> Question to the Other Old Man: If I am tempted and happen to transgress the command, what should I do?
>
> Response. If you receive a command from the saints and happen to transgress it, then do not be disturbed or stressed to abolish it. Remember what is said of the righteous: that "though they fall seven times a day, yet they will rise again" (Prv 24:16), and also the words of the Lord to Peter: "Forgive your brother seventy times" (Mt 18:22). Therefore, if he commanded mortals to forgive so many times, how many more times would he forgive everything, when he is rich in mercy and compassion? He cries out every day through the Prophet: "Return to me and I shall return to you; for I am merciful" (Jl 2:13, Zec 1:3), and again: "Now, O Israel" (Dt 10:12). Be careful that, upon hearing that the command has not actually been abolished, you do not become indifferent and reach the point of neglect; for this is indeed a grave sin. Furthermore, do not despise the command for the sake of what appear to be small details; even if you happen to be neglectful in these details, you should still strive to correct yourself. For through indifference to such small details, one is later led to greater sins. (*Letter* 371)

Such sensibility on the part of the spiritual elder to the vulnerability of the spiritual disciple is not the result of abstract anarchy but derives from a deeper aversion to uniformity or conformity:

> Question to the Great Old Man: I ask you, dear father and teacher, not to be angry with my faults, but instead to give

---

[7]See, for example, Poemen 86, in Benedicta Ward, *The Sayings of the Desert Fathers: The Alphabetical Collection* (Kalamazoo, MI: Cistercian Publications, 1975). See also the translation by John Wortley, *Give Me a Word: The Alphabetical Sayings of the Desert Fathers* (Yonkers, NY: St. Vladimir's Seminary Press, 2014).

me a rule about how I must behave in fasting, psalmody, and prayer. Are there distinct rules for different days?

Response by Barsanuphius. Brother, had you paid attention to the words of your questions, you would have understood the power of wisdom. If I am truly your father and teacher, why do you want me to be angry? For a father is compassionate and has no wrath at all. And a teacher is long-suffering, foreign to any wrath. But as for the rule about which you inquire, you are going around in endless circles in an effort to "enter through the narrow gate that leads to life" eternal (Mt 7:13). Behold, Christ tells you very concisely how you must enter.

Leave aside the rules of people and listen to him, who says: "Whoever endures to the end will be saved" (Mt 10:22, Mk 13:13). If one does not endure, one will not enter into life.

So do not look for a command. I do not want you to be "under the law, but under grace" (Rom 6:14). For it is said: "The law is not laid down for the righteous" (1 Tm 1:9). Retain discernment, like a helmsman steering the boat according to the winds. When you are sick, act accordingly in all things as you have written; and when you are well, again act accordingly. Because when the body is unwell, it does not digest food normally. Thus, a rule would prove worthless in that case.

And as far as the variety of days, treat them all as equally holy and good. Do everything with understanding, and this will prove to be for you unto life in Christ Jesus our Lord. (*Letter* 23)

This engaging exchange is reminiscent of the fluidity and spontaneity of the initial, formative period of monasticism, when sensibility to the particular situation and peculiar circumstances of each person meant far more than adherence to any hardened rules or codified regulations. What matters to Barsanuphius and John are not rules but persons, not changing external circumstances but focusing on internal transformation in the here and now. The two elders constantly try to inject something of the immediacy and mysteriousness of God's presence in the spiritual adventure. They repeatedly cite Deuteronomy 4.1, which emphasizes embracing each situation in its own right. From the outset, Barsanuphius writes:

Do not set any decrees for yourself. Become obedient and humble; and be demanding of yourself each day. For the prophet also indicated what should be done daily, when he observed: "And I said, Now I have begun" (Ps 76.10); and Moses also said: "So now, O Israel." (Dt, 4.1 and 10.12) Therefore, you too should keep this "now." (*Letter* 21)

As Benedictine scholar Columba Stewart puts it: "Barsanuphius, the great solitary of Gaza in the early sixth century, often refused to lay down a rule when asked to do so; he recognized that laws and obligations could short-circuit the growth he was there to encourage."[8]

It is this sensitivity and subtlety on the part of the two elders that attracted the attention of pilgrims and readers through the centuries. Their invigorating admonitions and transformative recommendations reveal an inimitable ability to relate the inner world to the outer circumstances as well as pursue the extraordinary in the very ordinary by discovering clarity in chaos and beauty in the most disagreeable or disordered aspects of life.

The Text: Manuscripts and Translations

Surviving manuscripts reveal that the correspondence of Barsanuphius and John found early appreciation and steady circulation. Although the Arab invasions of Palestine left little or nothing reminiscent in that region of the monastic presence or Byzantine influence,[9] nevertheless the correspondence was definitely known in early ninth-century Constantinople.

The earliest manuscripts originate on Mt. Sinai and date from the tenth century.[10] Several manuscripts are preserved on Mt. Athos from

---

[8]Columba Stewart, "The Desert Fathers on Radical Self-Honesty," *Sobornost/Eastern Churches Review* 12 (1990), 25–39 and 143–56. Reprinted in *Vox Benedictina: A Journal of Translations from Monastic Sources* 8.1 (1991), 7–54.

[9]J. Pargoire, *L'Église Byzantine de 527 à 847* (Paris: Librairie Victor Lecoffre, 1905), 274f.

[10]They are Georgian translations, containing some seventy-nine letters. [The 1971 edition of the Abbaye Saint Pierre de Solesmes translation includes letters translated from the Georgian by B. Outtier.] One Sinaite manuscript is entitled: "Teachings (Διδασκαλίαι) of the Blessed Barsanuphius and John" (Sinai 34), while another (Sinai 35), dated 907, is entitled: "Questions and Answers" (Ἐρωταποκρίσεις). Cf. G. Garitte, *Corpus Scriptorum Christianorum Orientalium*, vol. 165, *Subsidia* 9 (Louvain: Peeters Publishers, 1956), 97 and 116–17.

the eleventh through the fourteenth centuries, as well as in libraries of monasteries or universities in Paris, Oxford, Athens, Moscow, Munich, Jerusalem, and Patmos. Some manuscripts contain only a few letters; others preserve mere fragments. And while we have no manuscripts from the fifteenth to the seventeenth centuries, a number of manuscripts exist from the eighteenth century.[11]

From the late eighteenth century, several translations appeared in Moldavian,[12] Slavonic,[13] and Russian,[14] albeit sometimes partial to begin with, but complete by the end of the nineteenth century. Clearly, the influence of the two Palestinian elders, while not necessarily decisive, was nonetheless extensive through the centuries in both East

---

[11]J. Grinaeus first published nine of the letters by John the Prophet in Basel (1569), together with the works of Abba Dorotheus. In Paris (1715), B. Montfaucon published the letters pertaining to Origenism. In Volume 86 (columns 892–901) of *Patrologia Graeca*, published in Paris during the mid- to late-nineteenth century, J.-P. Migne included *Letters* 600–4 dealing with Origen, Evagrius, and Didymus, while Volume 88 (columns 1812–20) contains the letters addressed to Dorotheus of Gaza.

[12]Neamț Monastery possesses one of the oldest manuscripts of Barsanuphius and John. In the mid-eighteenth century, Paissy Velichkovsky sent Gregory of Neamț to Mt. Athos to secure a copy of their *Letters*. Makarios of Corinth informed Gregory of Neamț that two Athonite manuscripts were in existence, one in Vatopedi Monastery and the other in the Skete of St. Anne, both of which were very corrupt— an indication that they were regularly read in the monasteries. Makarios sent the manuscript from St. Anne's skete to Paissy for translation. In the nineteenth century, Ignatii Brianchaninov (1807–67) and Theofan the Recluse (1815–94) recommended the *Letters* as the finest spiritual reading, the latter including excerpts of the *Letters* in his *Philokalia* and influencing the tradition of startzi.

[13]The Moldavian and early Slavonic translations were directed by Paissy Velichkovsky on the basis of an Athonite manuscript dated 1794. The reason for the delay in translating the *Letters* of Barsanuphius and John—the texts are entirely unknown from 988 to the Kievan period in the mid-thirteenth century—probably lies in the controversy surrounding the two Palestinian elders, who for centuries were suspected of monophysitism. Even after their names were cleared by Sophronius of Jerusalem in the seventh century, their reputation remained tainted. In the fifteenth century, Joseph of Volokolamsk (1440–515) and Nil Sorsky (1433–508) cite excerpts from Barsanuphius but make no mention of John.

[14]Vladimir Solovyev mentions the "two ancient hermits" Barsanuphius and John in his *Three Lectures on War, Progress, and the Antichrist* (St. Petersburg, 1890), 123; the book first appeared in English in 1915 under the title *War, Progress, and the End of History* (University of London Press. At 105). In a brief entry to the *Konversationslexikon* of Brockhaus and Efron, vol. 6, 21f., Solovyev mentions an edition of the *Letters*, together with the *Life of Barsanuphius and John* by Nikodemus, on Mt. Athos in 1803, as well as a translation of the correspondence published by the Moscow Academy in 1855, which he may have consulted.

and West. Perhaps one reason for this gradual impact and growing interest was the sheer magnitude of the correspondence compared to the more concise *Apophthegmata* of Egypt or *Ladder* of Sinai. In my translation of the *Letters* of Barsanuphius and John for the Fathers of the Church Patristic Series, published by the Catholic University of America Press,[15] I consulted both manuscript and contemporary sources, including Bodleian Cromwell 18 (B) from Oxford as well as Vatopedi 2 from Mt. Athos. I also benefitted from the critical text adopted in the most recent French edition,[16] the partial English edition by Derwas Chitty,[17] and the modern Greek publication by the Monastery of St. John the Forerunner in Kareas, Athens.[18] The edition by Nikodemus of Mt. Athos—containing the first complete edition of *Letters* of Barsanuphius and John based on manuscripts at several Athonite monasteries and published in Venice in 1816 just after Nikodemus' death in 1809—was reprinted by S. Schoinas in Volos in 1960.[19]

* * *

[15]See n. 4 (above). This translation is the first complete English translation from the original Greek. A partial translation by Seraphim Rose (1934–82) appeared in 1990, along with a translation of the biography of the two Gaza elders by St. Nikodemus of Mount Athos, but was based on the Russian edition of 1855. See Fr. Seraphim Rose, *Guidance Toward Spiritual Life: Answers to the Questions of Disciples* (Platina, CA: St. Herman of Alaska Brotherhood, 1990).

[16]See *Barsanuphe et Jean de Gaza, Correspondance*, Critical text and notes by François Neyt and Paula de Angelis-Noah, trans. by Lucien Regnault, 5 volumes (Paris: Éditions du Cerf, 1997–2002). *Sources Chrétiennes*, volumes 426–7, 450–1, and 468.

[17]Chitty translated and published 124 letters in 1966, not long prior to his death in 1971. He compared Coislianus 124, Vatopedi 2, Nikodemus, and Sinaiticus 411S for his critical edition. He had also prepared a draft translation of *Letters* 125–249. A copy of this former exists in the library of St. Gregory's House in Oxford, England. See *Barsanuphius and John: Questions and Answers* in *Patrologia Orientalis* XXXI, 3 (Paris: Librairie de Paris, 1966), 445–616. See also the reprint in *Saints Barsanuphius and John: Questions and Answers* (Blanco, TX: New Sarov Press, 1998).

[18]Another Greek translation was published in Thessalonika by Byzantion Editions in 1988–9.

[19]Nikodemus' text contains repetitions, errors, and *lacunae* partly corrected by Schoinas. Chitty notes that St. Nikodemus was "engaged on a critical edition," observing that, in the early sixth century, for a brief period of at least eighteen years, the curtain of monasticism rises on the remarkable community at Thawatha. Derwas Chitty, *The Desert a City: An Introduction to the Study of Egyptian and Palestinian Monasticism under the Christian Empire* (London and Oxford: Mowbrays, 1966), 132–3.

The vibrant and personal tone of the correspondence is arguably what has always appealed to readers. This is why I have chosen to "allow" the two elders to speak verbatim and at length in this book, providing the reader with the license and liberty to communicate directly with the elders by listening to their inspired and inspirational words, which are unequivocally refreshing in the monastic and spiritual tradition.

When Anglican priest and Oxford theologian Derwas Chitty delivered the Birkbeck Lectures at Trinity College, Cambridge in 1959–60, the only printed edition of the *Letters* of Barsanuphius and John in the original Greek was that prepared by St. Nikodemus of Mt. Athos, who died before it was published in Venice in 1816. It was Chitty who introduced Barsanuphius and John to the English-speaking world. And it was his student, Kallistos Ware, who shared this treasure with his students at Oxford.

This book is a humble expression of gratitude and respect to Metropolitan Kallistos of Diokleia—a sincere affirmation of admiration and modest dedication for introducing these unique elders, whose uncommon and unparalleled wisdom merits more than just academic consideration and scholarly examination. By pursuing the extraordinary in the very ordinary and connecting the solitary to the social through ingenious common-sense and lighthearted astuteness, these two sixth-century elders of Thawatha in Gaza demonstrate an uncanny way of peeling away the accrued layers of a hardened soul as well as the obscure film of an undiscerning mind to reveal the promise of wonder and potential of beauty inside every human heart and every human person.

PART ONE

The Desert Blossoms
Setting the Scene

1

Monasticism in Egypt and Palestine

A Historical Framework

Palestine and Gaza

Palestine is divided into two distinct monastic regions: the first is centered around the Holy City and incorporates the territory around Jerusalem as far as the Dead Sea; the second lies in the southern province around Gaza.

Monastics in Palestine were generally conscious of their *biblical roots* owing to the historical significance of the region in the development of Jewish and Christian Scriptures. Barsanuphius is convinced that it is here that "God revealed the way of life through the prophets and the apostles" (*Letter* 605). This is, after all, the land where the prophets once wandered, the desert where Jesus personally retreated in prayer, and the soil where Christianity was first planted.[1]

Monastics of Palestine have a keen recollection of the *martyrs and confessors*, who offered the ultimate ascetic sacrifice, beginning with the death of Stephen in Acts 7. Barsanuphius delights in drawing connections between the monk and the martyr: "To

---

[1]See the comprehensive study of the monastic movement in Palestine during the Byzantine period: John Binns, *Ascetics and Ambassadors of Christ: The Monasteries of Palestine, 314–631* (Oxford: Clarendon Press, 1994).

renounce one's own will is a sacrifice of blood. It signifies that one has reached the point of laboring to death and of ignoring one's own will" (*Letter* 254).[2]

On account of its privileged status and strategic location—geography, climate, and history—the region of Gaza, where Barsanuphius and John would ultimately settle, proved a remarkable place of welcome and embrace for Christian monasticism after the fourth century. Its accessibility by sea and road, its proximity to Egypt, Syria, and the Holy Land, but also its prominence in Hellenistic and Roman times, rendered Gaza a significant and suitable haven for emerging models of ascetic life in its spiritual and intellectual expressions. Indeed, as a major commercial area from biblical times, this southern coastal region would remain coveted territory across centuries to our time.

Thus, in the southern parts of Palestine, Gaza soon begins to enjoy its own proper history of monasticism, the origins of which are recorded by Jerome and Epiphanius. Hilarion (292–372) lived here for almost twenty years. Born in Thawatha, five miles south of Gaza, he was schooled in Alexandria, where he encountered Anthony the Great, the celebrated father of monasticism. Upon returning home, Hilarion moved into a small cell near the port of Maiouma where he received numerous visitors. Around 356—coincidentally the year of Anthony's death—he decided to spend his final years in Cyprus in order to avoid the increasing number of pilgrims traveling to Palestine.

It is in the same tradition and in the same region, not far off in the desert, that a remarkable monastic community appears at the beginning of the sixth century, centered around two elders living in strict seclusion—Barsanuphius the Great and John the Prophet—who quickly acquired a reputation as charismatic counselors.

The *Sayings* and the *Letters*

The *Letters* of Barsanuphius and John, which date to the first half of the sixth century, frequently evoke and regularly quote from the

---

[2]See Edward E. Malone, *The Monk and the Martyr: The Monk as the Successor of the Martyr* (Washington, DC: Catholic University of America Press, 1950; repr. Literary Licensing, 2011).

wisdom of the *Sayings of the Desert Fathers*. There are at least eighty direct references to the *Apophthegmata*, while numerous phrases suggest them as the foundation of spiritual progress, "leading the soul to spiritual satisfaction and humility" (*Letter* 547). Their disciple, Dorotheus of Gaza, repeatedly cites the *Sayings* and is the first writer to designate the *Apophthegmata* by the conventional name that they have come down to us, namely, *The Gerontikon* (*The Book of the Old Men*).[3] Might Dorotheus be one of those actually associated with or responsible for the collection of these sayings?

Beyond explicit and extensive similarities between Egyptian and Palestinian practices and principles, the letters of Barsanuphius and John—especially those addressed to Dorotheus of Gaza (*Letters* 252–338)—retain an element that gradually recedes from the *Sayings of the Desert Fathers*, as these begin to be collated and edited. The original, oral transmission of the Egyptian wisdom invariably preserved the spontaneity of the advice and actions of the desert fathers and mothers. However, during the transition from a verbal culture to a written text, the sayings become more static and readers inevitably lose sight of the personal element that originally sparked and spurred these aphorisms.

More particularly, readers and listeners begin to misplace the process and struggle that initially spawned and shaped these words. What is "received" of course is the culmination or consummation of wisdom, though without any insight into the various stages and struggles that led to the final product. What is missing however is the ongoing process—all the traces of contention, hesitation, and limitation—that characterized the spiritual aspirant approaching the desert sages. What is therefore sometimes misplaced is the internal grind that initiates the informed support, the transpiring conversation behind the transcribed correspondence. These letters are the longer narrative that inherently sustains the personal story. They make sense of the bad in light of the good, perpetually grounding the experience and deepening the perspective. Ultimately, the letters expose recipients and readers alike to a wider screen picture that contains and simultaneously explains the adventure of tribulation in the context of transformation.

---

[3]See Dorotheus, *Teachings* 1,13 PG88.1633C in *Sources Chrétiennes* 92 (Paris: Les Editions du Cerf, 1952).

Briefly put, the correspondence of Barsanuphius and John provides a personal and cultural framework for the *Apophthegmata* of the desert elders. *The Sayings of the Desert Fathers* presents the spiritual reality in *the way it should be*, rather than in *the way it is*—with all its denial, doubt, and distress. More often than not, the *Sayings* conceal the intense and interminable struggle that is not always transparent in their brevity and conciseness. Whereas the *Letters* of Barsanuphius and John allow us to witness each of the painful phases as they unfold—almost in slow motion. What might normally take place on a face-to-face level is recorded in writing, with all of the mutuality and back-and-forth of a personal relationship. Neither the authors of the letters nor the compiler of the correspondence attempts to conceal the innate challenges and tensions of the spiritual process. As the French translator of the correspondence, Lucien Regnault, so eloquently, writes: "What the *Sayings of the Desert Fathers* allows us to glimpse only in the form of fleeting images, is here [in the *Letters* of Barsanuphius and John] played out like a film before our very eyes."[4]

The following exchange of letters is one among many examples that highlight this spiritual progress and literary progression in analyzing the intricacies and vagaries of the spiritual way:

> Question from the same brother to the same Old Man: If a brother does something insignificant, but I am afflicted by this act on account of my own will, what should I do? Should I keep silent and not give rest to my heart, or should I speak to him with love and not remain troubled? Moreover, if the matter afflicts others, and not just me, should I speak for the sake of the others? Or would this appear as if I have merely taken on a cause?
>
> Response by John. If the matter is not sinful but insignificant, and you speak simply to give rest to your heart, then it is to your defeat. For you were not able to endure it as a result of your weakness. Just blame yourself and remain silent. However, if the matter afflicts other brothers, then tell your

---

[4]Cf. *Barsanuphe et Jean de Gaza*, 6. Jennifer Hevelone-Harper remarks: "The 'sayings' of the desert fathers found a new mode of expression with these anchorites. The 'words' of Barsanuphius and John were given in the form of letters" (34).

Abbot; and whether he speaks personally or else tells you to speak, you will be carefree. (*Letter* 293)

Question from the same person to the same Old Man: If I speak to the Abbot for the sake of the others, I suspect that the brother will be troubled; so what should I do? Furthermore, if he afflicts both the others and me, should I speak for the sake of the others, or should I keep silent in order not to indulge myself? If I suspect that he will not be grieved, should I also speak for myself, or should I force myself against doing this?

Response by John. As far as the turmoil of the brother is concerned, if you speak to the Abbot, then you have nothing to worry about. Whenever it is necessary to speak for the sake of others, and you are worried about it, then speak for them. As for yourself, always force yourself not to speak. (*Letter* 294)

Question from the same person to the same Old Man: But my thought tells me that if my brother is troubled against me, he will become my enemy, thinking that I slandered him to the Abbot.

Response by John. This thought of yours is wicked; for it wants to prevent you from correcting your brother. Therefore, do not prevent yourself from speaking, but do so according to God. Even sick people that need to be healed will speak against their doctors; yet the latter do not care, knowing that the same people will thank them afterward. (*Letter* 295)

Question from the same person to the same Old Man: If I examine my thought and notice that it is not in fact for the brother's benefit that I wish to speak to the Abbot, but with the purpose of slandering him, should I still speak or keep silent?

Response by John. Advise your thought to speak according to God and not for the sake of slander. If your thought is conquered by criticism, then speak to your Abbot and confess your criticism, so that both of you may be healed—the one who was at fault as well as the one who was critical. (*Letter* 296)

Question from the same person to the same Old Man: But if my thought does not allow me to confess to the Abbot because I would be speaking to him with the purpose of slandering the brother, what should I do? Should I speak or not?

Response. Do not say anything to him, and the Lord will take care of the matter. For it is not necessary for you to speak when it harms your soul. God will take care of the brother's correction as he pleases. (*Letter* 297)

Other similar series of letters reveal the same gradation of reasoning or graduation of deliberation: on prayer (*Letters* 438–47), good deeds (*Letters* 401–13), spiritual thoughts (*Letters* 448–9), conversations with friends (*Letters* 469–76), blessings at meals (*Letters* 716–19), personal relationships (*Letters* 489–91), doctrinal issues (*Letters* 694–704), and almsgiving (*Letters* 617–36), as well as bad habits (*Letters* 433–7), treatment of servants (653–7), legal issues (*Letters* 667–73), and even real estate negotiations (*Letters* 486–8).

Much like his predecessor Isaiah of Scetis and his successor Dorotheus of Gaza, Barsanuphius displays *certain characteristics both in common with and in contrast to* the desert dwellers of Egypt. For instance, all three of them are balanced and non-polemical in their disposition and counsel. They scarcely reveal any traits of confessional bias and rift that plagued so much of Christendom during this volatile period, preferring instead to remain cautiously and consciously reticent on the numerous divisive and complex doctrinal debates of their time.

In this regard, Barsanuphius and John are far less militant and far more moderate than their sixth-century colleagues in Chalcedonian and non-Chalcedonian circles alike.[5] Moreover, nowhere in the vast correspondence of Barsanuphius and John is there any clear or explicit denunciation or defense of the Chalcedonian definition. Their disciples are equally encouraged to abstain from participating in such debates as well as from reproaching those who choose to take sides.

Surprisingly, the elders even allow room for disputation of advice received and for disagreement on opinions expressed (*Letter* 607). In fact, Barsanuphius and John will sometimes offer diverging or dissimilar advice: the former prefers his disciples to avoid excessive theological reading (*Letters* 600–7), while the latter recommends discernment in selecting theological books (*Letters* 600 and 604).

---

[5]The Council of Chalcedon, convened in 451 and recognized as the Fourth Ecumenical Council, defined two natures (divine and human) in the person of Jesus Christ but resulted in a schism within Eastern Christianity.

Nonetheless, the teaching of the two elders should be neither amalgamated nor conflated in any simplistic or sweeping manner;[6] after all, Barsanuphius is convinced that his God is exactly the same as the God of John (*Letters* 20 and 224).

It is no wonder, then, that while iconographic depictions of the two Palestinian elders are generally uncommon, even virtually nonexistent, an icon of the "great old man" graces the altar-cloth in frescoes dating from the tenure of Patriarch Tarasios (784–806) in the Great Church of the Holy Wisdom in Constantinople, alongside monastic pioneers like Anthony of Egypt and Ephraim the Syrian.[7] This may also be why Theodore the Studite (759–826) was subsequently anxious to defend the orthodoxy of Isaiah, Barsanuphius, and Dorotheus.[8] Certainly Barsanuphius himself is clear about his priority and preference for monastics: it is to pray for the salvation of the whole world, orthodox and nonorthodox, pious and pagan alike:

> There are three men, perfect in God, who have exceeded the measure of humanity and received the authority to loose and bind, to forgive and hold sins. These stand before the shattered world, keeping the whole world from complete and

---

[6]See for example François Neyt, "La formation au monastère de l'abbé Séridos à Gaza," in *Christian Gaza in Late Antiquity*, ed. Brouria Bitton-Ashkelony and Aryeh Kofsky (Boston: Brill, 2004), 151–63; and Alexis Torrance, "Barsanuphius, John, and Dorotheos on Scripture: Voices from the Desert in Sixth-Century Gaza," in *What is the Bible? The Patristic Doctrine of Scripture*, ed. Matthew Baker and Mark Mourachian (Minneapolis, MN: Fortress Press, 2016), 67–81.

[7]From the tenth century, icons of Barsanuphius and John appear in Cyprus and Meteora.

[8]Even the *Life of Barsanuphius and John* by Nikodemus of Mt. Athos endeavors to handle this problem by referring to two Barsanuphii and Dorotheii, one set being heretical and the other orthodox. Barsanuphius chose to adopt the rhetoric of the non-Chalcedonian party, while urging his disciples to follow a Chalcedonian bishop. See the *Testament* of Theodore the Studite in PG88.1813–16 and PG99.1028. These three were anathematized by Patriarch Sophronius of Jerusalem in a synodical letter to Patriarch Sergius of Constantinople in 634: see PG87, iii.3192–3. The orthodoxy of Barsanuphius was in question because of his reference in *Letter* 701 only to the First Ecumenical Council in Nicaea (325), without however making any mention of the Fourth Ecumenical Council in Chalcedon (451). The iconographic tradition, however, is also particularly interesting in light of the fact that the two Old Men permitted so few people to meet them in person.

sudden annihilation. Through their prayers, God combines his chastisement with his mercy.

And it has been told to them, that God's wrath will last a little longer. Therefore, pray with them. For the prayers of these three are joined at the entrance to the spiritual altar of the Father of lights. They share in each other's joy and gladness in heaven. And when they turn once again toward the earth, they share in each other's mourning and weeping for the evils that occur and attract his wrath. These three are John in Rome and Elias in Corinth, and another in the region of Jerusalem.[9] I believe that they will achieve God's great mercy. Yes, they will undoubtedly achieve it. (*Letter 569*)

Is it possible that Barsanuphius was bold enough to imagine himself as the third of these charismatic ascetics?

The Practice of Writing Letters

Stanley Stowers concludes his introductory chapters on letter writing in antiquity with the following observation:

> Since monasticism began in Egypt, there are also a considerable number of letters to and from abbots concerning the day-to-day life of monastic communities. These date mostly from the fifth century. Holy men are sometimes petitioned for prayer and healing or approached as patrons in papyrus letters. The papyrus letters help us to catch a sound from the voice of the common Christian, which has been all but lost in the glory of the great letter writers of the golden age.[10]

It is true that Christianity evolved from a movement based on letter-writing. Twenty-one of the twenty-seven books of the New Testament adopt the form of letters, the most obvious ones by

---

[9] While somewhat implausible, the foreword to the *Letters of Barsanuphius and John* (Volos: S. Schoinas, 1960) by Nikodemus suggests that Barsanuphius was the third.
[10] S. K. Stowers, *Letter Writing in Greco-Roman Antiquity* (Philadelphia, PA: Westminster Press, 1986), 47.

Paul or his followers. The writings of the Apostolic Fathers, too, are primarily letters of admonition and exhortation. In the fourth and fifth centuries, letter writers include Athanasius of Alexandria, Ambrose of Milan, Gregory Nazianzus, Basil of Caesarea, Gregory of Nyssa, John Chrysostom, and Augustine of Hippo. Well over 2,000 and possibly up to 10,000 letters are attributed to Isidore of Pelusium alone! And while all of the abovementioned documents were composed as letters, they were generally intended for a wide audience.

However, the letters of Barsanuphius and John are vastly different, resembling personal communications or briefer rejoinders, rather than formal or familial letters. The responses of the Gaza elders certainly contain elements reminiscent of Greco-Roman letter writing, particularly in their more exhortatory (*paraenesis*) features though less so in their admonitory (*epitimesis*) aspects,[11] but Barsanuphius and John do not seem to follow any textbook of rhetoric or letter writing. As in Aristotle's famous *Protreptikos*, what matters most to them is not so much the expression of a teaching but the embodiment of that tradition.

Of course many of the correspondents of the two "old men" remain anonymous. The compiler of the correspondence appears to enjoy ready access to the letters (especially the responses by the two elders), but he likely did not possess all the questions (which are often merely summarized) and may have been unaware of their provenance. Moreover, while thanksgiving is a genuine form of Hellenistic epistolary, Barsanuphius might well have adopted his emphasis on this concept from Paul's reference to thanksgiving (1 Thes 5:18). The indeterminate distinction by Adolf Deissmann between letters and epistles—where the former indicate private communications (Stowers likens them to "a telephone call today") while the latter imply epistles intended for wider publication and general readership[12]—may in fact be helpful in understanding the genre of the correspondence by Barsanuphius and John.

---

[11] See A. Malherbe, *Moral Exhortation: A Greco-Roman Sourcebook* (Philadelphia, PA: Westminster Press, 1986); and R. C. Gregg, *Consolation Philosophy* (Cambridge, MA: Philadelphia Patristic Foundation, 1975).

[12] Stowers, *Letter Writing*, 16–20. Deissmann's famous dictum was: "The letter is a piece of life; the epistle is a product of literary art." Cf. A. Deissmann, *Light from the Ancient East: The New Testament Illustrated by Recently Discovered Texts of the Graeco-Roman World* (London: Hodder and Stoughton, 1927), 230.

The style of letter-writing represented by Barsanuphius and John betrays a literary sensitivity and cultural exposure, perhaps even an aristocratic and well-educated background. In this respect, Claudia Rapp advances the role of the "holy man" by adding the specific features of intercessory supplication and spiritual direction. The holy man, she claims, is more than merely an arbiter or exemplar—the role and model promoted by Peter Brown—a person whose power depends on the perceived efficacy of his prayer and patronage.[13]

Nonetheless, the letters of the "great old man" and the "other old man" remain unique in the history of letter writing. While earlier documents principally emphasize the impact of the elder as *mediatory in—mostly—an upward direction*, namely, as trustworthy intercessors for people before God (Jas 5:16), the letters of Barsanuphius and John primarily underline the influence of the elders as *mediatory in—mostly—a downward direction*, namely, as compassionate counselors of people for God (Gal 6:2). Therefore, just as Rapp complements Brown's interpretation of the holy man as *arbiter and exemplar* through her emphasis on the holy man as intercessor and supplicant, we should additionally insist on the distinctive feature and gravity of the concepts of *counselor and director* in order to appreciate the antique holy man more thoroughly.[14]

It seems, then, that the letters of Barsanuphius and John enjoy a certain uniqueness within the epistolary literature of the early Near East in late antiquity from both a literary and a spiritual perspective. The two elders may not qualify as "holy men" by the conventional, even prevailing criteria of scholarship relating to hagiography. Moreover, their letters are neither primarily didactic[15] nor predominantly intercessory or again exclusively interventional.

---

[13]Claudia Rapp, "'For Next to God, you are My Salvation:' Reflections on the Rise of the Holy Man in Late Antiquity," in *The Cult of Saints in Late Antiquity and the Middle Ages: Essays on the Contribution of Peter Brown*, ed. James Howard-Johnson and Paul Antony Hayward (Oxford, UK: Oxford University Press, 1999), 63–81. See the articles by Peter Brown, "The Saint as Exemplar," in *Representations* 2 (Spring 1983), 1–25; and Peter Brown, "The Rise and Function of the Holy Man in Late Antiquity," *The Journal of Roman Studies* 61 (1971), 80–101.

[14]Barsanuphius, too, makes such a distinction. In *Letters* 567–9, he distinguishes his own function in instructing his disciples from those inspiring the world.

[15]The *Life of Antony* may be a deliberate effort by Athanasius of Alexandria to inform his contemporaries about the life and virtues of the desert elder, in the manner of Gregory of Nyssa's "Letter on the *Life of Macrina*" and, earlier, Jerome's *Letter* 108 on the life of Paula. See Rapp, "For Next to God," 80–1.

They serve, rather, to prolong and promote the vividness and spontaneity of the precious interpersonal contact, conversation, and communication encountered in the fourth-century sayings and setting of the desert fathers and mothers in Egypt. At the same time, they provide an alternative form of spiritual authority on the margins of Palestinian life to the more established form of ecclesiastical authority in the sacred center of Jerusalem.

The Structure of the Letters

The *Letters* of the two "old men" clearly comprise the largest collection from late antiquity, encompassing a private compendium that was probably not intended for publication but only circulated for spiritual edification. These were personal letters that were never destined to be spread or shared.

The correspondence begins with fifty-four questions addressed to and answers dictated by Barsanuphius, with the exception of one letter conveyed by the "other old man" (*Letter* 3). The opening letters are a series of queries communicated by John of Beersheba, anxiously investigating his gradual transition to the eremitic life in Thawatha. Toward the end of the first letter, Abbot Seridos expresses nervousness about whether he can remember all that Barsanuphius transmits in response to the opening question by John of Beersheba. He regrets not recording the words of the Old Man by dictation. Barsanuphius comforts him, assuring him that the Holy Spirit will enable him to remember exactly what was said:

> And I, Seridos, tell you something else wonderful. As the Old Man said this, I thought to myself: "How can I remember these things in order to write them down? Had the Old Man wanted, I could have brought here ink and paper, heard his words one by one, and then written them down." Yet he knew what I was thinking and his face shone like fire. So he said to me: "Go and write; do not be afraid. Even if I tell you ten thousand words, the Spirit of God will not let you write down even a single letter whether too much or too little. Not because you so choose, but because the Spirit is guiding your hand to write in a coherent manner." (*Letter* 1)

And so the correspondence proceeds, with Seridos now prepared for whatever might ensue.

In all, depending on the internal division adopted in some of the longer documents, the correspondence contains approximately 850 letters dictated by the two elders in response to a host of issues from a very diverse group of individuals. Neither Barsanuphius nor John spoke face-to-face with those who sought their guidance. Instead, enquirers would submit their questions or concerns in writing, and in due course they would receive a written reply from one—or, occasionally, both—of the Old Men through their respective secretaries in the nearby monastery.

Almost 400 letters (typically the longer ones) belong to Barsanuphius, while around 450 letters (usually the shorter ones) belong to John. Moreover, whereas the study and literature of spiritual direction traditionally address the spiritual formation of monks, Barsanuphius and John redress this imbalance by also engaging with lay persons. The overall structure of the text is thus organized with letters to monastics found in the early sections of the correspondence (comprising around two-thirds of the document), followed by letters to lay people (consisting of about one quarter of the compilation), and concluding with letters to bishops (containing about fifty letters).

In general, the correspondence is not arranged chronologically, with the exception of certain letters constituting a series—or string—of related questions and answers. Preliminary efforts to organize the letters in a systematic way—in order to ascertain or apply a vague structure—usually occur in manuscripts as late as the fourteenth century where the letters are divided into the following rudimentary categories:

1 *Letters* 1–223: Responses to hermits about the way of stillness

2 *Letters* 224–616: Responses to various brothers of the community headed by Seridos, especially to questions addressed by Dorotheus

3 *Letters* 617–848: Responses to lay people and other leaders in church and society

The letters are sometimes starkly brief (*Letter* 437), at other times markedly longer (*Letter* 256), almost to the point of constituting individual treatises (*Letter* 604).

A more detailed subdivision of the letters might be as follows:

1–54	Correspondence with John of Beersheba
55–71	Letters to elders and hermits
72–123	Questions from Andrew, an elder who is ill
124–31	Letters to monk Theodore
132–251	Questions from brothers and priests
252–338	Correspondence with Dorotheus
339–98	Letters from various monks, including Dorotheus
399–570	Questions from various brothers and laypersons
571–99	Letters to Aelianos on succeeding Seridos
600–7	Questions about Origenism
608–787	Correspondence with laymen of various professions
788–848	Letters to bishops and other people in Gaza

In other words, the letters "call to center stage more or less all of the main actors of the *societas christiana*"[16] of the period. A glaring exception to this picture is the absence of any letters from women.

Women: The Inconspicuous Factor

While there are no letters from women in the correspondence, women are neither extraneous nor exceptional to the monastery circles of Thawatha. Indeed, Barsanuphius is not at all exclusive in his attitude toward women (*Letter* 61), at least by comparison with contemporary standards elsewhere. For instance, unlike conventional practices in other contemporary Palestinian monasteries or Western monastic sources,[17] the community at Thawatha welcomed female visitors (*Letter* 595) for instruction and edification as well as to provide donations or receive support.[18]

---

[16]Cf. L. Perrone, "Monasticism as a Factor of Religious Interaction," in *Between Personal and Institutional Religion*, 91.
[17]See *Life of Euthymius*, chap. 54 and *Rule of Benedict*, chap. 54.
[18]On the Desert Mothers, see Laura Swan, *The Forgotten Desert Mothers: Sayings, Lives, and Stories of Early Christian Women* (Mahwah, NJ: Paulist Press, 2001). On women in early monasticism, see Susanna Elm, *"Virgins of God": The Making of Asceticism in Late Antiquity* (Oxford: Clarendon Press, 1994).

The women would assemble in specially constructed and consigned cells outside of the monastery walls. One reason for admitting women on monastery grounds was because Barsanuphius and John are disparaging of monks who abandon their spouses or families, expecting them to support their more vulnerable dependents. The two elders perceived the social responsibility and financial accountability of those renouncing civilization for solitude—with regard to regulation, distribution, or restitution of property—particularly where children are involved. Such matters were also of special concern to the Emperor Justinian as he reformed civil legislation in the mid-sixth century.[19]

One letter deals explicitly with relationships of monks with women visiting the monastery at Thawatha. Aelianos, the abbot who succeeded Seridos in the administration of the community, seeks Abba John's advice on the proper procedure for dealing with his own spouse and family that come to the monastery:

> Question: There are times when faithful women visit us, or else mothers of the brothers, and we receive them in the outside cell. That cell has windows opening up to the monastery; should I converse with them through the window, or not? Moreover, my elderly wife did not want to stay with her nephews, and so she gave me all of her belongings. Do you direct me to speak with her whenever she comes in order to meet her financial needs? What do you think that should I do? What should happen?
>
> Response by John. If there is any reason for these women to visit you for God's sake, not simply in order to see the place or for their own pleasure, but specifically to hear the word of God or to bring something here; if it is necessary to converse with them, then do so but always guard your eyes. For: "Everyone who looks at a woman with lust has already committed

---

[19]See Rosa Maria Parrinello, "The Justinianean Legislation Regarding the Wives of the Monks and Its Context: The Letters of Barsanuphius and John of Gaza," in *Männlich und weiblich schuf Er sie. Studien zur Genderkonstruktion und zum Eherecht in den Mittelmeerreligionen*, ed. Matthias Morgenstern, Christian Boudignon, and Christiane Tietz (Goettingen: Vandenhoeck und Ruprecht, 2011), 193–204. See also B. Flusin, "L'essor du monachisme," in J. M. Mayeur et al. (ed.), *Histoire du christianisme*, vol. 3 (Paris: Les églises d'Orient et d'Occident, 1998), 545–608 [at 553].

adultery with her in his heart" (Mt 5:28), while everything that happens according to God will be protected by God. Do not do this to please people or to seek praise, but out of a pure heart (cf. 1 Tm 1:5), extending your thought toward God. If it happens to be the mother of one of the brothers and she comes here for some need, then speak with her in accordance with the commandment that you have received. However, you should not see her unless it is necessary. For her son is able to inform her, while you can simply prepare whatever she needs, not giving to her in a wasteful manner, but again only what is necessary.

As for your elderly wife, for as long as she lives, you should speak to her from time to time and meet her needs, whether she wants to live in the city or in the nearby town. As for your children, however, you should not accept to do their favors, until they are settled in their lives. Direct them with godly fear. Feed and dress them carefully in order to avoid both prodigality and scorn, in order that they may not ask for more. Examine their needs and rebuke them, saying: "Give regard to yourselves; for you are no longer slaves but free people (Cf. Gal 4:7). How fortunate you are to be carefree and enjoy more rest than even the rich!" And, when your elderly wife dies, give them their freedom as well as their share of property, always with balance, whether here in the town or wherever else you want. For there is no law regarding this. But if you threaten them, they will become estranged from you, although the property will still be counted as yours. (*Letter 595*)

Aelianos was still a layman when he was appointed abbot. So the advice from Abba John is clear: take care of your wife, talk to her, and meet with her; as for your children, continue to raise and provide for them. Aelianos is not to be estranged from the family that he renounced for the sake of a solitary life. After all, his family is regarded as a microcosm of his community, while the monastery is an extension of his wife and children.[20] Ascetic renunciation was never to be associated with social resignation. What a refreshing

---

[20]Here the Gaza tradition echoes the advice of Basil of Caesarea, who encouraged monastics to provide for their parents and siblings. See *Longer Rules* 32. See W. K. Lowther Clarke, *The Ascetic Works of Saint Basil* (London: SPCK, 1925).

and inclusive conception of monasticism! How radically different to the mainstream tradition through the ages and to this day! Again, centering on the heart is never severed from contribution to the community.

On another occasion, a lay pilgrim asks the "great old man" whether he should leave his wife for the purpose of becoming a monk. Barsanuphius replies unwaveringly and unequivocally:

> Child, do not assume the responsibility of leaving her, because otherwise you are transgressing the commandment of the Apostle, who says: "Are you bound to a wife? Then, do not seek to be free" (1 Cor 7:27). For if she sins and becomes a sinful woman, the responsibility for that sin lies with you, since the decision was not taken by mutual agreement (cf. 1 Cor 7:5) or counsel. Simply leave the matter to God, and his loving-kindness will do as he wills. (*Letter 662*)

It is clear to the two elders that, above and beyond any monastic rule, there is always the Gospel law. Barsanuphius and John recognize that the commandment to love must be applied without discrimination and without exception to all men and women. Thus, while no letters in this collection are actually dictated by women, nonetheless the presence of women is palpable in the letters. And it could not be otherwise since, much as in the desert of Egypt, the virtues of hospitality and charity were never reserved for men, especially in the monastery of Seridos that candidly encouraged contact and communication with the wider, outside society.

Conversation and Communication

Notwithstanding any physical accessibility of the monastery to the general public and the inconspicuous visibility of women in the correspondence, all the letters are directly and distinctly to celibate monastics or clergy and lay men. The recipients include monks from the adjacent monastery of Abba Seridos and laypersons from nearby Gaza, through to high-ranking political officials and ecclesiastical leaders in more distant urban settings. There are bishops asking about ordinations (*Letter 815*). There is one letter, or possibly more, from Patriarch Peter of Jerusalem (*Letter* 821). Another letter relates to "the Duke, who has recently converted to Christianity" (*Letter* 834). Sometimes, letters simultaneously address both the recipient and scribe (*Letters* 207 and 484).

As already noted, a monk from the nearby community originally compiled the letters. This editor transcribed the correspondence, introducing each letter and occasionally naming the correspondent, while briefly delineating the context or purpose of the question addressed to the elders. However, the correspondence also remains somewhat incomplete: Dorotheus refers to a question that he once addressed to John as well as to the specific response by John, yet no such letter survives.[21] Other letters begin with the phrase: "This is the second"—and, on some occasions, "the third"—"time that I write to you," though there is no record of any preceding correspondence. Sometimes the question is quoted in full; at other times, it is summarized in brief. Regrettably, however, we are not explicitly informed about the identity of the editor, though he reveals that he was present when a visitor once speculated whether Barsanuphius was real person or whether his cell was empty. On that occasion, as we are told, the "great old man" came outside his cell and, without uttering a word, washed the feet of the doubting visitor in order to allay any skepticism and returned to his cell.[22]

Every detail of every question is considered worthwhile and warranting of a response. John the Prophet reflects: "Brother, in his responses to you, the [Great] Old Man left no question unanswered" (*Letter* 306). The *written means* of communication promoted and preferred by these remarkable elders clearly favors a *more comprehensive* answer, while the *dual ministry* of the elders facilitates a *more complete* response through the scribe (*Letter* 783). Sometimes, one advises the correspondent to consult a second opinion (*Letters* 361 and 504) or to search for answers within himself, rather than depending on others: "Do not seek answers from anyone with regard to yourself, but rather create the answers for yourself" (*Letter* 347b). At other times, the elders tender silence as the only fitting and healing response (*Letter* 148). This alone is hardly a suggestion or recommendation echoed too commonly in monastic or hierarchal circles.

---

[21] See Dorotheus of Gaza, *Discourses* II, PG88.1640.
[22] See *Letter* 125. *Letter* 226 responds to someone suspecting the origin of the letters.

We should also remember that letters do not simply reflect passive sources of information and instruction; above all, they represent active exchanges of conversation and communication. So they frequently reveal a picture of contemporary everyday life overlooked or ignored in many literary sources. Indeed, no other document from the early Christian era shows us in such vivid detail how spiritual direction was understood and exercised in practice. What might arguably have involved minimal editing, the Letters reveal the actual voices of the inquirers and their respondents with immediacy and intimacy, as well as with vividness and verve.

Inquirers came from all levels of society: not only from the members of the community where Barsanuphius and John dwelt, but also from those outside, bishops and monastics, clergy and laity. The topics are highly varied. As we would expect, many of the questions concern the life of prayer: for example, "Tell me, father, about unceasing prayer" (*Letter* 87). Other questions address concerns about physical illness: the elders, for instance, have to assure a novice who cries out that he cannot "bear the affliction of his illness" (*Letter* 613). Often the questions are specific and practical: "How much should I eat?" (*Letter* 154); "If one enters the church during the time of the Liturgy and leaves before the end, is this a sin?" (*Letter* 736); "The locusts ravage my fields. If I drive them away, my neighbors grow furious with me"—presumably because the locusts then move on to their fields—"but if I leave them, I suffer loss. What should I do?" (*Letter* 684).

Moreover, the letters are wide-ranging not only in regard to their recipients, but also with reference to their circumstances. People approach the elders to inquire about very ordinary, mundane matters. As a result, their questions touch on such everyday quandaries as the interpretation of dreams, the treatment of slaves, or relations with non-Christians (*Letters* 686, 732–5, 776–7, 836, and 821–2). They address slavery, debt, disease, and trade (*Letters* 648–9, 672–4, and 749–50). They even deal with burglary, murder, and bribery (*Letters* 667–9, 671, and 785). Laypeople inquire about illness and healing; in response, they are encouraged to consider the additional importance of spiritual health (*Letters* 637–44, 753–5, and 778–81; see also *Letters* 72–123 to a monk in illness). Other questions relate to legal and fiscal matters (*Letters* 667–72 and 749–56), family relations and daily chores (*Letters* 764–8), marriage and death (*Letters* 646 and 676), property and charity

(*Letters* 617–20, 625–6, 629–35, 649), proper interaction and appropriate boundaries between monks and laypersons (*Letters* 636, 681–2, 727–9, 736–42, and 751), and above all the practice of ascetic discipline in the context of city life (*Letters* 764–74).

In all, the letters divulge a diverse community, with concerned Christians seeking earnest guidance about daily life in sixth-century Gaza. For their part, Barsanuphius and John are fully conscious that they are facing new concerns and unprecedented challenges. No longer are their disciples—ordained, monastic, or lay—able to disregard or disdain their neighbors. In fact, the two elders prove far more open in their appreciation of and advice on contacts with non-Christians than many imperial authorities of the time.[23] In this regard, their counsel is modest, moderate, and mild (*Letter* 26). Perhaps the two elders were themselves experienced in the secular life before assuming a monastic life. In any case their seclusion hardly denies them the possibility and opportunity of experiencing and expressing compassion for the dilemmas of mundane exchange and social entanglement.

Rules and Regulations, Roles and Responsibilities

These letters were never intended to constitute or compete with any monastic rule. They differ tremendously from the *Pachomian Rule* or *The Rule of Benedict*. They also bear no comparison or correspondence to the *Longer and Shorter Rules* of Basil the Great, which arguably come closest to the style of Barsanuphius and John inasmuch as Basil was reacting to specific concerns addressed by superiors of communities within his diocese.[24] The letters of

---

[23]After Justinian's decree against pagans in 528–9, relations between Christian and pagan grew tense and confused, sometimes violent. See F. R. Trombley, *Hellenic Religion and Christianization c. 370–529*, 2 vols. (New York and Leiden: E.J. Brill, 1994), 267.

[24]See A. Veilleux, *The Life of Saint Pachomius and His Disciples* (Kalamazoo, MI: Cistercian Publications, 1980); *The Rule of Benedict* (Dublin, UK: Four Courts Press, 1994); and M. Monica Wagner, *St. Basil: Ascetical Works* (Washington, DC: Catholic University of America Press, 1962).

Barsanuphius and John are far more subjective in style and intimate in content. As the Prologue of the correspondence clearly asserts:

> The same teachings are not suited to all alike ... Therefore, we must not receive as a general rule the words spoken in a loving way to particular individuals for the sake of their weakness; rather, we should immediately discern that the response was surely addressed by the saints to the questioner in a personal way.

If anything, the letters pay very little if any attention to monastic regulations,[25] but focus and dwell instead on spiritual requirements or presuppositions. They describe the entire spectrum of the spiritual life, all the "ages" (ἡλικίαι) of the ascetic way (see *Letter* 1). These stages are not accidental, however; they are developmental. And the two elders are also able to detect various gradations within each stage, discerning individual shades within each gradation, with a

FIGURE 1 *Hermit cells in Palestine.*

---

[25]*Letters* 571–98 addressed to Aelianos, future abbot of the monastery of Abba Seridos, provide insights into how a monastery should be organized and administered. However, even in this case, the letters offer more spiritual direction than managerial directives.

view to reconciling and integrating them all within each particular person and within every specific context. So "the great old man" will field speculative questions about scriptural interpretation and allegory, whereas the "other old man" will confine his responses to more pragmatic liturgical or devotional matters.

Around 100 questions are submitted by Dorotheus (*Letters* 252–338, and some others); over 70 of these responses are crafted by John, while the rest are dictated by Barsanuphius. Dorotheus' letters expose readers to a biographical and spiritual exposition of the inner life of this exceptional novice and then monk, later possibly even abbot of a monastery and author of several influential treatises. For instance, we learn of his temptations (subtle and sexual), his duties (spiritual and medical), his obedience (as a monk among fellow monks), his service in positions of authority (responsible for a younger monk, named Dositheus),[26] as well as his close relationship with our two elders. Dorotheus of Gaza is undoubtedly the most prominent and renowned disciple of Barsanuphius and John, in some ways better known than his own spiritual masters.[27]

The most immediate and striking feature of the letters is without doubt their spontaneity and freshness, as well as their astute shrewdness and inimitable wit. Sometimes inspiring and uplifting, at other times agonizing and painful, the advice proffered is regularly lighthearted but unfailingly supportive and consistently receptive because the elders always speak from the heart to the heart:

> Let us not neglect to render thanks to God, like the one about whom you once told the story, that he used to go and pray in church in order that he might secure food for sustenance. But when he met someone who said: "Have breakfast with me today, and then you can go pray," he replied: "I cannot go; for I am supposed to be praying to God for food." (*Letter* 6)

---

[26]*Letters* 220–3 may be addressed to Dositheus, who was placed under the spiritual direction of Dorotheus (*Letters* 66 and 78).

[27]Possibly because the Jesuits, and the West in general, very early discovered his writings, which they recommended to novices in preparation for entry into the Society of Jesus. The letters to Dorotheus appear—at length, though not in full—in *Patrologia Graeca* volume 88 (columns 1611–844).

Another Christ-loving layperson asked the same Old Man: I want to press some Jewish wine in my presser.[28] Is this considered a sin?

Response by John. If, when God rains, it rains in your field but not in that of the Jew, then do not press his wine. But if he is loving-kind to all and rains upon the just as well as upon the unjust (cf. Mt 5:45), then why would you prefer to be inhumane rather than compassionate; for he says: "Be merciful, even as your Father in heaven is merciful" (Lk 6:36). (*Letter* 686)

Another characteristic of the correspondence is the inimitable humor of the two elders, which is inseparably combined with their profound humility and a good measure of realism. If Barsanuphius and John take themselves less seriously, it is because they are neither obsessed with their asceticism nor preoccupied with their virtue. They constantly recognize that frailty and failure come with the territory of being human; God's perspective differs immeasurably.

Thus to a monk suffering from rheumatism and asking whether this might derive from demonic temptation, Barsanuphius offers unsentimental consolation: "Do not grieve, my beloved one. For this is not of the demons, as you think, but it is merely a draft from the outside" (*Letter* 78). To another monk wondering whether he has the authority to advise his brother, the "great old man" provides reassurance that, "if necessary, God can even speak through the mouth of an ass (Nm 22:28)" (*Letter* 203). And to a layman asking whether crossing himself with his left hand on account soreness in his right hand would be disrespectful, Barsanuphius responds almost tongue-in-cheek: "Whenever I want to perform the sign of the cross on my right hand, I definitely need to use my left hand!" (*Letter* 437). Finally, to a layperson inquiring about the intricate subtleties of personal relationships,

---

[28]Gaza wine was historically renowned for its taste. The sixth-century Roman statesman and scholar Cassiodorus once praised the wine of his native Calabria by boldly asserting that it rivaled the wine of Gaza. See Michael Press, "Sudden Change or Gradual Transition," *The Tel Aviv Review of Books* (Autumn 2020). https://www.tarb.co.il/sudden-change-or-gradual-transition/ Accessed September 15, 2021. To this day, the region is known for its vineyards, orchards, and olive groves.

Abba John offers advice condensed in a single word: "Just do good (ἀγαθοποίησον)!" (*Letter* 679)

The elders are further distinguished by authenticity and originality. Their correspondence is more than just a manual on the spiritual life. Each of their letters is actually a personal provocation eliciting a distinctive response to a specific problem. The writing is always direct and simple, unpretentious and ordinary; the result is endlessly informative and edifying, inspiring, and even extraordinary. In fact, because the letters are written rather than spoken responses, they weave every minute detail of each question into the response. In this way, the correspondence clearly reflects *a text of a particular time*, albeit with far-reaching influence on readers through the centuries. And it clearly remains *a text of a particular place*, with far-reaching implications on a variety of cultures, which may explain why we hear so little about Barsanuphius and John beyond their generation and outside the region.

Still, the personalities of the two elders are very conspicuous in the correspondence and among their contemporaries. Barsanuphius comes across as kind, understanding, and warm; his language is clear, prayerful, and prophetic. The "great old man" reveals a strong and supportive personality, undeterred by crisis and unwavering in conviction. By contrast, John is less direct, more guarded, and not as ardent; his language is concise, precise, and conventional. The "other old man" reveals a sensitive and sympathetic personality, often referring and deferring to Barsanuphius as his mentor.

Moreover, the style and language of the correspondence are very personal, profound, and powerful. While the correspondence comprises 850 letters, in actual fact we should envisage it against the setting of countless visitations to the two Old Men. While some of the letters begin with the phrase: "Write to [so and so] ... " (*Letters* 1, 4, 6, 8–9, 16, 22, 27, and 31), others replace the word "write" with the word "tell [so and so] ... " (*Letters* 2–3, 7, 12–15, 19, 26–30, 39, 42, 47, and 54).

Finally, the tone of the letters is friendly and familiar, befitting that between master and disciple (*Letters* 56, 62, 68–9, 72–4, 86, 90–3, 96–8, and 126). In fact, the correspondence is reminiscent of the relationship between parent and child that forms the basis of monastic life in fourth-century Egypt, where the words that frequently instigated a conversation were: "Abba, speak a word to me [about how I may be saved]" or "Abba, pray for me."[29] This very approach is faithfully transplanted to Gaza:

> A certain elderly Egyptian man ... requested the prayer and counsel of the Great Old Man.
>
> [Barsanuphius responds:] As for what you ask, namely that I pray for your sins, I also ask the same of you, that you should pray for my sins. For it is said: "As you would that others do to you, so also do unto them" (Mt 7:12; Lk 6:31). Now I, though wretched and the least of all, do whatever I can for the sake of him who says: "Pray for each other that you may be healed" (Jas 5:16) ... Trust me, beloved one, that compelled by God's love, I transcend my boundaries in saying this to your love. Who am I, the least of all? So I ask forgiveness. "Forgive my babbling for the Lord's sake, and pray for me." (*Letter 55*)

---

[29]See, for instance, *Sayings*, Anthony 16 and 19.

2

Luminaries of Gaza

Prominent Personalities and Identities

Two Extraordinary Elders

We do not know exactly when—or, indeed, exactly why—an Egyptian monk named Barsanuphius[1] enters the hilly region of Thawatha (*Letter* 61) and chooses to live as a recluse in a local cell. From this position, however, he offers counsel to a number of ascetics, who gradually gather as the Old Man develops a remarkable reputation for spiritual discernment and pastoral compassion. One of these monks, Abba Seridos, who serves as personal attendant to Barsanuphius, is at some point appointed abbot of a community created specifically to cater for and administer the increasing number of monks attracted to Barsanuphius as their mentor and guide.[2]

The monastery is actually located in Thawatha, near Gerara, where the biblical patriarchs Abraham and Isaac once lived

---

[1] The monastery of Seridos included a significant number of Egyptian monks (*Letter* 228), although the language spoken there was Greek. The name "Barsanuphius" is the Latinized for of Βαρσανούφιος, a Hellenized form of a Coptic name, whose meaning is unknown.

[2] Some scholars argue that Seridos may already have directed a monastery in the area, which was privileged—indeed, may even have competed with other monastic centers—to lure Barsanuphius to the region.

(Gn 20; cf. *Letter* 257). It assumes the form of a loose community with many cells, where monks enjoy varying degrees of enclosure and independence. This monastery rapidly becomes a center of interest and magnetism for many monastics and visitors during the sixth century, largely due to the presence and prestige of the two Old Men, but partly also due to the brotherhood's far-reaching activities and services, which included workshops (*Letters* 553–4), two guesthouses (*Letters* 570, 595–6), the first recorded hospital in a monastic context (*Letters* 327 and 548),[3] and a large church (*Letter* 570).

In addition to these edifices, the monastery boasted sprawling property and premises with ample space for the construction of the cells inhabited by Barsanuphius and John. The abbot of the monastery, Seridos, is the only person permitted to communicate with Barsanuphius, acting as liaison and mediator for those submitting questions in writing. Barsanuphius explains how, as his personal ascetic rule, he has determined that he should not write by his own hand, but only and always by way of Seridos:

> Question. A certain elderly Egyptian man came to dwell in the monastery where the fathers were, and addressed a letter in Egyptian to the Great Old Man (for he too was Egyptian), requesting prayer and counsel for the benefit of his soul, and asking whether it would be possible to meet him.
>
> The holy Old Man wrote his response in Greek, as follows: Since I have promised myself not to write to anyone directly, but only through the Abbot [Seridos], this is why I have not written to you in Egyptian as you wrote to me, but was compelled to tell him to write to you in Greek; for he does not know Egyptian. If you rank me in your letters as your beloved father in the Lord, who understands the labor and the needs and the dangers of your soul, then if I am your father as you write, I give you a commandment not to bother me about a meeting. For I do not show favor to anyone in my life. Indeed, if I open my door to you, then I open it to all; but if I do not

---

[3] On hospitality for guests and care for the sick in the Monastery of Seridos, see Hyung-Guen Choi, *Between Ideals: Charity and the Letters of Barsanuphius and John of Gaza* (Macquarie Centre, NSW: Sydney College of Divinity Press, 2020), chapters 5 and 6, 141–209.

open my door to you, neither do I have to open it to anyone else. (*Letter* 55)[4]

Certain aspects of the solitary lifestyle characteristic of Barsanuphius and John are of course reminiscent of earlier models in Judean monasticism, which is geographically very close and spiritually very familiar to Barsanuphius. In the *Life of Euthymius*, Cyril of Scythopolis describes how Euthymius (d. 473) sought a life of solitude and silence but was also concerned about the welfare and guidance of those who chose to live near him. Euthymius would, therefore, organize his monks into a small community, and then proceed to a more remote region, where—once again discovered by other pious followers—he would repeat the process.[5]

Furthermore, the practice of Barsanuphius to relate only through one person, as a measure of protecting his solitude, echoes another precedent in the lifestyle of Abba Isaiah of Scetis, who regularly preferred to communicate through Peter the Egyptian during his fifty years of seclusion in the same region.[6] However, Isaiah never quite reached the same degree of exclusion or reclusion as Barsanuphius and John; nor again did the method of contact and conversation with his disciples constitute a central element of his own spiritual ministry. Still, the fact that we encounter a similar form of lifestyle in earlier monastic pioneers and ascetic authors leads us to believe that this was not altogether exceptional and unfamiliar, at least in the region of Gaza.

Subsequently, sometime between 525 and 527, a hermit by the name of John comes to live beside Barsanuphius, who surrenders

---

[4]Since Seridos did not know Coptic, he would record the words of Barsanuphius in Greek. Seridos, it seems, was Greek, although he may have been Syrian. The correspondence offers more biographical information about Seridos than about the two elders (*Letter* 570). The concept of "opening the door" echoes the early Desert Fathers: see Arsenius, *Saying* 8: "If I open my door to you, I open my door to everyone."
[5]See E. Schwartz, ed., *Cyril of Scythopolis, Life of Euthymius* (Leipzig: J.C. Hinrichs Verlag, 1939). Translated in R. M. Price, *Cyril of Scythopolis: The Lives of the Monks of Palestine* (Kalamazoo, MI: Cistercian Publications, 1991).
[6]The community of Seridos recommended the reading of Abba Isaiah to its monks (see *Letter* 240), while Barsanuphius appears closely connected to the teaching of Isaiah (*Letters* 98, 245, and 612). John the Prophet speaks about Abba Isaiah as if he were very personally familiar with his community and practice (*Letter* 252).

his cell to him in order to adopt a newly constructed cell nearby. Abba Barsanuphius becomes known—in the correspondence and in posterity—as the "holy old man" or the "great old man," a Coptic phrase familiar among Egyptian circles and formerly ascribed by Palladius to Anthony. Abba John is simply called the "other old man" or the "prophet." The two share the same way of life and support one another's ministry (*Letters* 224–5 and 571–2). Emulating Barsanuphius, who is his model and mentor, John procures the services of Dorotheus to be his disciple, attendant, and mouthpiece over the next eighteen years.[7]

We know very little about the early years of Barsanuphius. *Letters* 74 and 512 reveal that he was often ill, while *Letter* 258 admits the manifold and intense temptations experienced in his youth. In *Letter* 13, he tells John of Beersheba:

> If I were to write to you about the temptations that I have endured—nevertheless I tell you that your ears could not bear it, and perhaps neither the ears of anyone else in this time.

He is a wise and respected ascetic. He eats three loaves of bread a week (*Letters* 72 and 97), although allegedly he does not have to eat at all (*Letter* 78). He is respected for his humility (*Letter* 192), discernment (*Letter* 170), foresight (*Letters* 1, 27, 31, 54, 163, and 800), love (*Letters* 110 and 17), illumination (*Letter* 10), and sharing his gifts (*Letters* 10, 111 and 212). He forgives sins (*Letters* 212, 10, 145, 147, 235, and 166)[8] and even assumes upon himself the sins of others (*Letters* 59 and 235). He is known for working miracles through prayer (*Letters* 1, 43, 47, 171, 174, 227, 510, and 581), but what characterizes him above all else is "the gentleness that rests in his heart" (*Letter* 20) and the generosity that characterizes his relationships. He is always ready to offer a word,

---

[7]Dorotheus of Gaza would approach the door of John's cell "as one would venerate the precious cross." See L. Regnault and J. de Préville, eds., "*Dorotheus of Gaza: Didascalia*," in *Sources Chrétiennes* 92 (Paris: Les Editions du Cerf, 1963), IV, 56, 240.

[8]We are not certain as to whether Barsanuphius was ordained, although it is clear that John was not (*Letters* 44 and 138). On forgiveness of sins in the East, especially with regard to Symeon the New Theologian, see L. Petit, "Bibliographie," *Echos d' Orient* 3 (1900), 316–18.

a prayer, a counsel, a morsel of bread, a glass of water, or a piece of clothing as demanded by the situation at hand (*Letters* 1, 63, 72, 166, 173).

We know still less about the life of the "other old man," John. He is probably a Palestinian monk, since—unlike Barsanuphius—there is nothing to indicate Egyptian provenance. What we do know is that, while John stays for the most part in the shadow of Barsanuphius as his disciple (*Letter* 130), Barsanuphius nonetheless claims that John holds the same authority as his master:

> With regard to the conduct of my child who is of a single mind with me, that blessed and humbly obedient one who has completely renounced all of his desires, even to the point of death, what can I say? For the Lord said: "The one who has seen me, has seen the Father" (Jn 14:9); and about the disciple he said: "He is like his teacher" (Lk 6:40). "Let the one who has ears listen" (Mt 11:15). (*Letter* 188)

Institution and Inspiration

The authority of Barsanuphius is more inspirational, responding to principles of a spiritual nature. By comparison, John reflects more an institutional approach, responding to matters of an ordinary practical nature. Yet the two elders never compete against each another; in fact, they seem to complement one other. Together, they maintain an integrity of authority-in-charity, supporting one another's commitment and compassion. They recognize that they share the same God (*Letters* 20 and 224) and the same virtue (*Letter* 780).

> Question. If all of us are one (Jn 17:21)—the Old Man in God and I in the Old Man—then I dare to say that, if he gave you his word, I too give you mine through him. I know that I am weak and the least; yet I cannot separate myself from the Old Man. For he is compassionate on me so that the two of us are one ... (*Letter* 305)

The inspiration and influence of these elders is genuinely refreshing and deeply fascinating. At a time when monastic life in the West is becoming increasingly regulated and codified, adhering to Roman legal norms and forms, Palestinian monasticism retains the flexibility and fluidity of the earlier Egyptian ways reflected in the *Sayings of the Desert Fathers*. Therefore, while the emphasis in Western monasticism gradually focuses on the importance of *discipline*, Eastern monasticism consistently highlights the importance of *discernment*. Spiritual direction in the Christian East has invariably been more personal, less institutional. In the West, one becomes attached to a community or, in later centuries, to an order; in the East, one always seeks out an elder or *geron*, an *abba*, or *amma*. Indeed, the chief social role of monastic centers in the East is to provide spiritual directors; the fundamental expectation upon entering a monastery has always been to discover men or women of prayer and holiness, rather than learned scholars or committed missionaries.[9]

Curiously, the inaccessibility and invisibility of Barsanuphius and John become the very reasons for their attraction and accessibility. These elders function as alternative sources of authority, independent of and beyond the civic and ecclesiastical leadership of the time. Of course, the relationship between bishops and monks has never been straightforward or smooth in the history of the church's institutional organization.[10] Yet inasmuch as it was also never formally resolved, it has resulted in a creative tension for the life of the church. In some ways, then, there seems to be a progression—or succession—from the authoritative influence of the "holy man" (Peter Brown) through the formative instruction of the "mediator and master" (Philip Rousseau) to the charismatic inspiration of the "old men" in

---

[9]On spiritual direction in Gaza and Palestine, see Jennifer Hevelone-Harper, *Disciples of the Desert: Monks, Laity, and Spiritual Authority in Sixth-century Gaza* (Baltimore, MD: Johns Hopkins University Press, 2005). Cf. also Peter Brown, *Authority and the Sacred: Aspects of the Christianization of the Roman World* (Cambridge, UK: Cambridge University Press, 1995); John Chryssavgis, *Soul Mending: The Art of Spiritual Direction* (Brookline, MA: Holy Cross Press, 2000); and Lorenzo Perrone, *La Necessità del Consiglio: Studi sul Monachesimo di Gaza* (Abbazia del Praglia: Edizioni Scritti Monastici, 2021).

[10]See Peter Brown, *Power and Persuasion in Late Antiquity: Toward a Christian Empire* (Madison, WI: University of Wisconsin Press, 1992); Philip Rousseau, "Ascetics as Mediators and as Teachers," in *The Cult of Saints in Late Antiquity*, 45–59; and George Demacopoulos, *Five Models of Spiritual Direction in the Early Church* (Notre Dame, IN: University of Notre Dame Press, 2007).

Gaza, where we discover an alternative focus of power and almost para-ecclesiastical form of leadership, orchestrating ecclesiastical and civil affairs[11] from the silence and solitude of their cells (*Letters* 788–839).

While themselves likely not ordained, the two elders are nonetheless involved in matters of ordination (*Letter* 807). Barsanuphius even grants John the specific charge and task of directing bishops (*Letters* 788–9). In fact, it is not uncommon for bishops to submit to the counsel of the Old Men (*Letters* 794–801)—though not habitually, and not always enthusiastically. At the same time, the elders normally refrain from publicly challenging church hierarchy (*Letter* 792)—though not always, and not always eagerly. In general, Barsanuphius and John intervene less directly in episcopal matters in Gaza than their contemporary Sabas, whose monks assume a militant stance against heresy in Jerusalem.[12] Barsanuphius and John prefer to encourage lower clergy and laity to exhaust the institutional process and system in order to resolve problems and, above all, to trust in the sovereignty of God. Their spiritual authority serves not to eliminate human authority but to illuminate divine authority. Their role was not to impinge on established institutional structures but to inspire individual institutional leaders. This is why they are equally as comfortable ordering secular leaders to stand up for the rights of the poor (*Letters* 823–30) as they are rebuking church leaders for not standing up to secular governors (*Letters* 831–3).

As noted, the "other old man" bears the additional title of "prophet," a reflection and recognition of his exceptional spiritual discernment (*Letters* 785–9). In a legend that is more hagiographical than historical, Abba John even delays his death (*Letter* 224) at the request of Abbot Aelianos, who succeeded Seridos as head of the community. John remains alive for an additional two weeks in order to respond to questions by Aelianos about the administration and organization of the monastery.

The "other old man" also has the gifts of foresight (*Letter* 777) and tears (*Letter* 565), of discernment (*Letter* 805) and miracles

---

[11]See Bitton-Ashkelony and Kofsky, *The Monastic School of Gaza* (Leiden-Boston: Brill, 2006), 85–8.
[12]See E. Schwartz, ed., *Cyril of Scythopolis, Life of Sabas* (Leipzig: J.C. Hinrichs Verlag, 1939), 125.

(*Letter* 781). Nonetheless, sensational miracles and exceptional charismas are neither the most striking nor the most appealing feature of these elders. While Peter Brown tends to emphasize the more "extraordinary" characteristics of the Old Men,[13] Barsanuphius and John are in fact far less "spectacular"—one might even say "ordinary." They defy what is sometimes criticized by contemporary scholarship as the idealized or homogenized hagiographical image of the late antique holy man. Thus, whereas contemporary lives of the saints are full of miracles, spectacular healing stories are almost entirely absent from the correspondence of the two elders of Gaza.

There is, for example, little on fear of the supernatural or reliance on the superstitious; the advice is realistic and down to earth. Often it is expressed in brief and somewhat riddling phrases. "Forget yourself and know yourself," they say (*Letter* 112); "Let us weep in order that we may laugh" (*Letter* 196); "Die completely, that you may live completely" (*Letter* 37). For the two elders, it is up to the recipient to work out the riddle and apply it to himself.

There is also little on theoretical mysticism or speculative theology; the emphasis is on ascetic moderation. The objective is reaching inward; the inner is far more important than the outer; what goes on inside is what can influence and change what goes on outside (see *Letter* 77). "Labor" and "violence" (*Letters* 239 and 340), along with "pain" (*Letters* 256 and 267) and "suffering" (*Letter* 703), are inseparable from "bearing the cross" (*Letters* 45, 191, 243, and 519) and "restraining the will" (*Letters* 16, 121, 232, and 243) in imitation of Christ Himself (*Letters* 20, 106, 150, 191, and 239).

Barsanuphius and John can therefore write without evasion or compromise, but at that the same time with profound compassion. They are humane and generous. Avoiding extremes, they caution against excessive asceticism and austerity in eating and fasting, sleep and vigilance (*Letters* 146 and 570); instead, they insist, "Always keep the middle way" (*Letter* 314). While conscious of the authority that they have received from God, they display a sensitive respect and responsibility for the freedom of others: "Do not force

---

[13]See Peter Brown, *The Body and Society: Men, Women, and Sexual Renunciation in Early Christianity* (New York: Columbia University Press, 1988), 213–40.

the will," they affirm in characteristic terms, "but only sow in hope" (*Letter* 35). They do not offer elaborate rules, but echo the paradigm of Paul (Rm 6:14): "Do not look for commands. I do not want you to be under the law but under grace" (*Letter* 23). "It is always beneficial to practice freedom," they state (*Letter* 378); "the two go together: the free will of the human being and the power of God" (*Letter* 763).

Yet this respect and responsibility for the freedom of others did not signify that the two Old Men were in any way distant or indifferent. On the contrary, one of their favorite Scriptural texts is Galatians 6:2: "Bear one another's burdens." They regard the spiritual father or mother not as a legislator, but *par excellence* as a burden bearer, a companion, and a fellow-sufferer. "Hold my hand and walk," they write (*Letter* 31); "I have spread out my wings over you and bear your burdens" (*Letter* 239). Again and again, in moving terms, they emphasize how closely they feel involved in the joys and sorrows of their disciples: "The Lord has bound your soul to mine," they affirm (*Letter* 164). "There is not a blink of the eye or a moment that I do not have you in my mind and in my prayer" (*Letter* 113). "I will never abandon you, even in the age to come" (*Letter* 239).

At the same time, however, the two elders refuse to provide wisdom on request, nor do they attempt to solve all problems presented before them. Their purpose is to inspire rather than impress; their aim is to exhort rather than excite. Most of the time, their counsel is quite practical; they simply say: "Do what you can; do whatever comes naturally" (*Letter* 302). And their counsel is quite balanced: "Not wounding one's neighbor, that is the way of Christ" (*Letter* 26). Their counsel is never formalized or merely conventional, but consistently situational and full of compassion. They understand the weakness and vulnerability of others, their secret pain and insecurity, yet they are also acutely conscious of the greatness of human nature, of its boundless possibilities. They seek to encourage and enable their spiritual directees by gently guiding them on the way that they have already envisioned or embarked, rather than discouraging them by denouncing their actions or distracting them from their path: "Simply do your best, and God will come to your assistance in everything" (*Letter* 343)

The Age of the Old Men and their *Letters*

As far as dating the text itself, the correspondence contains certain historical details that prove helpful. *Letters* 568–9 allude to a plague that spread through the Roman Empire between 542 and 543. *Letters* 600–7 deal with the controversy over Origenism, the first indications of which we know reach the monks of Palestine as early as 514 and the final resolution of which takes place in 553 at the Fifth Ecumenical Council in Constantinople. And *Letter* 821 refers to a decree, issued by Emperor Justinian in 528–9 regarding pagans and schismatics. Therefore, with known dates spanning 514 to 543, the timeline within which the correspondence was most likely transmitted is the early part of the sixth century.

There is an interesting legend that comes down to us in the writings of Evagrius Scholasticus about the death of Barsanuphius. In his *Historia Ecclesiastica*, Evagrius dedicates an entire chapter to Barsanuphius, noting that at the time of his own writing—that is to say around 593, some fifty years or so after Barsanuphius' unknown date of death—the "great old man" is still believed to be alive. Although no one has actually seen the Old Man or even brought him food in a very long time, popular opinion nonetheless maintains that he has not died. When the patriarch of Jerusalem—presumably Peter of Jerusalem (524–52), whom *Letters* 813–30 mention—orders that the door of the cell be pried open, a consuming fire is said to flash out of the cell, causing everyone present to flee.[14] It was a subtle reminder of the elder's undiminished influence, long after he was actually deceased. Barsanuphius never really died; he just further retired from the world, retreating to a place of utter seclusion and ultimate silence. He simply no longer dictated letters; or, as Bitton-Ashkelony and Kofsky put it: "[H]e simply faded away"![15]

---

[14]See Evagrius, *Historia Ecclesiastica* IV, 33 in PG87, ii.2764.

[15]Bitton-Ashkelony and Kofsky, *The Monastic School of Gaza*, 105. On the monastery of Seridos in Gaza, see Yizhar Hirschfeld, "The Monasteries of Gaza: An Archaeological Review," in *Christian Gaza in Late Antiquity*, ed. B. Bitton-Ashkelony and A. Kofsky (Leiden-Boston: Brill, 2004), 61–88 [at 76–7]. More recent excavations have been conducted by the École Biblique on the site of a monastery in the same area. See E. René-Hassoune Ayman, "Le monastère de St-Hilarion à Umm-el-`Amr. Bande de Gaza," *Comptes rendus de l'Académie des Inscriptions et Belles-Lettres* (2004), 359–82. Also https://journals.openedition.org/syria/474?lang=fr. Accessed September 15, 2021.

We hear very little about Barsanuhpius and John in later years, just as the testimony about the monastery of Seridos in subsequent years is scant. We know, for example, that the monastery existed in the seventh century. Indeed, there is little evidence of their influence anywhere outside Gaza and Palestine during their lifetime. A late twelfth-century text, *Vita Barsanuphii*, was composed by a priest in Oria, near Brindisi in southern Italy; extracts of this biography appear in the *Acta Sanctorum*.[16] The *Vita* contains certain hagiographical details, including the translation of the relics of Barsanuphius to southern Italy in the ninth century. Local tradition claims that the relics are still preserved in the cathedral of Oria, where to this day two modern statues—one of them hovering over the city as a patron and protector—and a mural attest to the popularity of the saint, whose name is also popular as a Christian name in the region. Barsanuphius is remembered on April 11 in the West and on February 6 in the East. The Eastern Church also commemorates Abbot Seridos on August 13, the same day devoted to Dorotheus of Gaza.

Other Key Personalities
John of Beersheba and Abbot Seridos

The opening letters of the correspondence are questions directed to Barsanuphius by John of Beersheba, a devout monk hailing from the city of Beersheba in the nearby Negev desert. Were it not for *Letter* 3 by the "other old man" to John of Beersheba, as well as a reference in *Letter* 9 where Barsanuphius forwards greetings from himself, Seridos, and "our brother John," it would be very tempting and unassuming to identify John the Prophet with John of Beersheba. Another token of evidence against such a theory is found in *Letter* 13, which indicates that Seridos is acquainted with "three [distinct] individuals," namely, Barsanuphius, John the Prophet, and John of Beersheba.

Scholars have long held that John of Beersheba was a distinguished ascetic, living in a local monastery—perhaps serving

---

[16]See Chitty, *The Desert a City*, 140, and the introduction to the French edition in *SC* 426 (Paris: Les Editions du Cerf, 1997), 31–2.

as its abbot—or else as a hermit in a nearby cell. It is generally assumed that John was well known in Beersheba as an anchorite, later choosing to enter the community of Seridos under the spiritual guidance of Barsanuphius, perhaps attracted there by the fluidity and flexibility of the brotherhood overseen by Seridos. Barsanuphius would sometimes communicate individually—albeit still through Seridos—with a number of monks in the monastery (*Letters* 250 and 503).

That John was not originally a member of the Seridos community is apparent from the opening question of our correspondence. From the outset of their epistolary relationship, Barsanuphius speaks to John with a tone of familiarity that hardly reflects a long-distance exchange. It may be that John chose the Seridos community at a mature age out of respect for and devotion to the "great old man." It was here that he gradually proved to be a gifted monk of discernment and discipline—another confirmation that the free spirit of the Barsanuphian network did not stifle individual growth, but instead encouraged spiritual formation at a personal rhythm and rate. It was inevitable that—upon attaining a certain degree of spiritual maturity—a charismatic monk like John would steadily exercise considerable authority and leadership within the community.

However, John's charismatic presence in the monastery rapidly becomes a cause of tension with the abbot (*Letters* 17, 24, and 49). Seridos was probably appointed by Barsanuphius to lead the community on the basis of his administrative skills rather than any spiritual qualities. The spiritual authority enjoyed by Seridos derived predominantly from his relationship with the "great old man," whom all of the brothers in the community and in the vicinity universally revered.

So the correspondence describes the period through which John adopts a life of stillness beside Barsanuphius, moving from the monastery of Seridos to a cell beside the "great old man." The transition reflects the familiar pattern of Palestinian monasticism, a movement *within* the community to a higher level of solitude and seclusion. To begin with, Barsanuphius permits John of Beersheba to assume a semi-eremitic life within the confines of the monastery (*Letter* 32). With time, however, he permits him to adopt a life of complete silence and stillness (*Letter* 36), even delegating the responsibility of directing others (*Letters* 37–43). In the correspondence, Barsanuphius waits a period of time before granting this authority to John (*Letter* 51), subsequently advising him to meditate on the letters he has received (*Letters* 32, 36, and 49) during his early period as a member of the community of Seridos.

It appears that the loose style of paternal direction promoted by Barsanuphius in his letters and inside the nearby community inevitably fostered tensions, albeit all too human, occasionally arising from ambition or arrogance. Some letters therefore deal with conflicts arising between elders and their disciples (*Letter* 503). Two poignant and painful instances of such difficulties affect the entire community. In the first case, an elder mistreats a monk; as a result, the younger monk decides to leave the monastery. When approached on two separate occasions about whether the elder is at fault or whether the other brothers should find the monk and convince him to return, Barsanuphius displays an unwillingness to take sides; he neither chooses to intervene nor again does he permit others to interfere (*Letters* 489–91). Instead, he seems to admit and even approve a degree of autonomy in the relationship between the elder and the monk. He believes that when both individuals resolve their pride, the relationship will also be reconciled.

On another occasion (*Letter* 504), Abba John is sufficiently open-minded and progressive to recommend to one of the monks, asking whether he would be permitted to consult an elder other than his own, that he can do so even without informing his own elder. John assures the young monk that, over time, this would only lead him to discover the distinct gift of his relationship with his own spiritual director. I will return to this instance later, in Chapter 4 on spiritual direction.

What is important to highlight here is that, in all that he says and does, Barsanuphius consistently portrays a distinct form of leadership.[17] Presented here for posterity, indeed in such a matter-of-

---

[17]While apparently unique in their balance between spiritual and administrative authority, as well as in their breadth of mutual and collaborative authority, Barsanuphius and John may reflect a practice not unfamiliar to monasticism in the region. See the *Lives* of John and Cyriacus by Cyril of Scythopolis, *Lives. Kyrillos Von Skythopolis*, ed. E. Schwartz, TU 49/2 (Leipzig: J. C. Hinrichs Verlag, 1939). See A.McCray, "Between the Judean Desert and Gaza: Asceticism and the Monastic Communities of Palestine in the Sixth Century," *LSU Doctoral Dissertations* 5214 (2020), https://digitalcommons.lsu.edu/gradschool_dissertations/5214. Accessed September 15, 2021.

fact way, are the practical implications of an open-ended structure of spiritual authority and spiritual direction. This flexible formation is best described as *an open process* rather than *a closed system* because it points to spiritual direction as a tentative and delicate exercise, always very much "a work in progress." It is a structure that heavily relies on mutual honesty and spiritual transparency. Barsanuphius constantly and persistently encourages the freedom of the brothers. If he chastises a deacon rebelling against his abbot (*Letter* 239), this only indicates the space and license that all of the brothers should enjoy in the community. If on another occasion he criticizes a brother prematurely seeking the external conditions of solitude (*Letter* 233), it is because this opportunity was already partially available to all the monks within the community.

This open process or overt structure does not, however, imply that master and disciple are on equal footing. There are times when Barsanuphius and John strictly recommend following the counsel of only one spiritual elder (*Letter* 358). And those who approach Barsanuphius and John certainly consider them to represent exceptional models of authority and authenticity. The elders themselves address their disciples with clarity, attending to every detail of the disciples' written questions and unspoken intentions. Yet their openness is grounded in their ability to discern the value and valor of the spiritual struggle, which they perceived not so much as a way of achieving particular merits but of discerning the presence of God in the tentative relationship between two mortals.

It was inevitable, then, that such an open-ended dynamic would challenge the individual monks of the community, while at the same time challenging the very process of spiritual authority. The relationship between the Seridos and Barsanuphius, as well as between Dorotheus and John, is undoubtedly far more problematic than the partnership between Barsanuphius and John. Even when some of the brothers express reservation, envy, and hostility (*Letters* 226, 125, 231, and 235–40), Barsanuphius would insist that the abbot is an integral part of a unique triangle or spiritual triumvirate (*Letters* 132–7). In the unique community at Thawatha, the inherent structure or reciprocal chain depends on personal contact and communication on three levels: the monks of the community → Abbot Seridos (and, to a degree, Dorotheus) → as well as Barsanuphius and John. Seridos is a man committed to obedience and a man endowed with authority, at once a disciple and an abbot. These roles are not in danger of conflict, so long as the two supportive poles of the triarchic structure are maintained (*Letter* 570).

Dorotheus of Gaza

John the Prophet, the "other old man," is not the only example of a gifted monk progressively promoted within the community. Dorotheus of Gaza presents the very same dynamics and tensions as John of Beersheba (*Letter* 248 and 286–8), except that the younger Dorotheus is in the long term capable of forging a more fruitful relationship with his abbot, Seridos. Indeed, Dorotheus is intimately and idiosyncratically associated with all three of the key figures in the community at Thawatha: Barsanuphius, John, and Seridos.

An aristocrat, both intelligent and well-educated, trained as a lawyer but engaged by Barsanuphius as the director of the monastery infirmary, Dorotheus is characterized by an unusual sensitivity in relation to his brothers. It comes as no surprise, then, that Abbot Seridos harnesses Dorotheus's secular affluence and spiritual influence to his advantage in the administration of the monastery. For instance, with the financial assistance of Dorotheus' brother, Seridos establishes an infirmary inside the community and places Dorotheus—who is experienced in medical training and nursing skills—in charge of attending to the health of the brothers. From this position of responsibility and authority, Dorotheus regularly finds himself in direct consultation with the abbot. Subsequently, Seridos appoints Dorotheus to one of the most noble and enviable services within the monastery, namely the personal care of the "other old man," John the Prophet.

Much like the connection that John of Beersheba enjoyed with Barsanuphius, Dorotheus had prior communication with the two Old Men (*Letters* 252–4). However, as a result of his prosperous upbringing in society as well as his privileged position in the monastery, Dorotheus frequently becomes the target of envy and hatred on the part of his brothers (*Letters* 286 and 313). So intense is the emotional pressure that Dorotheus considers abandoning his duties and leaving the monastery. Only the unfailing support of the two elders eventually sustains him during this difficult period (*Letters* 259 and 314). As in the case of John of Beersheba,

Dorotheus' own relationship with Abbot Seridos is occasionally strained (*Letter* 288). Nevertheless, Seridos is able to recognize the young monk's gifts, elevating him to higher levels of responsibility while entrusting other monks to his care. Perhaps the relationship between Seridos and Dorotheus is delicately balanced by the common task of both in serving as scribes to the Old Men and in transmitting their directives to the rest of the community. They are the only ones permitted to meet with or speak directly to Barsanuphius and John. Dorotheus serves for nine years in this capacity, until the deaths of Seridos and John (*c*. 543). Based on the fact that Dorotheus frequently recalls John's words by memory, it may be argued that—unlike Seridos who merely serves as a scribe for dictation, Dorotheus actually becomes a broker of relationships.[18] Still, there is no reason to deny the equivalence in the functions of Dorotheus and Seridos. After all, Seridos also records a great deal from memory, even expressing apprehension about whether he will remember the elder's words with accuracy (*Letter* 2).

After the death of the two Old Men, Dorotheus leaves the monastery—possibly to enjoy the quiet of solitude that he witnessed in his renowned elders or else to found a new community near Gaza based on the model of monasticism that he had experienced at Thawatha. The likelihood of the second option is supported by the sudden, almost total absence of Seridos's community in subsequent historical sources as well as by the full title of Dorotheus's works: "Discourses from our holy father Dorotheus to his disciples when he withdrew from that of Abba Seridos and, with [the grace of] God, founded his own monastery, after the death of Abba John the Prophet and the complete silence of Barsanuphius."[19] Whether addressing his disciples in solitude or in community, Dorotheus and his writings represent the spiritual succession and historical sequel of the community in Thawatha and the correspondence of Barsanuphius and John.

Little or nothing is known with any degree of certainty about Dorotheus's life after his departure from the community of Seridos. Outside of his spiritual writings, no other remainder or reminder

---

[18]Cf. F. Neyt, *Les lettres à Dorothée dans la correspondance de Barsanuphe et de Jean de Gaza*, Doctoral Dissertation, University of Louvain (1969), xlvii.
[19]See Regnault and de Préville, ed. *Dorothée de Gaza*, 73 [English translation].

survives: no physical or material relic, no knowledge or evidence of a grave, and almost no information or recollection about the monastic community that he founded. So could Dorotheus be anonymously and silently present in the collection and preservation of the letters of Barsanuphius and John? Is it coincidental that his personal letters to the two old men are scattered throughout the correspondence, sometimes preserved without any attribution?

There is surely validity to the hypothesis that Dorotheus is the compiler of the correspondence. Seridos could not possibly be just an editor, since many letters deal with events surrounding his own death. Moreover, not only is Dorotheus the most famous disciple of the two Old Men, but he is also the only well-known disciple to survive the elders. Dorotheus would surely have had access to the manuscripts of the letters, but he would also have recalled the circumstances surrounding the questions in order to fill any apparent gaps.[20] Moreover, the absence of Dorotheus's name in some of the earlier manuscripts—coupled with Dorotheus' motivation to exclude reference to his own name out of humility for the sake of posterity—further suggest the likelihood of this hypothesis.[21]

Several letters (*Letters* 570–99) present us with information about the lives of John, Seridos, and Aelianos—the successor to Seridos as abbot of the monastery. At some point between 543 and 544, the monastery undergoes a number of significant changes: Abbot Seridos dies and the "other old man," John, follows suit; Barsanuphius himself enters a life of complete seclusion, thereafter devoting his life to total silence in a sealed cell. This is the point at which Dorotheus leaves the community.

---

[20]See Dorotheus, *Instruction 1*, *Sources Chrétiennes* 92, 288 (PG88.1697). See also John Moschus, *Spiritual Meadow*, ch. 166, PG87.3033. It has also been suggested that, as Barsanuphius' closest friend, John of Beersheba may be the editor of the correspondence. However, while John of Beersheba is the recipient of around fifty letters (all of them from Barsanuphius), Dorotheus is the recipient of almost 100 letters (addressed to him by both of the elders). It would, therefore, be reasonable to conclude that, more than anyone else, Dorotheus was well acquainted with the two elders and the letters addressed to their numerous visitors. See Hevelone-Harper, *Letters*, 37.

[21]Ibid., 91–7.

Aelianos: The New Abbot

When Seridos and—just two weeks later (*Letter* 599)—John die (*c.* 543), the delicate structure of authority and spiritual direction in the community appears to collapse. The sense of continuity and stability provided by Barsanuphius, John, and Seridos is replaced by a sense of vulnerability and fragility. A series of twenty-nine letters (571–99) describes the ensuing dramatic adjustments in the monastery as administrative authority changes hands. For several decades prior to this, Barsanuphius and John had directed the community at Thawatha. Seridos left behind a will that included a list of monks who might conceivably replace him. A layman (*Letter* 574) by the name of Aelianos is finally appointed, after first being tonsured monk, ordained priest, and installed as abbot (*Letter* 575). Aelianos is a wealthy man (*Letter* 571), himself also previously in correspondence with the two Old Men about the possibility of retiring to the monastery in the future.

Perhaps Aelianos was a good candidate because, as an outsider, he was not enmeshed in the intense triangle of spiritual relations that had shaped and sustained the community's leadership up to that point. We know that all other candidates proposed by the brotherhood declined out of modesty (*Letter* 574), though possibly also out of trepidation for the internal rivalries that such a role innately fostered. But Aelianos faced the added burden of leading a community now bereft of both Seridos the Abbot and John the Prophet. He was moreover deprived of the inspired guidance of Barsanuphius, who decided to withdraw into complete seclusion soon after Seridos's death.

Above all, however, the common denominator—the fatherly figure of Barsanuphius, who for an entire generation had united everyone inside and around the community—had suddenly disappeared. The new abbot would strive to maintain the same policy established by Seridos and John. But now there was a glaring vacuum. The spiritual outlet and protection that Seridos enjoyed—able at any time to defer to another, a higher authority that would resolve difficult decisions and absorb divisive tensions—were no longer at his disposal. Aelianos was not simply elected abbot; he succeeded and inherited an entire network of authority. Now, one person alone was obliged to exercise an authority and responsibility previously shared on all levels by three people. Perhaps this was the invisible, albeit inherent weakness of the exceptional system at Thawatha.

Brief note should be made here of the overall influence of John the Prophet on Barsanuphius himself as well as on the entire community. It may well be that John is actually Barsanuphius' alter ego.[22] There is a possibility that the correspondence conceals John's role; instead it seeks to emphasize the supremacy of Barsanuphius and the secondary, derivative, significance of John. Nonetheless, the sudden departure of Barsanuphius—like the utter disappearance of Seridos's community from the sources—suggests the prospect of John possessing a more central and influential role, both with regard to the emergence of Barsanuphius in particular as well as to the reputation of the community in general. This deference of John to Barsanuphius parallels that of John the Baptist to Jesus Christ (Mt 3:11)—an intimate form of humility that also reflects the relationship between Timothy and Paul.

Certainly the distinctive characteristics of Barsanuphius imply a shyer man, who may have been encouraged to surface from his seclusion and silence by a more outgoing John, who early recognized in him a man of profound discernment and exceptional charisma. It is the more extroverted personality of John that handles communications with the hierarchical and institutional world of the time. After the death of Seridos, Barsanuphius continues to communicate with letters, whether through Aelianos or some other monk. Upon the demise of John, however, Barsanuphius understandably returns to a life of seclusion and silence, one with which he would have been more accustomed and which he presumably preferred prior to John's arrival at Thawatha.

Either way, these end-of-life developments affirm that Barsanuphius and John brought out the best in each other (as well as in others), resulting in a truly remarkable force—two elders, pursuing the extraordinary in the very ordinary and drawing life-changing associations between monastic seclusion and social integration.

---

[22]L. Regnault, *Maîtres spirituels au désert de Gaza: Barsanuphe, Jean et Dorothée* (Sable-sur-Sarthe: Abbaye de Solesmes, 1967), 19.

3

Fundamental Concepts and Principles

Looking through a Window Frame

What did the world look like inside the community at Thawatha? Or, more precisely, how do the two elders—and their neighboring community—view the outside world in the nearby city of Gaza, the Holy Land in the region surrounds them, and the universe around the broader Mediterranean?

Before exploring some of the more definitive and foundational teachings of Barsanuphius and John, it may be helpful to conduct a panoramic survey of the historical pedigree, theological worldview, and spiritual cornerstone that inspires and supports their mindset and outlook.

Scripture and Sacraments

The Word of Life

The two elders cite profusely from the Hebrew and Christian Scriptures; indeed, as with the writers of the New Testament, Barsanuphius and John have access to the translation of the Seventy.

The Bible is their principal source and basis. In fact, they quote from every single book of Scripture, including many of the deutero-canonical texts, while spontaneously composing devotional prayers based entirely on passages from the Old and New Testaments. In this respect, their letters are like breathing concordances of written Scripture. For them, the Gospel is the sacred and quintessential vehicle for transmitting the monastic message.

Firmly rooted in the classical tradition of the Church Fathers, particularly in the Alexandrian emphasis on the primacy of the divine Word, Barsanuphius likes to adapt and incorporate Scripture—both allegorically and spiritually—as he responds to the particular needs of each individual. For him, as indeed for the earlier monks in Scetis, the Word of God is always the word of life. Unlike theological abstraction, which can be a source of self-indulgence, the use of Scripture is considered a wellspring of self-subsistence. It is not that contemplation in itself is objectionable or unreliable; but scripture is always preferable to speculation, while silence is clearly preferable to both scripture and speculation (*Letter* 547).

The list of scriptural passages cited, either directly or indirectly, in this sixth-century document is indeed impressive and inspiring. The Book of Psalms has of course always been a favorite among monastics through the ages, and the "great old man" has some distinctive preferences. Moreover, he frequently quotes from the Wisdom literature: especially from Job, Proverbs, and Sirach; he also refers, though less frequently, to the Song of Songs and the Wisdom of Solomon. Of the prophetic writers, Isaiah is cited most extensively, followed by Jeremiah and Ezekiel.

The New Testament is overall afforded a place of priority. Barsanuphius cites all four of the Gospels, particularly delighting in the Sermon on the Mount. His predilection with Paul includes the Letter to the Romans and the Letters to the Corinthians; above all, however, he borrows heavily from the Letter to the Hebrews. Another standard favorite in monastic circles is the Letter of James, and Barsanuphius is no exception here. Finally, the general tone pervading the correspondence is that of the heavenly kingdom, as portrayed in the Book of Revelation.

So Barsanuphius knows the Scriptures very well. The Word of God is what provides him with nourishment. He preaches—with the authority of a spiritual master—through both experience and explication. For the Gaza elders, the Word of God informs the mind and transforms the heart. Their purpose is to provide moral commentary and personal application. Some letters resemble complete treatises with protracted strings—or sequences—of scriptural passages reminiscent of Origen of Alexandria.

On the whole, their appreciation of the Bible is strikingly refreshing. One letter (*Letter* 10) describes Christ as light, shelter, way, power, crown, speed, master, and savior. *Letter* 31 recalls the great biblical figures: Joseph (for chastity), Moses (for meekness), Noah (for poverty), Abraham (for humility), Job (for endurance), Joshua (for courage), David (for submission of passions), Solomon (for wisdom), Jonas (for risking all), Daniel (for discernment), and so on. This is how Barsanuphius and John may have acquired and assimilated the scriptures from Anthony and the Egyptian elders.[1]

Perhaps more importantly, there is no clear line of demarcation between the *Word of God in scripture*, the *interpretive word of a spiritual guide*, and the distinctive *application of this word by the disciple*. Barsanuphius appropriates and interiorizes the Bible; this is what allows him to share it with others. It is precisely the authoritative role of the biblical word that presents Barsanuphius with a license to affirm the validity of his own words while at the same time admitting the deficiency of his own role:

> Ruminate on my letters, and you will be saved. In them, you have the Old and the New Testaments, if only you can understand. Indeed, if you understand them, you will not need any other book. (*Letter* 49)

> I have written more than enough to you. These words are sufficient to lead a person from the beginner's stage to perfection. Study and remember them so that you do not forget them. For they contain an entire library. (*Letter* 32)

---

[1] Cf. Athanasius, *Life of Antony*; and *Apophthegmata Patrum*, ed. J. Cl. Guy, in *Sources Chrétiennes* 387 (Paris: Les Editions du Cerf, 1993), chap. 1, no. 23, 114–15.

The disciple should strive to remember the elder's words about scripture (*Letters* 20, 32, and 49):

> Response from the same Great Old Man to the same person, advising him continually to remember the things he wrote for his benefit and for the support of his heart. Solomon said about his parents: "They taught me and told me, let our word be established in your heart" (Prv 4:4). So, then, I also say the same to you, brother. Let my words be firmly established in your heart. And meditate continually on everything I have written to you; just as God said through the mouth of Moses: "Bind them on your right hand, and they shall remain steadily before your eyes at all times; and study them when you are asleep and awake, when you travel and sit at home" (Dt 6:7–8). Demonstrate the same progress in the perfection of your works, and my God will be with you to the ages. (*Letter* 11)

FIGURE 2 *Icon of Sts Barsanuphius and John.*

This illustrates how, when Barsanuphius dictates to—and through—Abbot Seridos, a veritable ritual unfolds. Moreover, throughout this process, the distinction becomes somewhat blurred between the inspiration of the living book and the inspiration of a living elder. After all, it is one and the same Spirit that breathes in both. This is what accounts for Barsanuphius' extraordinary humility, on the one hand, since he is aware of his limitations; and, on the other hand, it explains the striking boldness that calmly asserts his authority. "You have sufficient divine food [in the letters] from me to last you for a long time (*Letter* 17)." "Whoever drinks of the water" which I send through my letters, "will never thirst to the age" (Jn 4:14) (*Letter* 43).

In his letters, Barsanuphius—and it is normally the "great old man" who responds to more delicate matters by offering elaborate commentaries on Scripture—searches for deeper spiritual meaning, discerning the face of Christ in the Bible. For him, after all, it all makes sense "today," "now" (*Letter* 167). This is why "the Son of God became human for you" (*Letter* 199). His typology is fundamentally Christocentric, centering primarily on the Cross (see *Letters* 45–8, 62, 70, 106, 124–6, and 182). The Crucifixion leads Barsanuphius to an intense sensitivity and compassion for human frailty and mortality as well as to an acute sense of hope and anticipation for the heavenly kingdom: "Who does not know that we are in the final hour?" (*Letter* 36) While clearly distinguished from and comparatively critical of Origenism as an exegetical methodology,[2] the interpretive style of Barsanuphius is indebted to his Alexandrian predecessor with regard to this emphasis on the kingdom, as well as to the Letter to the Hebrews. After all, as I discuss below in Chapter 4 where I explore his teaching on spiritual direction, the "great old man" feels personally obligated to and responsible for his disciples, for whom he will also be accountable on that final day of judgment: "Here am I and the children whom God has given me (Is 8:18; Heb 2:13)" (*Letter* 607).

---

[2]See *Letters* 600–7. *Letter* 604 introduces a refreshing way of addressing theological *heresy*, linking its transmission to the critical role of spiritual lineage and inferring that it is the result of an interruption in the succession of spiritual leadership. The softer approach to Origen in the correspondence reflects its composition before the condemnation of Origenism in 543 and 553.

Life-giving Mysteries

Many monastic texts are curiously silent about the sacramental life of the early hermits and communities. For instance, in his *Life of Antony*, Athanasius—fourth-century Archbishop of Alexandria and clearly concerned about the liturgical life of his district—provides no explicit testimonial as to whether "the father of the monasticism" ever received holy communion during his countless years in what he called his "outer" and "inner" deserts. His contemporary Evagrius of Pontus—a monk commonly considered "the theoretician of monasticism"—makes little if any reference to the sacraments in his influential treatises. And in his undisputable masterpiece of monastic literature, *The Ladder of Divine Ascent*, John Climacus—seventh-century hermit and abbot of the renowned monastery on Mt. Sinai—mentions the sacrament of communion only in his chapter on insensitivity and the sacrament of baptism only in his chapter devoted to tears.[3]

Such a reticence about the sacraments obviously neither constitutes an established rule nor implies that these authors in any way undermine their significance or centrality for the ascetic life. Indeed, even as prominent a pope of Rome as Gregory the Great does not refer at all to the Eucharist in his famous *Moralia*. Perhaps these authors take the sacraments for granted, or perhaps they do not consider themselves obliged to spotlight them in their writings.

Whatever the case, there are many significant exceptions to this rule of silence. For instance, in the early fifth century, Mark the Monk emphasizes the sacrament of baptism as the quintessential cornerstone for his entire teaching. And in the sixth century, our own Barsanuphius and John undoubtedly stand out as brilliant rarities and unique advocates of the sacramental life.

Several letters, then, refer to the importance of baptism into the faith of the Nicaean Fathers (*Letters* 58 and 694), to salvation deriving from baptism as deliverance from death to life (*Letters* 62 and 211), and to the baptism of heretics (*Letters* 820–2). A number of letters refer to forgiveness through the prayer (Jas 5:16) and power (Jn 20:23) of the saints, who can bind and loose sins

---

[3]See, for instance, John Climacus, *The Ladder of Divine Ascent*, trans. C. Luibheid and N. Russell (Mahwah, NJ: Paulist Press, 1982), *Steps* 18 and 7, respectively.

through the sacrament of confession (*Letters* 10, 107, 194, 220, 226, 233, 240, 277, 345, 359, 399, 404, 444, and 543), while they cite holy unction as the sacrament of healing and reconciliation (Jas 5:14–15. See *Letter* 211).

Beyond this explicit mention of sacraments, other letters refer to liturgical customs and rituals (*Letters* 4, 241, and 742), liturgical cycles and offices (*Letters* 32, 50, 143, 169, 178, 209, 334, 427–8, 519, 739, 751, and 821), as well as participation in the sacrament of the Eucharist itself (*Letters* 241, 334, 404, and 463–4), which Barsanuphius describes as an "incorruptible sacrifice, offered for the life of the world. The one who truly eats thereof is also sacrificed and not dominated by spiritual corruption" (*Letter* 137b). A monk is to approach communion with fear of God, faith, and love (*Letters* 170, 241, and 244), but also with humility and without vainglory (*Letters* 742 and 821), in order to participate without condemnation (*Letters* 170 and 570b) in the sacraments of the church. Ever conscious of and compassionate toward human frailty and everyday reality, the two elders are careful to explain that, if a monk is unwell or incapacitated, he may even partake of the sacred mysteries in his own cell rather than being obliged to attend a church (*Letter* 212).

Overview and Worldview

Before exploring some of the central principles of the ascetic teaching and spirituality of Barsanuphius and John, it may be helpful to offer two parenthetical though fundamental comments on their understanding of 1) the relationship between ascetic practice and abstract theology, and 2) the distinction between monastic life and secular life. These observations relate to commonplace assumptions and misconceptions about monasticism through the centuries.

First, it is often tempting to separate *ascetic practice from abstract theology*, categorizing the former as the experience of saintly, albeit manifestly less scholarly representatives of the mystical way, and the latter as the expression of more intellectual, albeit not necessarily less spiritual representatives of the contemplative way. Certainly the two Palestinian elders encourage their disciples to imitate the "ways" rather than merely iterating the "words" of the patristic tradition (*Letter* 604). Still, it is hazardous to establish priorities in the spiritual life, exalting seemingly more abstract matters, while denigrating more practical activities. I am not sure that Barsanuphius and John would feel comfortable advancing any distinction between prayer and practice, or between asceticism and theology; Barsanuphius speaks of the wisdom of silence.[4] For the two elders, work is inseparable from prayer, and work is not a distraction from prayer (*Letter* 150).

Moreover, while the letters offer balanced and practical advice about the spiritual life, they nonetheless contain remarkable nuances and theological insights. For instance, *Letters* 600–7 deal with doctrinal questions—especially related to Origen of Alexandria, Evagrius of Pontus, and Didymus the Blind—posed by a monk in the community. As a rule, however, whenever the elders respond to such theological questions, it is primarily in benevolent deference to queries from their disciples.

> God does not demand these things [i.e., questioning doctrinal matters] from us. Rather, he demands sanctification, purification, silence, and humility. Nevertheless, since I do not want to leave your thoughts unanswered, and I have been afflicted in my prayers to God in order that He might assure me in regard to this matter, I am constrained by this dilemma, yet choose instead to endure affliction in myself in order to relieve you of your own affliction ... For you will not be asked about these matters on that day [of judgement], as to why you do not understand them or why you have not learned about them. (*Letter* 604)[5]

At the same time, while in most of their responses, Barsanuphius and John normally describe the toilsome journey of the ascetic

---

[4]See *Letters* 8–9, 22, 119, 163, 213, 247, 311, 565, and 582.
[5]Doctrinal and ecclesiastical issues are also treated in the correspondence: general issues (*Letter* 370), the Trinity (*Letters* 169 and 600), the Council of Nicaea (*Letters* 58 and 701), martyrdom (*Letter* 433), the Canons of the Church (*Letter* 170), the teaching of St. John Chrysostom (*Letter* 464), deification (*Letter* 199), and relationships of bishops *vis-à-vis* heretics (*Letters* 694–702, 733–5, 775, and 792).

struggle, they sometimes define—while at the same time being very careful not to devalue—the mystical goal of the spiritual life and sheer delight of arriving there:

> Having arrived at this point, [the saints] attained to that degree where there is no agitation or distraction, becoming all intellect, all eye, all life, all light, all perfect, all god. They toiled, they were magnified, they were glorified, they shone, they were perfected; they lived, because first they died. Now they rejoice, and so they make others rejoice, too. (*Letter* 207)

The second distinction that sometimes poses a false dilemma is between *the monastic life and the secular life*. Under the umbrella of monastic life, people typically include all the diverse practices of discipline identified with those renouncing the world and assuming the cross, following Christ in total obedience, to the point of death. By the same token, under the classification of secular life, we generally subsume all of the virtues to be acquired and vices to be avoided by every Christian. Once again, the tendency is to imagine that monasticism is somehow exceptional, beyond the ordinary experience and expectation of other Christians. Yet Barsanuphius and John refuse to distinguish between the way of the desert and the way of the world. Most of their correspondence may be addressed to a monastic audience, but a significant portion of it comprises responses to laypersons asking personal questions and receiving practical responses.

It is helpful here to recall the words of Basil of Caesarea, for whom the life of monasticism is none other than "the way of the Gospel."[6] In the spiritual life, there can be no sharp demarcation between monastics and non-monastics; the monastic life is simply the Christian life lived out in a particular way. The external circumstances of the response to our vocation to wholeness and holiness may vary, but the internal path is essentially one and the same. Monks are baptized Christians who have discovered alternative possibilities of imitating Christ; but Christians in the world encounter the same challenges and have the same goals. The

---

[6]Basil, *Letter* 207, 2 PG32.761.

benchmarks and impediments of monastics and lay Christians may be distinct, but they are not different.

In fact, Barsanuphius and John scarcely distinguish between monastics and lay people. In their letters, lay Christians ask about the ascetic life, while questions posed by monastics relate to the spiritual life. Each is called to do whatever one is doing, to be whatever one is supposed to be, to "follow one's particular ways" (*Letter* 840). The only prerequisite for everyone is to "examine one's ways"—variously designated as an injunction to study (μελέτησον), pay attention (πρόσεχε), search (ἐξέτασον), and on two occasions in the same letter (838), grope in the darkness of one's heart (ψηλάφησον).

Barsanuphius makes it perfectly clear that he professes the universality of God and espouses salvation through a God addressed to all and achievable by all. The internal structure of the correspondence provided by the editor suggests the same: it dedicates the first section to hermits (*Letters* 1–223), devotes the next section to monastics in community (*Letters* 224–616), and directs the final section to bishops and laity in cities (*Letters* 617–850). Indeed, the monastery of Seridos seems to be a unique institution combining and adapting—within one and the same brotherhood—the three forms of monastic life originating in early Egypt: the eremitic (adopted by hermits or recluses), the semi-eremitic (observed in sketes or groups of cells), and the cenobitic (found in larger monasteries or communities).[7] Monks could gradually progress from one (the normal starting-point is the community) to another level, always with the blessing of Barsanuphius, while simultaneously remaining in the same setting (*Letters* 36, 121, and 239).

Mindset and Approach

The letters therefore reveal the mindset and outlook of the two Old Men as they advise those seeking understanding and wisdom, irrespective of whether they are monastic or secular Christians. Often they aim to awaken their listeners from despondency or

---

[7] See Bitton-Ashkelony and Kofsky, *The Monastic School of Gaza*, 5 and 225.

lift them from despair. At one point, surprisingly striking because of its conventional and conversational style, the "other old man" remarks: "Awaken the Jesus that lies asleep within" (*Letter* 182). This is a striking example of the very ordinary language of the letters revealing the extraordinary insight of the elders, who are equally capable of penetrating the soul of the specific recipient as well as the heart of the contemporary reader.

In this regard, the elders advise their disciples never to be overwhelmed by, but always to welcome temptations:

> You should give glory to God for demonstrating the truth of Scripture. For it is said: "God is faithful, and he will not let you be tested beyond your strength" (1 Cor 10:13). He allows you to be tested according to your strength; while those who are great, he tests according to their own strength with diverse temptations, and they rejoice in this. For temptation brings us to progress; and wherever there is good, there also temptation occurs. So do not be afraid of temptations, but rejoice that they are leading you to progress. Simply scorn them, and God will assist you and protect you. (*Letter* 496)

The two Old Men offer strength and support. This is what they do, and it is what they enjoin others to do as well:

> What you should do is endure with thanksgiving whatever comes your way and suffer with everyone in the community. In this way, you are fulfilling the command of the Apostle (see 1 Cor 12:26): namely, to grieve with the person who is grieving, in order to comfort and console that person. That is what compassion is; and it is a good thing to suffer with the weak in order to contribute to their healing. Indeed, if a doctor is rewarded for caring for patients, how much more so will you be rewarded when you suffer as much as you can with your neighbor in everything?[8] (*Letter* 315)

---

[8] On healing in Palestinian literature, see Kyle Schenkewitz, *Dorotheos of Gaza and the Discourse of Healing in Gazan Monasticism* (New York: Peter Lang Publishing, 2015).

And the elders are always positive: "Listen, my child, for every passion there is a medicine, and for every sin there is proper repentance" (*Letter* 226). They completely identify with their spiritual children and fully empathize with their suffering:

> If I could, I would fill these letters with tears and send them to you, since you have afflicted yourself; this would have been of greater benefit to you. (*Letter* 229)
>
> I have written to you as if to my own soul. (*Letter* 16)

Ten Spiritual Principles

With such a compassionate and encouraging approach, it is easy to see why people flocked to the cells of Barsanuphius and John. Receiving a response to an enquiry was attended by a full immersion into their profound insight and wisdom: vigilance in temptation, gratitude and joy, humility and love, and above all prayer.

The following ten fundamental points or spiritual principles serve as a window frame displaying the fundamental contours of their worldview. By allowing the elders to speak in their own words, my purpose here is to provide readers with a sense of their openness and freshness, as well as the breadth and depth of their instruction that inspired with numerous and heterogeneous visitors.

1. Constant Vigilance

> Pay attention to yourself with vigilance, that you may set God before you at all times, that the words of the prophet may be fulfilled: "I beheld the Lord ever before me; for he is on my right hand, that I may not be shaken" (Ps 15:8). Stretch out your hands with all your soul to the things that lie before you, and meditate on this continually, that you may hear God's voice saying to you: "Behold, I am sending you my angel, to prepare the way that lies before you" (Mt 11:10). (*Letter* 7)

We are always supposed to "make a new beginning," say the two Old Men.[9] But this beginning is forged in light of the end. The reason for vigilance is the unfading certainty of one's impending death, which should become the focus for one's attentive life.

> Be vigilant, brother; for you are mortal and ephemeral. Do not consent to lose eternal life for a fleeting moment. (*Letter* 256)

> Pay attention to yourself, and expect your impending death. Repeat to yourself the words of the blessed Arsenius: "Arsenius, why did you leave the world?"[10] (ibid.)

2. Unabating Temptation

The struggle against the passions is powerful and persistent, but it is also productive and promising. Barsanuphius will often reply: "The untempted is also untested" (*Letters* 248, 258, and 499). However, the fact that one's struggle to remain focused through constant vigilance is unnatural in a world of distraction is highlighted by the word "force": "For the kingdom of heaven is taken by force" (Mt 11:12).

> Brother, "forcing oneself in all things" and humility brings one to progress. Even the Apostle says this: "We are afflicted in every way, but not crushed" (2 Cor 4:8) ... This is why a person should not hold to one's own will but in everything blame oneself; then that person will find the mercy of God. However, if the devil fools someone into arrogantly presuming one has done well, then everything that has been achieved is lost. Therefore, as you do whatever you do, humbly say: "Lord, forgive me; for I have burdened the Abbot, by casting on him my burden." And the Lord Jesus Christ will save you. (*Letter* 243)

---

[9] This phrase—reflective of a peculiar Egyptian colloquialism—is henceforth established in ascetic terminology. See *Letters* 55, 257, 266, 276, 493, 497, 500, 562, 614, and 788.
[10] Arsenius 40, in *Sayings*.

The ascetic continually struggles against the "eight passions" (*Letter* 44), or "seven nations"[11] (*Letter* 209), in order to purify the "five senses"[12] (*Letters* 208 and 612). This is how to achieve results in the spiritual life. The correspondence constantly emphasizes the importance of harvesting the consequences to one's actions: "You shall know them by their works" (Mt 7:16) or fruits (cf. *Letters* 22, 23, 94, 238, 401, 405, 453, and 455).

3. Persistent Gratitude

The words "give thanks in all circumstances" (1 Thes 5:18) constitute an order. (*Letter* 267)

Let us never lose our thanksgiving. (*Letter* 366)

Question. How is it possible to give thanks to God worthily?
Response. People who are frivolous forgive one another for the slightest thing, and even relieve others of terrible affliction, so that these confess their gratitude and proclaim to all the benefit procured. How much more so, then, should we give thanks, when we receive benefits from God in every way? With what words can we ever sufficiently thank Him, who above all else created us and offered us assistance against our enemies by giving us prudence of heart, health of body, light in the eyes, breath of life and especially a place for repentance and the possibility of receiving his body and blood for the forgiveness of our sins and establishment of our heart? ...

---

[11]The concept of eight thoughts (sometimes condensed to seven passions, especially in the West) derives from Evagrius of Pontus, who probably inherited it from the desert fathers in Egypt and originally from Origen of Alexandria. Evagrius was the first to order these thoughts in monastic theology. See *On the Eight Thoughts*, in *Evagrius of Pontus: The Greek Ascetic Corpus*, trans. Robert E. Sinkewicz (Oxford: Oxford University Press, 2003).

[12]The concept of five spiritual senses is also derived from Evagrius, who in turn again inherited it from Origen of Alexandria. See Karl Rahner, "The Doctrine of the 'Spiritual Senses' in Origen," in *Theological Investigations: Experience of the Spirit*, vol. 16 (New York: Seabury, repr. 1979), 81–103.

> Let us, therefore, thank Him as much as we can, with our mouth and heart. He is so loving-kind toward us that he will count and number us with the copper coins of that widow (Mk 12:42). That is why sinners are obliged to give thanks; because the righteous give more than thanks, even when they are torn up and put to death, according to St. Paul, who says: "Give thanks" (1 Thes 5:18) to God. (*Letter* 404)

We are called to offer thanks to God in all things (*Letters* 2, 6, 29, 45, 191, 201, 351, 384, 574, and 682), including illness (*Letters* 174, 182, 197, 211, and 515). Such gratitude comprises an act of sacrifice, which can even intercede to God for us: "In all things give thanks to God. For thanksgiving intercedes to God for our weakness!" (*Letter* 214)

4. The Mark of Joy

One of the most definitive and delightful legacies of these Palestinian elders is their emphasis on joy. The sense of hopefulness and cheerfulness consistently opens and closes their correspondence (*Letters* 10 and 848), while at least twenty responses convey a sense of balance and equilibrium by stressing the need for light and grace, along with hope and joy, in the spiritual life (*Letters* 220–3 and 569).

This teaching is an assurance by the elders that the light of the kingdom overcomes any fear of the judgment. Moreover, the endless joy of the spiritual life prevails over the temporary pain in life (*Letter* 115). Such joy stems from the conviction that God never abandons us (*Letter* 77). Barsanuphius repeatedly exclaims: "Rejoice in the Lord; rejoice in the Lord; rejoice in the Lord" (*Letter* 10). "Rejoice in the Lord, brother; rejoice in the Lord, beloved; rejoice in the Lord, fellow heir" (*Letter* 87). This threefold repetition is at the heart of his message that true joy comes from above:

> May the God of our Fathers bring you into this joy. For it contains ineffable light, and it is brilliant and sweet. It does not remember earthly nourishment, but reaches out only to what is above, meditating with what is above, where Christ is seated at the right hand of the Father. (*Letter* 98, Athens ms.)

However, despite the divine origin of joy, it is a state to which everyone without exception should aspire: "May you rejoice in the Lord when you have reached the goal, and when you are about to reach it, as well as when you are still awaiting to reach it" (*Letter* 137).

5. Applied Humility

> Question to the Great Old Man: Tell me, father, what does humility mean? ...
> Response by Barsanuphius. Humility means regarding yourself as "earth and ashes" (Gn 18:27) in deeds and not just in words, and saying: "Who am I?" (2 Sm 7:18). "Who counts me as anything?" "I have nothing to do with anyone." (*Letter* 100)
>
> Humility means not reckoning yourself as anything in every situation, cutting off your own will in everything, and calmly enduring whatever occurs from outside. This is true humility, in which there is no room for vainglory. The person who feels humble does not need to seek to speak humbly; it is enough for that person to say: "Forgive me and pray for me." Nor is it necessary for that person to pursue humble matters relating to oneself. For both of these create vainglory and do not allow one to make progress. Nevertheless, when you receive an order and consequently contradict this in practice, then you are certainly led to progress. There are two kinds of such disregard: one derives from within the heart, and the other arises from injuries received from the outside. The second is greater, namely the one that comes from the outside. For the one that comes from the heart takes less labor than the one that comes from people; whereas the latter creates more pain in the heart. Guarding one's own heart is compunction of heart. (*Letter* 278)

Humility is a form of self-emptying that recalls and even resembles death. The process of dying implies learning to prioritize and sympathize. However, in order to learn something new, one needs first to surrender and be emptied. Transformation involves a form of dying, always however in the context of new life.

6. Not Reckoning Oneself as Anything
(τό ἀψήφιστον)

> Be carefree from all things; then, you will have time for God. Die to all people; for this is true exile. Moreover, retain *the virtue of not reckoning yourself as anything*; in this way, you will find your thought to be undisturbed. And do not consider yourself as having achieved done anything good; thus, your reward will be kept whole. (*Letter* 259)

> You should keep your tongue from idle talk, your stomach from pleasure, refrain from irritating your neighbor, remain modest, do not reckon yourself as anything, love everyone, and always have God in your intellect, always remembering the time when you will appear before God's countenance. Keep these things, and your soil will yield a hundredfold (Mt 4:8) in terms of fruits for God. (*Letter* 271)

Barsanuphius is specifically asked to explain this complex notion, which is so central to his teaching.

> Question to the Great Old Man: Father, what does it mean not to reckon oneself as anything?[13]
> Response. Brother, not reckoning oneself as anything means not equating oneself with anyone and not saying anything with regard to any good deed that you may have achieved. (*Letter* 227)

He is of course hardly innovating here; in fact, he attributes the concept to the desert fathers of Egypt:

> We are called to strive for these things, for which our Fathers also strove in the past, especially those around Abba Poemen and the others with him who struggled in this way. This struggle includes not reckoning oneself as anything, not assessing oneself as something special, and simply regarding oneself as earth and

---

[13]Dorotheus of Gaza develops this theme in his *Spiritual Works*, Letter 2.

ashes (Gn 18:27). By contrast, the struggle of those living in the world involves regarding oneself as knowing everything, causing oneself to puff up in arrogance, reckoning oneself and assessing oneself in everything, and ultimately avoiding humility. (*Letter* 604)

7. Pretense to Rights (τό δικαίωμα)

This is another virtue that the "great old man" is asked to explain and whose origin he ascribes again to Egypt. It is defined as the "pretense to rights"; it relates to the notion of self-justification and reinforces the concept of personal responsibility.

> Question. What is the notion of pretense to rights?
> Response. The notion of pretense to rights is something that does not contain arrogance, but rather contains the denial of fault, in the way Adam and Eve and Cain and others sinned, but later denied their sin in order to justify themselves. (*Letter* 477)
> The desire that comes from demons is what we call pretense to rights and trust in oneself. Through these, one is entirely taken captive [by sin]. (*Letter* 173)
> Nothing that occurs with turmoil is good, but always comes from the power of the devil through our pretense to rights. (*Letter* 724)

Barsanuphius is clearly drawing here on his long experience and spiritual engagement with the desert tradition, where a hermit avoids blaming other people or difficult circumstances but always assumes the burden of personal accountability. In the *Sayings of the Desert Fathers*, "Abba Anthony said to Abba Poemen: 'This is the great work of a person: always to take the blame for one's own sins before God and to expect temptation to the last breath.'"[14]

---

[14]Anthony 4, in *Sayings*.

8. Labor of Love (*ascesis*)

Barsanuphius and John recognize of course that all of our spiritual discipline is the result of divine synergy; in this way, they are able to reconcile an age-old conundrum of the ascetic tradition by offering the following explanation of the mystery:

> If a person inclines one's heart toward good and invokes the assistance of God, God will consider the good desire of that person and bestow the power necessary for that person to accomplish the task of asceticism. So the two move forward together: the free will of the human being and the divine power of God. (*Letter* 763)

Labor, therefore, is not laborious; the Greek term adopted by Barsanuphius is ἔργον, which implies industriousness and creativity. Certainly, the struggle will be difficult; after all, everyone resists change, pain, passion, and especially death. Nevertheless, the result is productive and constructive suffering; it is always a labor of and for love:

> Labor, brother, so that you may find all the more love and rest. For before the boat reaches the harbor, it is beaten and tossed by the waves and the storms. But once it reaches the harbor, it finds itself in a state of great calm. (*Letter* 9)

> No one can be saved from the passions and please God without labor of heart. (*Letter* 256)

> Pay attention to yourself; for it is impossible to be saved without labor. (*Letter* 240)

If the Old Men were to summarize what this labor of love entails, here is what they would say:

> Pay close attention to yourself, and struggle against your thoughts in order not to be negligent, not to have vainglory, not to uphold your will in anything, and not to receive the thoughts sown in you from the right. Otherwise, you will suffer a great fall. And be assured that wherever you go, from one side of this world to the other, you will

not benefit as much as you will in this place. Let the prayer of the Fathers here be to you as an anchor is to a boat. Acquire discipline and it will dispel the boldness that brings every evil ...

Brother, without labor it is not possible to live; and without struggle, no one can be crowned. Struggle to be saved by engaging in spiritual battle and God will help you; for "he wants all people to be saved and come to the knowledge of truth" (1 Tm 2:4). May he have mercy on you, child, so that you may commit yourself to work with longsuffering. (*Letter* 259)

Brother, unless your heart labors in everything in search of the Lord, you cannot make any progress. If you spend time on these matters, you will make progress. For it is said: "Be still" (Ps 45:11), and so on. May the Lord grant you to understand these things and to labor in them. (*Letter* 277)

9. "Bearing One Another's Burdens"

The clearest evidence that one is genuinely laboring for love lies in the fulfillment of the commandment to "bear one another's burdens" (Gal 6:2), which is nothing less than a reflection and imitation of the example set by Christ (see Mt 11:28–30). This Pauline phrase is repeatedly and regularly quoted in the correspondence[15]— their favorite expression and most frequently cited passage from Scripture. The Old Men themselves are profoundly aware that they bear the burdens of their disciples—sometimes promising to carry only half the burden,[16] at other times up to two-thirds of the burden,[17] while on occasion even the entire burden![18]

> I admire your love, brother, but you do not understand the affairs of love that are according to God ... Yet if I say something to someone beyond my measure, or beyond my power, I speak moved by the love of Christ, knowing—as I said—that I am

---

[15]See, for instance, *Letters* 94, 96, 104, 108, 123, 239, 243, 483, 575a, 579, and 604.
[16]See *Letters* 70 and 72.
[17]See *Letter* 73.
[18]See *Letters* 73, 553, and 833.

nothing but a worthless slave. Since then you did not understand what I told you, namely that I bear half your sins, I have made you a partner with me. For I did not say to you: "I bear one third," leaving you to bear more and be burdened more than I. And again, I said what I have said in order to banish self-love; this is why I did not speak to you of bearing two thirds, showing myself to be stronger than you; for such conduct would be vainglory. And I did not say: "I bear the whole." This belongs to the perfect, to those who have become brothers of Christ, who laid down His own life for our sake, and who loved those who have loved us with perfect love in order to do this … However, if you wish to cast on me the whole burden, then for the sake of obedience I accept this too. Forgive me that great love leads me to talking nonsense. (*Letter* 73)

10. Learning to Pray

Finally, if we were to consider the goal of the spiritual life, then the vast correspondence of Barsanuphius and John might well be condensed and crystallized into a single virtue, namely, *the power of prayer*—indeed, *the practice of unceasing prayer*.

> Question. If I am chanting the psalms or find myself in the company of other people so that my thought is afflicted, and I say the name of God in my heart since I cannot do so with my mouth, or even if I simply remember his name, is this not enough to receive divine assistance?
> Response by Barsanuphius. If you are standing in the choir while it is chanting the psalms or if you are in the company of other people, and you are inspired to say the name of God, do not suppose that because you are not saying it with your mouth you are not in fact addressing God. Remember that he knows people's hearts; he pays attention to your heart. Therefore, go ahead and repeat his name in your heart.
> This is why Scripture says: "Shut your door and pray to your Father who is in secret" (Mt 6:6). This means that we are to shut the mouth and pray to him in the heart. When you shut your mouth and invoke God's name, or else pray to him in your heart, you are actually fulfilling this Scripture. Even

if you do not mention his name in your heart, but simply remember him therein—because this is more powerful than merely uttering his name—this is sufficient for you to receive divine assistance. (*Letter* 430)

Question. Is it good for someone to meditate or pray constantly in the heart, even if the tongue does not fully participate? When this happens to me, my thought plunges deeply and I feel burdened, so that I think I am seeing things or beholding fantasies or even dwell on my dreams.

Response. This belongs only to the perfect, who are able to direct the intellect and keep it filled with fear of God, so that it does not deviate and plunge to deep distraction or imagination. However, one who is unable to enjoy godly vigilance at all times grasps hold of oneself and connects the meditation to the tongue as well. The same occurs with those swimming in the ocean. Some are experienced swimmers and confidently dive into the water, knowing that the sea cannot overwhelm those who with good swimming skills. But someone inexperienced in such skills, who feels the waters dragging him down and is afraid of drowning, moves out of the sea to the shore. And after regaining his breath a little, the same person might again enter the deep water and continue the effort to become competent in the skill of swimming so as to reach the level of those who have mastered this skill. (*Letter* 431)

Such prayer is the activity of the monk at all times and in all places (*Letter* 827):

Question. When I sit down, either to read or do my handiwork, and want to pray, I am not sure whether I should be sitting or standing. The same happens even when I have my head covered. Also, when I walk about and try to pray, my thought compels me to turn to the east. What should I do?

Response. Whether sitting down or walking about, whether working or eating, or whatever else you happen to be doing, even if you are performing your bodily need, whether you turn to the east or to the west, do not hesitate to pray. For we have been commanded to pray without ceasing (1 Thes 5:17) and, indeed, to do so in every place (1 Tm 2:8). Again, it is written: "Prepare the way for the one who rides to the west;

his name is the Lord" (Ps 67:5), which indicates that God is everywhere. And when you have your head covered, do not stop praying. Simply make sure you are not doing this out of contempt. (*Letter* 441)

The elders offer advice about how to pray without ceasing, especially in difficult situations, but also when prayer appears to be of no benefit. Moreover, with regard to "praying without ceasing" (1 Thes 5:17), the elders recommend the use of the Jesus Prayer (*Letters* 124 and 421).

> Question. How is it possible to pray unceasingly?
> Response. When you are alone, you should chant the Psalms and pray with your mouth and heart. But when you are in the marketplace or among others, you do not have to chant Psalms with your mouth, but only with your mind. It is also important to guard your eyes and lower them on account of the distractions and snares of the enemies. (*Letter* 710. See also *Letter* 182)
> Question. When I pray or chant the Psalms, I do not understand the meaning of the words because of the hardness of my heart. Of what benefit are they to me?
> Response. Even if you do not understand the meaning of the words you chant, yet the demons understand, hear, and tremble. So do not stop chanting the Psalms and praying; and gradually, God will soften your hardness. (*Letter* 711)

The Jesus Prayer

One area where the Gaza elders inherited a precious legacy from preceding generations, which they in turn transmitted as a living tradition to succeeding generations is the Jesus Prayer—the short formula probably conceived among monastic inhabitants of the fourth-century Egyptian desert, cultivated in the spiritual teaching of John Climacus, and culminated in the emphasis on unceasing prayer established in the anthology of the *Philokalia*.[19]

---

[19]See Chapter 8 on "Solitude, Silence, and Stillness."

There is actually no clear and unambiguous mention of such a technique of prayer, at least in the Greek tradition, until the late thirteenth and early fourteenth centuries.[20] Short prayers are mentioned in the *Sayings of the Desert Fathers*: "Abba Poemen said that Abba Paphnutius ... had recourse to short prayers."[21] Yet while Nilus emphasizes the invocation of the Name of Jesus, it is still peripheral in the spiritual practice of the period. Barsanuphius and John continue and expand the early desert tradition, citing the importance of short prayers with particular reference to the Name of Jesus and unceasing prayer.[22] While commending short prayers—with or without explicit invocation of "Jesus"—in general they attach paramount value to the holy name. Even when not referring specifically to the Jesus Prayer, their letters are replete with such remarks as:

> Cry out to Jesus until your throat becomes hoarse: "Master, save us; for we are perishing." (*Letter* 148)

> Learn what you have come here seeking. Run to Jesus, that you may win him. (*Letter* 256)

> Let us flee this fear and awaken the Jesus that lies asleep inside us, saying: "Master, save us; for we are perishing." (*Letter* 182)

However, there is one specific form of prayer, to which the Old Men attach particular attention and significance—namely, the remembrance of the divine name.[23] Barsanuphius responds to a question about the invocation of the name of God:

> In addition to all this, we learn that unceasingly remembering the name of God is like a medicine that dispels not only all the passions but even the sinful act itself. For just as the doctor recommends some medicine or perhaps a plaster for the wound

---

[20]The standard form of the Jesus Prayer is first found in *The Life of Abba Philemon*, a text about a monk in Egypt. While this document is difficult to date, it is perhaps more or less contemporary with the *Ladder* of John Climacus in the mid-seventh century.
[21]Cf. *Apophth*. Poemen 190 (ed. Guy, 30). Cf. also *Apophth*. Elias 7, PG65.184D-185A and Macarius 19, PG65.269C.
[22]Barsanuphius, *Letter* 446.
[23]On the remembrance of God, see Bitton-Ashkelony and Kofsky, *The Monastic School of Gaza*, 176–82.

of a patient, and this operates internally without the patient even realizing how it happens, so also the name of God dispels all the passions when invoked, without us even knowing how this actually occurs. (*Letter* 424)

In fact, Barsanuphius responds to a question about "captivity of the intellect" by suggesting that one should never leave the intellect idle, but constantly fill it with the repetition of God's name:

> This, too, is a form of captivity; for the enemy transfers the intellect from one place to another. Instead, pinch yourself when you notice this temptation arising; and reproach your intellect: "Where are you going, wretched thing? Remember your future torments, reserved for those who do or think these things." Did not Job make an inopportune offering for his children, declaring: "Perhaps my children have sinned in their hearts against God" (Jb 1:5). So with these words, apply your intellect to the words of the Psalms recited. If you notice this happening again, rebuke yourself; and do this on a third occasion as well. Of course, if it persists, remove your intellect from there. But do not leave it idle; think about the judgement and eternal hell. And pray the holy name of God, saying: "Lord Jesus Christ, have mercy on me." (*Letter* 446)

In this context, Barsanuphius and John propose a series of diverse, albeit standard scriptural texts that could be implemented during prayer, thereby clearly acknowledging that several alternative forms or formulas of prayer may be envisaged:

> Question from the same brother to the same Old Man: "Is it good for me to be occupied with the prayer "Lord Jesus Christ, have mercy on me," or should I repeat by heart certain passages from sacred Scripture and recite the psalms?"
> Response by John. You should really do both: a little of one and a little of the other. For it is written: "These you ought to have practiced without neglecting the others." (*Letter* 175)

Barsanuphius is in full agreement:

> Response from the same Great Old Man to the same person, when a brother even wanted to cut conversation with his own

attendant because he was told to be carefree when approaching the city ...

Tell the brother: Wait a little longer. For it is not time yet. Indeed, I care for you more than you care for yourself; or rather, it is God who really cares for you. Brother John, do not be at all afraid of temptations that rise up to test you. For the Lord will not abandon you to them. So whenever something like this occurs, do not waste time investigating matters, but cry out the name of Jesus, saying: "Jesus, help me," and he will surely hear you; for "he is near to all who call on him." Do not be faint-hearted, but run willingly and you shall win. (*Letter* 268)

Invoke the holy name of God to assist you, saying: "Master Jesus, protect me and help me in my weakness." And be confident that he will crush the arrow of the enemies. (*Letter* 659)

It is out of envy that the devil aroused this warfare within you. So guard your eyes, and do not eat to the point of satiation. Drink only a little wine, for the sake of the illness that you describe. Acquire humility; for it shatters all the snares of the enemy. And I, the least, will do whatever I can by praying to God, that he might protect you from every temptation and guard you from all evil. Neither surrender, brother, nor cast yourself into despair; for this is the great joy of the devil. Just pray without ceasing, saying: "Lord Jesus Christ, save me from dishonorable passions." And you will find mercy from God and thus receive strength through the prayers of the saints. (*Letter* 255)

These matters may sometimes appear trivial or technical. Yet they do not obscure—but rather serve to illuminate—the fact that an incessant and repeated invocation, whatever form of short appeal or entreaty it may assume, reflects the fundamental notion of prayer as a person-to-person relationship. Prayer does not even need to be articulated in linguistic structures and logical sentences: "We do not know how to pray as we ought, but the Spirit intercedes for us with sighs too deep for words" (Rom 8.26). This is precisely what lies at the heart of the timeless theory and practice of prayer found in the two elders of Palestine.

A Wisdom Distilled

Throughout their correspondence, Barsanuphius and John constantly stress vigilance and violence in the ascetic struggle, discernment, and humility in one's spiritual life, as well as gratitude and gladness in daily activity. A comprehensive and succinct summary of their teaching occurs in the following letter:

> Labor to receive these with toil of heart, and God will grant them to you continually; I am referring to warmth and prayer. For forgetfulness makes these things vanish, while such forgetfulness is caused by negligence. As for the protection of your senses, every gift is granted with toil of heart. The gift of vigilance does not allow evil thoughts to enter; but if they do enter, it does not allow them to cause any damage. May God grant you to be vigilant and alert. For the words "give thanks in all things" (1 Thes 5:18) constitute a command. Finally, searching your faults in order to acquire forgiveness is also beneficial. (*Letter* 267)

PART TWO

The Desert Beckons
Sitting by the Cell

4

Spiritual Direction

Two Extraordinary Models

Guides on a Journey

If there is a distinct legacy bequeathed by the two Old Men of Gaza, it is their exceptional, albeit unconventional model of spiritual direction. In one of his letters, Abba John provides an intensive introduction to spiritual guidance for the newly appointed Abbot Aelianos:

> When he heard this, he glorified God and said to the Old Man: "Father, since I am a beginner and know nothing, what do you direct me to say to the brothers?"
> Response. Tell them the following: "The Lord Jesus Christ, who cares for you, said: 'I shall not leave you as orphans; I am coming to you' (Jn 14:18). Pay attention to yourselves with all humility and love for God, and he shall bless you and become your protection and direction."
> Also tell them this: "Let no one conceal any thought, because the joy of the [evil] spirits comes when we conceal our thoughts in order that they might destroy our soul."
> Finally, if any of the brothers reveals his thoughts to you, say the following to yourself: "Lord, everything that you have for the salvation of the soul, grant it to me in order that I may speak to the brother, and especially that I might speak your word rather than my own." Then, say whatever comes to you,

believing within yourself that this is not your own word; for it is written: "Whoever speaks must do so as one speaking the very words of God." (*Letter 577*)

But what exactly is the vocation or function of a spiritual director? And how is spiritual direction exercised with insight and integrity?

In embarking on a journey, we often need a map of the landscape, a detailed survey of the pathways that someone has previously trodden in order to chart the contours of the territory. One thing is very clear in the spiritual life. We all need someone, a spiritual guide or special friend, before whom we can trustingly open up our heart, soul, and mind—someone with compassion, someone in whom we can rely with confidence.

The notion of spiritual direction by an experienced elder has been underlined from the earliest times of the apostolic community and, especially, from the first beginnings of monasticism. Deuteronomy 32:7 says: "Ask your father and he will tell you"; Proverbs 31:4 suggests: "Do everything with counsel."[1] Dorotheus, the spiritual protégé of Barsanuphius and John, even composed a series of spiritual instructions for monastics, conceding: "If it is my duty to get something done, I prefer it to be done with my elder's advice, even if I do not agree with him, and even if I get it wrong, rather than to be guided by my own opinion, even if it turns out right."[2]

Centuries of institutionalism and clericalism in the history of Christianity, followed by the "lay revolution" in patriarchal and

---

[1] See also Sirach 32:19. The basic study on spiritual guidance remains that by I. Hausherr, *Spiritual Direction in the Early Christian East* (Kalamazoo, MI: Cistercian Studies, 1990). See also Chryssavgis, *Soul Mending*; Kallistos Ware, *The Inner Kingdom* (Crestwood, NY: St. Vladimir's Press, 2000), esp. chap. 9, 127–51; Graham Gould, *The Desert Fathers on Monastic Community* (Oxford: Clarendon Press, 1993); Joseph Allen, *Inner Way: Toward a Rebirth of Eastern Christian Spiritual Direction* (Brookline, MA: Holy Cross Orthodox Press, 1999); Richard Valantassis, *Spiritual Guides of the Third Century: A Semiotic Study of the Guide-Disciple Relationship in Christianity, Neoplatonism, Hermetism, and Gnosticism* (Minneapolis, MN: Fortress Press, 1991); Daniel Caner, *Wandering Begging Monks: Spiritual Authority and the Promotion of Monasticism in Late Antiquity* (Berkeley, CA: University of California Press, 2002); and George Demacopoulos, *Five Models of Spiritual Direction in the Early Church* (Notre Dame, IN: University of Notre Dame Press, 2007).

[2] See Eric Wheeler, *Dorotheos of Gaza: Discourses and Sayings* (Kalamazoo, MI: Cistercian Publications, 1977), 252.

progressive circles alike, has regretfully rendered the concept of spiritual authority problematic, indeed a point of contention and almost a position of disdain. Therefore, any discussion about personal direction or mutual consultation may ring strange to contemporary readers, but they were commonplace in early Christian communities, where a spiritual father (*abba*) or mother (*amma*) was an inspired and enlightened elder, capable of guiding others in the intricate ways of the mystical life and advising people on complex challenges of everyday life.

Perhaps surprisingly for most, monastic teaching and tradition suggest that a spiritual guide does not have to be a priest. In fact, the spiritual elder illustrates the two fundamental levels on which the church exists and functions: the hierarchal and the spiritual, the outward and the inward, the institutional and the inspirational, ultimately the organizational on the one hand and the charismatic on the other. In this sense, a *geron* (Greek), *starets* (Russian), or *abba/amma* (Coptic) exists alongside the apostles and martyrs. Though not necessarily ordained a presbyter through the episcopal laying-on of hands, the spiritual father or mother is nevertheless a prophetic figure who receives his or her charisma directly from God. There is no formal act of appointment; on the contrary, it is the disciples who point to the elder as a spiritual authority and authenticity. There is no evidence, for example, that either Barsanuphius or John was an ordained priest. Yet they remain two of the most distinguished and definitive elders of Eastern Christian monasticism. Moreover, the questions and answers that constitute their remarkable correspondence demonstrate—with a depth and clarity unparalleled in so many other classical sources—the quintessential principles and fundamental practice of spiritual direction through the ages.[3]

Of course, these two Palestinian monks already have behind them centuries of tradition and experience pertaining to the institution and implementation of spiritual direction. As we have already seen in Chapter 1, Palestinian monasticism represents a

---

[3]Foreshadowing Dorotheus of Gaza, Abba John writes: "Doing something with counsel is always a lesser wrong; whereas doing something alone brings double trouble" (*Letter* 324). See also *Letters* 535, 551, and 693. See also Hevelone-Harper, *Disciples of the Desert*, 79–105.

link between the ground-breaking pioneering movements of early-fourth century Egypt (embodied by the desert fathers and mothers) and the subsequent reformative developments of late-seventh century Byzantium (with Maximus the Confessor and Theodore the Studite). Indeed, monastic life flourishes in Palestine until 638, when Jerusalem fell to the Muslim Arabs and the centers of monasticism shift to Asia Minor and the West.

So Barsanuphius and John understand well "the science" of spiritual direction (*Letter* 256). They assume that, from beginning to end, all people are intimately, intricately, and inextricably interconnected. We all depend on one another for nourishment, encouragement, and maturity. What happens to one of us affects all of us. For them, Paul's vision of "one body with many members" (1 Cor 12:12–31) indicates that such oneness is not optional and that wholeness or healing is contingent on the ability to share and receive counseling, to forgive and be forgiven, ultimately to "bear one another's burdens" (Gal 6:2). Thus, the two Old Men can state without reservation:

> Behold, this is the way of salvation. If it pleases you, walk it; and God will offer you a hand of assistance. If it does not please you, then it is up to you. For every person who desires also has authority over oneself. However, if you release this authority to another person, then you are carefree, and the other person bears your care. So choose what you want. (*Letter* 237)

Ways of Spiritual Direction
The Discipline of Obedience

The basic premise of spiritual direction is of course obedience—a foundational principle often misconstrued and misapplied in practice. Obedience is the way in which the community bonds and holds together. "Doing everything on the order of the Abbot and not according to one's own will is a sign of communality and equality with the brothers in the monastery" (*Letter* 250). The ascetic struggle may be arduous, but the spiritual journey is not supposed to be solitudinous. Obedience and submission, seeking counsel and cutting off one's will, are part and parcel of the spiritual way that a person should not undertake alone.

> Obedience cuts off the will, but without toil no one can acquire obedience. If you are sitting for the sake of obedience and not for bodily comfort, then this is not your will, nor are you sitting passionately but instead you are pleasing God. If you are sitting in order to receive pleasure from comfort, then you are not pleasing God. (*Letter* 249)

In this perspective, then, obedience is one of the most critical elements of asceticism, a crucial aspect of lifting the cross, and an indispensable tool for the monastic. Simply put, "a monk should not hold onto his own will *at all in anything*."

> Question. Should I cut off my will and conform to the Abbot in matters only which are good or even moderate, or else also in matters where it appears that God's commandment is almost being transgressed? And if his order happens to be beyond my ability, should I be relieved of it so as not to be overcome by sorrow and turmoil? Moreover, what happens if someone asks me to mediate about his problem with the Abbot but I refrain from doing so in order that it does not bring me honor because I might reckon within myself that I am something?
>
> Response. Brother, one who wishes to be a monk should not hold onto his own will at all in anything. Christ Himself taught us this when He said: "I have come into the world not to do my own will" (Jn 6:38). For someone who wants to do one thing and be relieved of another is either trying to manifest oneself as more discerning than the one who gave the order, or else is being mocked by the demons.
>
> Therefore, you must obey in everything, even if the matter appears to be sinful. For your Abbot who gave the order will bear the judgement, since he is responsible and accountable for you (Heb 13:17). If the order seems to be too heavy for you to carry out, then tell him and leave the matter to his discretion. If those who gave you the order are your brothers, and you see that the matter will bring you harm or else lies beyond your ability, again ask your Abbot and do whatever

he tells you. For if you want to discern matters yourself, you will bring afflictions upon yourself.

Confide everything to your Abbot and do whatever he discerns. For he knows what he must do and how he must care for your soul. Then you may be at rest, believing that whatever he tells you is according to God and will bring neither sorrow nor turmoil. "Every good tree brings forth good fruit" (Mt 7:17).

As for asking your Abbot about other people, if this is necessary, then do it as if fulfilling a commandment which you have heard and must carry out. For if your Abbot asks you to sit at the entrance-gate and tells you: "Report to me about every movement," will you decide on your own what to do, or will you carry out the order of your Abbot? Therefore, whether your Abbot tells you to report to him or not about your brothers, you bear no responsibility in this regard. (*Letter* 288)

In fact, one of the most striking elements in the teaching of Barsanuphius and John is the conviction that they bear responsibility for their disciples before God.

Question. Request from the same brother to the same Great Old Man, that he might bear his sins.

Response. Brother, although you are asking of me something that is beyond me, nevertheless I shall show you the limits of love, namely that it forces itself to move even beyond its own limits. Behold, I admire you as a person, and so I assume responsibility for you and bear you. Nevertheless, I do so on this condition, that you also bear the keeping of my words and commandments; for they will bring you salvation. In this way, you shall live without reproach. (*Letter* 270)

As already observed, the unique three-way relationship among Barsanuphius, John, and Seridos offers the local community a safety net allowing open expression and transparent exchange. All three elders perceive spiritual direction less as a gift for resolving some problem and more as a path leading the disciple to discover a solution. Obedience and spiritual direction work only when the relationship between elder and disciple is a two-way street, fostering a mutual and reciprocal relationship of faith and love. When obedience is balanced by prayer and trust, the spiritual relationship avoids disruption and distortion.

This is why Barsanuphius and John emphasize the importance of prayer in the absence of spiritual direction (see *Letters* 365–6 and 390). At the same time, however, they are careful not to interfere in or impose themselves on the spiritual development of their correspondents; they simply provide "counsel without compulsion" (*Letter* 368). In this regard, the spiritual director is more *identified with* than *authoritative over* the spiritual disciple: "The Lord has bound your soul to mine, saying: 'Do not leave him.' Therefore, it is not for me to teach you, but rather to learn from you" (*Letter* 164; see also *Letter* 553).

Barsanuphius and John are no ordinary spiritual directors; they perceive spiritual direction as an extraordinary opportunity to impart as well as to increase wisdom. They are prepared to apply the root definition of obedience—in both Greek (*ypakoē*, from *akoē* [whence "acoustics"]) and Latin (*oboedire*, from *audire* [whence "audio"])—quite literally as an invitation to listen more closely and more attentively.

The Spiritual Guide

There are examples in the lives of the saints when God illumines their life and intervenes directly; but for most of us, divine inspiration and intervention occur through other people (*Letter* 50), who serve as "advocates before the king" (*Letter* 139). For Barsanuphius and John, as for the entire Christian East, that is where a spiritual elder or guide comes in:

> He guides you toward the light; so do not seek the darkness. He guides you in the straight way; do not seek the way of falsehood. He guides you to the truth; do not deviate toward deceit. He guides you to peace; do not seek combat. He guides you to joy; do not run toward sorrow. He guides you to humility; do not turn to pride. He guides you to righteousness; do not seek injustice. He guides you to bear insults and injuries that come your way; do not seek praise or vainglory. He guides you to

mortification; do not seek rest ... He guides you to eternal life. (*Letter* 137b)[4]

Much of the Western approach to counseling that we are familiar with is—to adopt Jungian terminology—rooted in the *animus*, focused on consciousness. However, the "great old man" is quite uncomplimentary of "laborious investigation or excessive analysis" (*Letter* 39). The Eastern approach admits more of the *anima*, involving a more diffused awareness. And in this process, the spiritual guide recognizes "the specific weakness of particular individuals," "addresses the response in a personal manner," and "provides appropriate nourishment and remedy for various ages and stages" ("Prologue"; see also *Letters* 16–17). An experienced guide knows that there are multiple "letters" in the spiritual alphabet (*Letter* 98), many "stages" in the spiritual life, several "rungs" on the spiritual ladder:

> We should not desire at once to set our foot on the highest rung of all before placing it on the first rung of the ladder. (*Letter* 160)

Otherwise, the collateral damage will prove mutually disastrous:

> I am astonished at how some people, who have spent many years in school, are yet still learning the alphabet and syllables, when they really ought by now to be accomplished teachers. I am likewise astonished at how those who have spent much time in the monastic life, and ought to be able to discern the deeper thoughts of others, are nevertheless still subjected to the warfare of novices. You ought to be guiding into the straight way those who have gone astray, as if you were perfected; however, instead of bearing the burdens of the weak, you burden them to the point of drowning out of sorrow. (*Letter* 98)

---

[4]If the language of this chapter appears exclusive to men, it reflects the reality that spiritual guidance is often restricted to men in the Eastern Christian tradition. Nevertheless, it is helpful to remember that men and women alike can offer spiritual direction. The sacrament of engendering spiritual disciples transcends gender distinctions. In the Egyptian desert, as in ensuing centuries, women too offer spiritual direction, a reminder that in the realm of freedom, "there is no male or female" (Gal 3:28).

The spiritual guide should be "righteous" (*Letter* 139), endowed "with the authority to bind and loose, to forgive and retain sins, standing before the world, protecting it from annihilation ... and attracting God's mercy" (*Letter* 569). This charisma is what enables the spiritual guide to "forgive like God" (*Letter* 358), to "forgive sins from birth" (*Letter* 115), to "forgive the past allowing the disciple to assume responsibility for the future" (*Letter* 229), and even to "bestow a pledge for the salvation of the soul" (*Letter* 274).

Moreover, the spiritual guide should be humble (*Letters* 70 and 788) and honest (*Letter* 17), gentle (*Letter* 789) and joyful (*Letters* 10 and 87).

> You counted me as a great man and yourself as the brother of such a man. Do you not know that we are all children of Adam's transgression (Rm 5:14), that we are all earth and ashes? (Gn 18:27). (*Letter* 348)

> Brother, you are blessed if you are utterly conscious of your sins ... Part of repentance is becoming conscious of one's sins and requesting assistance from the elders. (*Letter* 498)

> If a person wants to bend a tree or a vine, then he bends them carefully so they do not break. However, if a person pulls it forcefully, it immediately snaps. (*Letter* 25)

> These three things contain our entire salvation: Always rejoicing paves the way of righteousness; but no one can truly rejoice unless one's life is righteous. Praying unceasingly is the aversion of every evil; for it allows no room for the devil to act against us. Finally, giving thanks in all circumstances is clear proof of our love for Christ. If joy and prayer regulate our life, then we shall give thanks to the Lord. (*Letter* 848)

As a result, then, the spiritual director is balanced (*Letter* 77) and positive:

> It is not so much saying or proclaiming something with our lips that constitutes faith; rather, perfect faith is revealed in the healing itself. Therefore, if you believe that you have been healed,

then walk and do not stumble. You have been healed; so do not limp. You have been healed; so do not carry any spot of leprosy. You have been healed; so show that your issue of blood has ceased. (*Letter* 59)

Rules and Roles

One thing is clear: The spiritual guide does not simply impose rules or enforce roles. While he may admonish and instruct, he does not prescribe directives but becomes a living model. "Be their example, not their legislator," advises Abba Poemen in the Egyptian desert.[5] Barsanuphius, too, is well aware that "people's rules" can sometimes "prove worthless" (*Letter* 23). The aim of the guide is to "become a model beneficial to all, neither criticizing nor condemning, but only counseling others as genuine brothers" (*Letter* 21).

Coincidentally or not, around the same period that Benedict of Nursia is founding a monastery in Monte Cassino outside of Rome and composing his influential *Rule*, Barsanuphius and John are exercising their vocation as spiritual directors in Thawatha outside of Jerusalem. This means that, at a time when Western monasticism appears to tighten restrictions on individual judgment and regulations on monastic activities, Eastern monasticism is exercising greater tolerance for personal discernment and flexibility.

This is why Barsanuphius and John are hesitant to institute or impose regulations. The only rule is that there are no rules. "Do not conceive in your heart that I have given you a rule; it is not a rule but a friendly opinion" (*Letter* 160). Barsanuphius claims "never to have placed a bond on anyone, including himself" (*Letter* 51). He is merely a friend offering fresh perspectives, not a master establishing harsh stipulations: "I have not bound you, brother, nor have I offered you a commandment but only an opinion. Therefore, do as you please" (*Letter* 56). "Do not believe in your heart that I have given you a command. It is not a command, but the opinion of a brother. The way is open before us" (*Letter* 64; see also *Letter* 92).

---

[5]Poemen 174, *Sayings*.

John, too, distinguishes between "instruction" and "indulgence" (*Letter* 547), between counsel and command:

> Simple advice according to God is one thing, but a command is another. Advice is counsel without compulsion, revealing the straight way of life; a command, on the other hand, is an inviolable bond. (*Letter* 368)

Paradoxically, then, as John professes, the purpose of spiritual direction is independence, not dependence: "Wherever there is no command, it is always beneficial to practice freedom" (*Letter* 378). For "God created human beings free in order that we may be able to incline toward good" (*Letter* 763).

Everything on the spiritual journey is an indication and reinforcement of our freedom, not a suggestion or reminder of our frailty. Change can only come through love, not by force; it can never be impelled or imposed. Change is always personal; and it comes with patience. As Abba Barsanuphius reminds Abbot Seridos: "If you milk the cow, it will produce butter; but if you press hard on the teat, it will produce blood (Prv. 30.33)" (*Letter* 25). This means that the spiritual director simply points to the light; the spiritual director should never block the light or steal the limelight. There must always be sufficient space in spiritual direction—enough room for freshness and forgiveness. The objective is always to lighten (not lade) any burden, to enlighten (not darken) the journey, to comfort (not crush) the disciple.

Of course, the spiritual guide remains a source of immense authority—a figure of power and prayer, of influence and intercession.[6] While John is "obliged to speak freely, he nevertheless speaks with godly fear" (*Letter* 503). And the reason the two elders prefer to give opinions rather than mandates is because they are profoundly conscious of their own limitations!

> It is very beneficial for us to recognize that there still remains within us that human factor, that we may come to know our

---

[6]Peter Brown, *Society and the Holy in Late Antiquity* (London: Faber and Faber, 1982), 103–52 [here at 121]. See Rapp, "'For Next to God, You Are My Salvation'", 63–81. Also Alexis Torrance, "Standing in the Breach: The Significance and Function of the Saints in the Letters of Barsanuphius and John of Gaza," *Journal of Early Christian Studies* 17.3 (2009), 459–73.

limitations, namely where we actually are, and be humbled in order to receive the grace of the humble. (*Letter* 811)

Know at least where you are and what power you have. (*Letter* 92)

Fully conscious of their own limitations, Barsanuphius and John are able to show understanding and compassion for the weaknesses of others. Fully aware that they are filled with human passions, they can communicate a word of healing to all those who approach. This self-awareness and self-knowledge—beyond other qualifications, spiritual (like fasting and prayer) or social (like education or maturity)—is what renders them eminently prepared and qualified to guide others.

Above all, however, the two elders prefer complete silence (*Letters* 36 and 69). Barsanuphius declares: "I do not want to become anyone's spiritual elder or teacher. I have the Apostle offering me reproof: 'You, then, that teach others, will you not teach yourself?' (Rom 2:21)" (*Letter* 66). The spiritual guide always examines the deeper motivation—"the slightest motion" (*Letter* 22) "and emotion" (*Letter* 21)—behind every instruction (*Letter* 21). John asks: "How can someone who does not construct one's own cell construct that of another?" (*Letter* 233)

In all situations, the spiritual guide is a mentor and tutor, "exceedingly forbearing and caring" (*Letter* 24), "showing no favoritism to anyone" (*Letter* 55), "adopting his children with genuine love" (*Letter* 573): "If I am your father and teacher, how can I be angry? For a father is compassionate, having no wrath at all. And a teacher is long-suffering, foreign to indignation. But as for requesting a rule, you are going around in endless circles" (*Letter* 23). "For a father weeps for the soul of his child more than for his own soul" (*Letter* 600):

> Since we are using words spoken according to God and not according to mortals, allow me to repeat the words of his servant Moses: "Either lead my spiritual son, who is writing to me, to eternal life with me, or else wipe me also from your book" (Ex 32:32). May I not be permitted to see the face of Jacob the father of Joseph unless I have Benjamin with me (Gen 44:34). I believe in his holy name, that he will not refuse my request. For the joy

of the Holy Trinity and of the holy angels is the salvation of those being saved. Therefore, I shall not cease praying to God until he grants me the joy of your salvation. (*Letter* 790)

"Hold My Hand and Walk" (*Letter* 31)

Mindful of the rungs comprising the spiritual ladder but above all conscious of his own limitations as a human being, the spiritual guide ultimately seeks a level of solidarity and identity with the disciple. In the *Tales of the Hasidim*, Rabbi Zusya observes: "I climbed down all the rungs until I was with the sinner and bound the root of my soul to the root of his."[7] This priority and principle of sharing is a distinct master-theme in the letters of Basranuphius and John: "Your holiness should suffer excessively with those who are afflicted" (*Letter* 844).

In approaching a spiritual elder, one is essentially saying: "Give me your hand for the sake of love, and draw me toward God; for through you he will save me" (*Letter* 63). And the spiritual guide responds: "I have spread my wings over you in order to bear your burdens ... Now you are like a person sitting under the shade of a tree" (*Letter* 239). Quoting his favorite scriptural passage (Gal 6:2), Barsanuphius contends: "There is no other settlement of our salvation than 'bearing one another's burdens'" (*Letter* 104).

One reason for the need to share is that most of us are harsher critics of ourselves, striking the most painful blows against ourselves at just the time when we most require tolerance and compassion—virtues that characterize Arsenius and Macarius in Egypt but also Barsanuphius and John in Gaza. People need others because often the wounds themselves are too deep to admit; sometimes the evil is too painful to confront alone. This is precisely why directives and dictates assume a back seat to sharing and love: "Leave these behind and follow my words; I shall bear your burden" (*Letter* 553). The sole inspiration and justification for a

---

[7]Martin Buber, ed., *The Tales of the Hasidim: The Early Masters* (New York: Schoken Books, 1968), 242.

relationship between elder and disciple is love, which transcends all barriers and overcomes all deficiencies:

> Although you ask of me something that is beyond me, nevertheless I shall show you the limits of love, namely that it forces itself to move even beyond its own limits. Behold, I admire you as a person, and I assume responsibility for you and bear you. But on one condition, that you also bear the keeping of my words and commandments; for these bring you salvation. In this way, you shall live without reproach. (*Letter* 270)

The concept of "bearing one another's burdens" is by no means exclusive to Gaza.[8] Grounded on the "model" (*Letter* 61) of the good shepherd, who "lays down his life for his neighbor" (Jn 10:11), and the Pauline conviction that "when one member suffers, all members suffer with it" (1 Cor 12:26), the conviction is that "we who are strong ought to bear the failings of the weak" (Rm 15:1). This sharing in suffering and bearing of burdens is fundamental to the worldview of Dostoevsky, for whom assuming responsibility for all people suggests no longer criticizing or controlling others but instead acknowledging the dignity of all. Rowan Williams draws a connection between Paul's "bearing one another's burdens" (Gal. 6.2) and Dostoevsky's variations of "being liable for everyone," "being responsible for everyone," and "being guilty for everyone."[9] "Responsibility is a bracketing and quieting of the self's agenda for the sake of another voice"[10]—eventually and ultimately, the voice of every person, but initially and immediately, the voice of one's spiritual guide.

So delicate and intricate is this responsibility and relationship in Barsanuphius and John that the spiritual guide may bear partial responsibility for the disciple, assuming liability for "one third" (*Letter* 73) or "one half" of the burden[11]:

> Since you did not understand what I told you, namely that I bear half your sins, I made you my partner. For I did not say to you: "I

---

[8]See Bitton-Ashkelony and Kofsky, *The Monastic School of Gaza*, 145–56.
[9]Rowan Williams, *Dostoevsky: Language, Faith, and Fiction* (Waco, TX: Baylor University Press, 2011), 168.
[10]Op. cit., 171–2.
[11]See *Sayings*, Abba Lot 2: "I will carry half of your fault with you."

bear one third," leaving you to bear more and be burdened more than I. And I said this in order to banish self-love; this is why I did not speak to you about bearing two thirds, suggesting that I am stronger than you; for such conduct would be vainglory. Nor again did I say: "I bear the whole." For this belongs to the perfect ... If we are brothers, let us share equally in our Father's property. (*Letter* 73)

At other times, the spiritual guide may accept responsibility for "the greater portion" (*Letter* 39) or even more:

> If you wish to place on me the entire burden, for the sake of obedience I will accept this, too. Forgive me that great love leads me to speak nonsense. (*Letter* 73)

> Since I am obliged to offer you whatever I have, I say to you: "I will respond on your behalf to the loving God in regard to all your sins." (*Letter* 231)

The "great old man" goes so far as to indicate that he would "bear the writ against the disciple" on the day of judgment and "never abandon the disciple even in the age to come" (*Letter* 239)!

"Work with Me a Little" (Letter 239)

There is, of course, also an obligation on the part of the disciple, who must contribute to the relationship or partnership:

> Do not be negligent in your obligation to labor a little yourself. For those who desire imperial grants, though they may have many superiors mediating for them, yet they must also endure affliction and peril at sea, undertaking journeys and labors until they achieve them. Therefore, you too should likewise contribute a little labor in order to find great mercy. (*Letter* 198)

> Work with me and sweat a little. (*Letter* 199)

What is astonishing is that the advice of the elders is not radical but reasonable, not rigid but moderate:

> No one ever says to another person: I bear your concern, and then remains without any concern; otherwise, one is found to be an impostor. Instead, the brother whose burden is being carried must also contribute some small effort and do his best with vigilance to keep the commandments of his elders. If he should fall, then he should rise up. Moreover, I trust in God that, even if he is caught out once and strives to rise up again, then he will not become accustomed [to falling] at all, nor will he be negligent. Instead, God will quickly lead him to the degree of nobility, to the degree of maturity. (*Letter* 268)

So the disciple is invited to "walk with the elder" (*Letter* 63), to "endure rather than elude the struggle" (*Letter* 563), to persist in rather than resist the journey:

> It is a good thing not to leave a place at the time of struggle." (*Letter* 563)

> You should care about nothing else except the direction of your journey. (*Letter* 38)

> Pay attention to where you are and where you want to go. (*Letter* 49)

> Ask nothing else of God or through his servants beyond assistance and patience. (*Letter* 90)

> A beginner's goal is as follows: to walk in great humility, without asking: "What is this?" or "What is that"? (*Letter* 92)

> The more one strains forward, there is no stopping, but one always considers oneself as lacking something, and therefore is continually making progress. (*Letter* 410)

> This is the true way. Outside of this, there is no other way. Let the one who wants run! Let the one who wants run! Let the one who wants run! (*Letter* 450)

Along this journey, as already intimated, one is never alone. The spiritual guide always accompanies the disciple. The two may not be quite "on the same footing" (*Letter* 469) but they invariably travel the same path: "I speak to you as to my soul-mates, desiring to travel the way that we have walked" (*Letter* 192). In fact, unless accompanied from beginning to end by a guide, "one will never reach the intended city" (*Letter* 126). Because obedience is not perceived as yielding to coercion or domination, it is a manifestation of solidarity and community. It is a circular movement, a reciprocal exchange that proceeds both ways—to and from the elder but also from and to the disciple.

The process of mutual consultation is a great leveler, an ultimate equalizer, a common denominator. Convinced that "a brother assisted by a brother resembles a city fortified with ramparts" (Prov 18:19), Barsanuphius emphasizes: "The Fathers have said: 'Obedience for obedience'" (*Letter* 144).[12] Doing everything at the instruction of the elder rather than according to a personal whim is the sign of communality and equality in the monastery (see *Letter* 250). Simply put, no spiritual guide can subjectively declare himself a spiritual authority or illumined oracle; by contrast, he is part of an ages-long tradition, a charismatic "succession,"[13] and a "pedigree"[14] of authority.

Engraving the Will of God

Many early ascetic texts highlight the submission of the will to the spiritual guide, but Barsanuphius and John distinctly stress that the will must be surrendered in order increasingly and eventually to be strengthened. Needless to say, this is an arduous and costly procedure:

> To renounce one's own will is a sacrifice of blood. It means that one has reached the point of laboring to death and of ignoring one's own will. The phrase "we have left everything and followed you" (Mt 19:27, Lk 18:28) is about perfection; it is not about property or money, but about thoughts and desires. (*Letter* 254)

---

[12] Also Abba Mius 1, *Sayings*.
[13] Alongside the institutional or apostolic succession or pedigree.
[14] Coined by Chitty, *The Desert a City*, 67–8.

The process is as paradoxical as it is profound:

> Show complete estrangement to acquire complete intimacy; shun adoption to receive adoption; surrender your will to perform your will; put yourself to death to give yourself life; forget yourself and know yourself. (*Letter* 112)

> Transition in your thought from this vain world to the other age. Leave behind the worldly, and seek the heavenly. Abandon the corruptible, and you shall discover the incorruptible. In your mind, flee from the temporary, and you shall reach the eternal. Die completely, that you may live completely. (*Letter* 37)

For the two elders, the will must be sharpened to conform to the will of God: "Cutting off one's own will is precisely what spiritual progress is all about. It implies cutting off one's will in all things and doing the will of the saints" (*Letter* 380). "Engrave the will of God in your heart" (*Letter* 331).

Russian Orthodox writer, Fyodor Dostoevsky, reflects on the role of such an elder, as he experienced this in Ambrose of Optina:

> What is such an elder? An elder is one who takes your soul, your will, into his soul and his will. When you choose an elder you renounce your own will and yield it to him in complete submission, complete self-negation. This novitiate, this terrible school of abnegation, is undertaken voluntarily, in the hope of self-conquest, of self-mastery, in order after a life of obedience, to attain to perfect freedom, that is from self; to escape the lot of those who have lived their whole life without finding their true selves in themselves.[15]

For Barsanuphius and John, the art of spiritual direction connects—or nails—the will to the cross:

> "Denying oneself and taking up the cross" means cutting off one's will in everything. (*Letter* 257)

---

[15] See *The Brothers Karamazov*, trans. R. Pevear and L. Volokhonsky (New York: Vintage Classics, 1991), 27.

If you do not want to walk with a limp, take up the rod of the cross, set your hand firmly on it, and die to yourself. Then, you will no longer walk with a limp; for a dead person does not walk with a limp. (*Letter* 61)

One is called to this kind of liberation by way of the margins of self-renunciation, in the paradox of self-subjection to a spiritual elder. "Those who seek to save their life will lose it, and those who lose their life will preserve it" (Lk 17:33). Leaving the city in search of the desert is the initial step in learning to lose, which is in turn the preliminary step in learning to love.[16] But surrendering one's self is no comfortable or convenient task. The ascetic may often choose to go to extremes, but this is because of the extremity of the fallen condition—a liminal state requiring limitless steps.

Holding on to the cross provides a sense of stability. Part of why we require spiritual direction is because we live our lives like a thermometer (*Letters* 204 and 483), with our temperament rising or sinking contingent on the actions of others:

> Instead, love those who test you. For I very often loved those who tested me. If we are prudent, it is such people who bring us to progress. (*Letter* 21)

> If we regard all people as one, and all days as equal, then God is truly with us. If we love those who hate us, insult us, abuse us, despise us, harm us and cause us grief in the same way as we love those who love us, praise us, benefit us and refresh us, then truly God is with us. The sign that a person has reached this degree is that one always has God within. (*Letter* 137b)

Trials and temptations invariably involve the will and are inevitable (*Letter* 248), perhaps even desirable (*Letter* 21); we must be grateful for the opportunity they afford us in our struggle for progress: "Temptation brings us to progress; and wherever there is good, there also temptation occurs. So do not be afraid of temptations, but rejoice that they lead you to progress"

---

[16]For a modern interpretation of the "interior" or "interiorized" desert, see Paul Evdokimov, *The Struggle with God* (Glen Rock, NJ: Paulist Press, 1966), esp. 111–30.

(*Letter* 496). The aim is not to resist them but to become like living fire! "Then, burning with this fire, you will always desire to be a companion, co-citizen, and co-heir of the saints, who have acquired the things 'that no eye has seen, nor ear heard, nor the human heart conceived, of what God has prepared for those who love him'" (1 Cor 2:9) (*Letter* 130).

Grounded in Love

"Identify unconditionally with those who suffer. This is the task of a spiritual father and teacher" (*Letter* 844). Such, then, is the vocation of the spiritual guide: to demonstrate a sense of intimate compassion with those are wounded by passion, and to do so "with pain of heart, with even greater love, and with copious tears" (*Letter* 57). Without this, one gains nothing from spiritual direction but a feeling of guilt. We should not consider spiritual direction in terms of remorse, but in terms of reconciliation, restoration, and reintegration. Grounded in love, spiritual direction exceeds anything that can ever be expressed through words: "If I could fill these letters with tears and send them to you, since you have suffered so much, it would have been of greater benefit to you" (*Letter* 229). Devoid of love, however, spiritual direction is no longer creative but destructive. Without love, spiritual guides cannot offer hope or healing.

The fact that the letters of Barsanuphius and John capture and crystallize their words for eternity is a supplementary element of their primary sensitivity in spiritual direction. Words matter; they contain power; they must be selected with consideration and compassion. And spelling out one's advice in longhand—dictating a response of instruction and direction—is yet another means of abstaining from imposition or insensitivity and protecting the disciple: "The trouble is that we do not pay close enough attention to what we say" (*Letter* 95).

The spiritual guide cares deeply and loves ... divinely:

> As God knows, there is not a blink of the eye or a moment in time that I do not have you in my mind and my prayer. And if I

love you so much, then the God who created you loves you still more. (*Letter* 113)

I have told you all these things so you may learn that I shall not cease praying for you until God brings you, with me, to the heavenly gates. (*Letter* 645)

For Jesus is the mediator, who presents [us] before the entrance gates. (*Letter* 153)

A Second Opinion

What is particularly refreshing about the letters of the two Old Men is, as previously noted, the triangular structure of their spiritual network. For them, spiritual direction is not a unilateral expression of authority or a unidirectional course of advice. It is not a one-way road, but an open-ended conversation, informed and enriched by director and disciple alike. There is no circumvention of any institutional or spiritual hierarchy here, but only an insight into the elaborate ramifications of forgiveness and reconciliation. This reciprocity and mutuality are foremost in their concept of spiritual direction, offering disappointed and disgruntled disciples a way out any arising impasse, the possibility of appeal on reaching a deadlock.

This is interaction at its best, healing at its most authentic. The unusual and unparalleled form of spiritual direction offered in consort and in collaboration by the two elders provides a safety net or escape that releases the pressure and relieves the tension that commonly accumulates in any close-knit hierarchal community. It also permits the uninterrupted flow of communication and confession *from* the disciple, while at the same time preserving reliability and security *for* the disciple. Here is how Abba John perceives it:

> If all of us are one—both the [Great] Old Man in God and I in the Old Man—then I dare say that, if he gave you his word, I too give you mine through him. I know that I am inadequate and insignificant; yet I cannot separate myself from the Old Man. For he is compassionate to me so that the two of us are one. (*Letter* 305)

The two elders regard spiritual direction not so much as a solution to some specific problem of a disciple, but rather as the path leading to a solution generated by the disciple:

> If you are unable to ask your elder about something, you should pray three times about it. Afterward, you should observe where your heart inclines, even very slightly, and act accordingly. For this assurance becomes quite clear and apparent to the heart. (*Letter 365*)

They are also well aware that their system is open to abuse:

> You should always ask the person you trust, knowing that he will bear your thoughts; trust in him as if in God. As for consulting another person about the same thought, this is a result of faithlessness and temptation. For if you believe that God has spoken through his saint, then why should you test God by posing the same question to someone else? (*Letter 361*)

However, Barsanuphius and John are convinced that the "open-ended" or "three-dimensional" system of spiritual direction is far less susceptible to abuse than the "one-sided" or "two-dimensional" approach in the traditional practice. So they work very hard to complement and complete each other:

> Someone asked Abba John about a certain matter. And after receiving a response, he addressed the same question to Abba Barsanuphius, without telling him that he had already asked the Other Old Man about this.
> The Old Man responded in this way: "Do as you were told by brother John."
> Again, sometime afterwards, it happened that the same brother asked Abba John about something and, having heard the response, directed the same question to Abba Barsanuphius. However, the Great Old Man replied as follows: "From now on, one response is sufficient for you. For the God of Barsanuphius and John is one." So that brother never again approached the two Old Men with the same question, being content with the response of the one. (*Letter 224*)

One specific letter sheds further light on the concept of spiritual direction as implemented by the two elders. The "other old man" is asked about a situation where a disciple considers consulting another elder because he feels that his own elder is incapable of providing the necessary counsel. The disciple therefore asks whether he is obliged to reveal to his elder that he will be approaching someone else. The question cuts to the core of the open spiritual direction practiced by Barsanuphius and John: If I think that my spiritual guide is unqualified to assist me in a particular problem, can I turn to someone else? And do I have to inform my spiritual guide that I am doing so? The response by Abba John is straightforward and striking, even shocking:

> If you know that your abba will benefit the soul, you should confide in him, saying: "I have these thoughts; what do you think I should do?" The elder, like someone with an ill child who hurries to take it to a doctor—in fact, even spends all of his income to care for his child—will gladly take his disciple to someone with the gift of healing, or else send him to find another elder. If you know that the elder cannot endure this, then you should not say anything but simply look for an opportunity, when God will provide an occasion, to ask another spiritual elder about your thoughts, entreating him not to inform your own elder because this would lead him to the passion of envy. (*Letter 504*)

It is remarkable that, not only does John consent to the request about consulting someone else, but he also concedes that it may even be beneficial to withhold this information from his own elder. Barsanuphius and John are clear about one thing: There is only one thing worse than a spiritual disciple persuaded that any advice received is magical or mystical, and that is a spiritual director presuming that his advice is irrefutable and infallible!

Lest, however, we jump too swiftly to any conclusion, that this response somehow enables exploitation of a spiritual relationship, Abba John promptly adds:

> This of course will create great affliction because one is asking another elder while not being scandalized at one's own elder for not possessing a particular gift; for not all gifts are given to everyone. Nevertheless, *if one searches carefully, one will in fact*

discover that one's own elder has another gift.[17] For the gifts of the Spirit are diverse and distributed variously among people, to one in such a manner while to another in a different manner. Finally, if you do not find the opportunity to ask someone else, then you should be patient, praying to God for assistance. (*Letter* 504)

It is noteworthy that Abba John is not intimidated by the question because he knows all too well that the purpose of all spiritual direction is ultimately to acknowledge and affirm the unique talent of each person, from whom we can learn and grow. The art of spiritual direction eventually contributes to the circle of community and is conducive to all of us in "bearing one other's burdens."

"Do Your Best" (*Letter* 343)

We often tend to highlight the extraordinary qualities and learned wisdom of early—or modern, for that matter—spiritual guides. Yet Barsanuphius and John are not spectacular gurus; they are not eccentric miracle-workers; they are not extreme ascetics or charismatic visionaries; they do not profess either expertise or experience. In fact, they avoid all the excessive quirks and austere idiosyncrasies personified by Peter Brown's diviner, magician, and exorcist.[18] Most of the time, they are simply trying to deflate fantasy and diminish drama; the bulk of their emphasis is placed on common sense. Abba Barsanuphius advises against making mountains out of molehills—in his words, "a camel out of a gnat, or a rock out of a pebble" (*Letter* 16). And Abba John quotes the desert fathers: "If you see a younger monk rising up to heaven through his own will, hold his foot and pull him back down" (*Letter* 693).

Ironically, that is precisely what renders the two elders extraordinary—that they are in fact ordinary advisers, providing simple teaching and steadfast encouragement to people in their daily struggle. They neither pretend to have nor presume to supply

---

[17]Emphasis mine.
[18]Brown, "The Rise and Function of the Holy Man," 80–101. Reprinted with additional notes in Brown, *Society and the Holy in Late Antiquity*, 103–52. [Here at 121–6].

answers on tap to spiritual challenges; they do not even profess to have solutions to every problem. They simply offer the assurance of God's abiding love and persistent mercy:

> My brother and soul-mate Andrew, do not grow weary. For God has not forsaken you; nor will he forsake you. This is the Master's promise. (*Letter* 105)

> Therefore, do not be sad. For God has not forgotten you but cares for you as a true child, not as an illegal child. (*Letter* 106)

In fact, their confidence lies not so much in any foresight or foreknowledge about the ways of the heart as it does in their farsightedness and firm knowledge of what happens to the heart when it is loved by God. The journey may be tenuous and the struggle uncomfortable, but if we recognize that God loves us, there is nothing to worry about, nothing to be anxious about:

> You should believe that everything that happens from God will have a good end; do not be anxious about anything else. (*Letter* 576)

> You are blessed if you are completely conscious of your sins … So do not relax, but do not collapse. (*Letter* 498)

> Simply do your best, and God will come to your assistance in everything. (*Letter* 343)

Such is the fundamental conviction of Barsanuphius and John; and it is the essential key to their appreciation and application of spiritual direction: that by receiving forgiveness, we learn to forgive. Accepting divine compassion is what allows us the space to be grateful, generous, and in the end forgiving. It enables us to experience someone else's predicament, to understand someone else's experiences and challenges. By being loved, we learn how to love. By embracing our darkness and weaknesses, we enlighten the hearts and lighten the burdens of others.

If Barsanuphius and John are filled with joy (*Letters* 10, 137, and 459) and thanksgiving (*Letters* 267, 366, and 404), it is because they are convinced about God's love, confident that God never abandons us—whoever we are and wherever we happen to be on the spiritual journey: "Pray also for me; for my slackening leads me to many evils. Nevertheless, I do not despair; for I have a merciful God" (*Letter* 512). This humility and humor transmit the assurance that "alone, it [may be] impossible; but with God all things are possible" (Mt 19:26).

> Do not grieve; for the mercy of God is nearby. I greet you in the Lord; be healthy, you cry-baby. (*Letter* 514)

This degree of joy enables us to give thanks for ordinary things without resentment, objection, or bitterness. When we have a wider perspective of life—a panoramic 30,000-foot view—joy becomes unconditional, independent, and undemanding. Then it is no longer contingent on more possessions or better circumstances. Nothing changes externally, but only internally. It is joy and thanks simply because we live and breathe; it is joy and thanks simply because!

5

Fasting and Feasting

Sustained by God in the Wilderness

It's Not about the Food[1]

On the one hand, the heart of the ascetic discipline frequently seems like it pertains to a profound spiritual struggle in the face of vice or in pursuit of virtue, but so often relates to the proper approach to ordinary routines and everyday activities—like eating and drinking. On the other hand, the most mundane exercises and material actions are filled with spiritual significance and mystical meaning—like eating and drinking. Nevertheless, in this remarkable correspondence, Abba John affirms the apostolic injunction that the kingdom of heaven is not about food:

> Advise them in all humility with the words of the Apostle: "Those who eat must not despise those who do not eat; ... and those who do not eat should not pass judgement on those who eat" (Rom 14:3–6). Both those who eat and those who do not eat are honorable in God's eyes; for each of them acts according to God's glory. In brief, each person should do what is necessary out

---

[1] From the title of a book on eating disorders: see Carol Emery Normandi and Laurelee Roark, *It's Not About the Food* (New York: Grosset/Putnam, 1998).

of love for God, saying: "I am weak and unable to do otherwise; please be compassionate with me." As the Apostle said: "The kingdom of heaven is neither food nor drink, but love and purity of heart" (Rom 14:17, 1 Tm 1:5). (*Letter* 584)[2]

And elsewhere, the same elder counsels: "Do not abstain [from food] altogether, but struggle instead against your thought" (*Letter* 162).

For many people today, food has become an enemy; but early monastic literature considered a different kind of enemy. In our age, we have demonized food in vain search for material comfort, emotional coping, and physical competence; today, the struggle against savory temptation gets waged in the fitness club or the weight loss program, not in the heart or the mind. In former centuries, however, food was the source of a more dangerous nuance or spiritual distraction. Gluttony was once a consequence of self-*adoration* or disrespect for *God*.[3] Today we perceive it as an aspect of self-*admiration* or disrespect for one's *self*. Despite a more secular approach to life, it is surprising that our relationship with food still readily translates into a language about God and the devil, or else about sin and repentance: We speak of overeating as "being wrong," of rich foods as "tempting" or "sinfully delicious," and of delight in food as creating "guilt" or causing "remorse."

After all, so much of the world's population goes hungry each day. Thus, no matter what the period or purpose, the struggle to control eating and limit consumption is always intense. Adhering to the Pauline approach (Phil. 4:5 and 1 Cor. 9:25), Evagrius of Pontus advised monks to maintain a sparse and moderate diet.[4] The sixth-century elders of Gaza attest to this permanent and persistent war waged against the vice of gluttony:

> When the passion of gluttony tempts you, struggle as much as possible not to give the body all that it requires ... Once you

---

[2] See also *Letter* 607.
[3] For a socio-cultural approach to temptation, see S. M. Lyman, *The Seven Deadly Sins: Society and Evil* (New York: St. Martin's Press, 1978).
[4] Evagrius, *On the Eight Thoughts: Gluttony* I, 14. See David Brakke (trans.), *Evagrius of Pontus, Antirrhetikos: A Monastic Handbook for Combating Demons* (Collegeville, MN: Liturgical Press, 2009), 56.

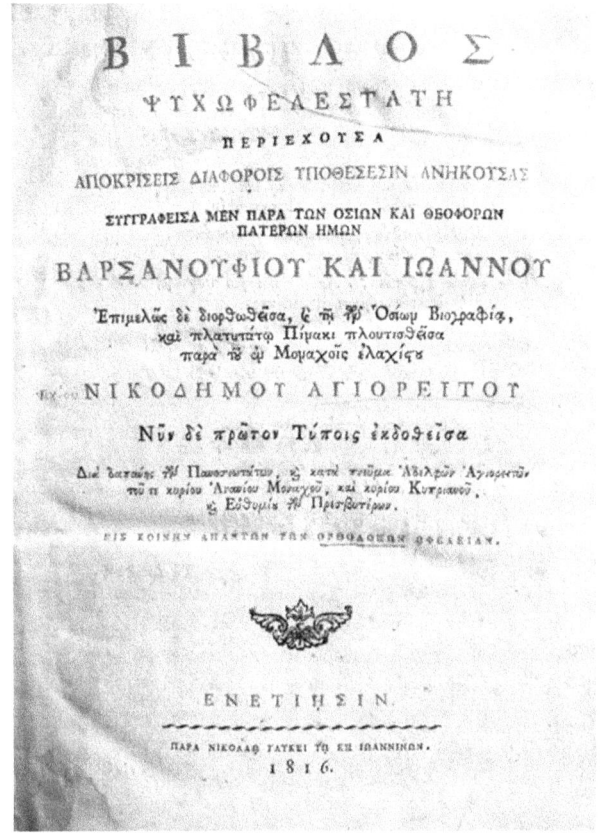

FIGURE 3 *First edition of Barsanuphius and John (Venice).*

have triumphed over the temptation with the grace of God, then you may acquire whatever you need. (*Letter* 502)

Struggle against gluttony as much as you can, and the Lord will assist you to understand and do whatever is beneficial for you. (*Letter* 328)

One who consumes many types of foods during meals is gluttonous. Whereas one who eats daily from only one food not only lacks greed, but in time also develops distaste for that food. (*Letter* 85)

It seems that, over the centuries, the notion of gluttony has generally evolved along with ideas about the body and food, about the individual and society, as well as about health and holiness. Still, whether one praises or condemns this seductive sin, it remains a mirror wherein we ultimately see a clear reflection of ourselves and our fears, our passions and prejudices, our darkest dreams and deepest desires. Indeed, our contemporary fascination with gluttony—along with our struggle to suppress or subdue it—discloses as much about our spiritual aspirations as it does about our never-ending attempts to define human nature.

Our struggle with food is, in the final analysis, an inherently metaphysical matter; if, according to the German philosopher and anthropologist Ludwig Feuerbach (1804–72), "we are what we eat,"[5] then what we believe about eating reveals our perception about who we are and what we want to become, about the hunger of our body and—above and beyond all else—the yearning of our soul. Whether fasting or feasting, food is ultimately a reflection of our passions and priorities.

So it is helpful to focus on the struggle to understand or overcome gluttony by first looking in the mirror, then confronting our desires, and eventually making honest choices about our behavior. Only then will we be sufficiently empty and thirsty to be filled with God's love and in humility to make the right choices according to his will. It is only after the fast that we will truly delight in the feast of grace and love.

The Face of Gluttony

But what does gluttony look like? After all, as Orson Wells puts it: "Gluttony is not a secret vice!" Moreover, gluttony does not have a single target; for Abba John: "The measure of gluttony applies not only to matters [related to food], but also to speech, sleep, dress, and all the senses. Each of these likewise has its own degree of abstinence" (*Letter* 155). In this regard, one can speak of various forms of a "visible" and "tangible" gluttony: there are the more apparent vices of overeating (the gluttony of filling our stomach);

---

[5]Feuerbach, *Sämtliche Werke*, vol. 10 (Leipzig, 1846–1866), 5.

there is the vice of compulsive activity (the gluttony of filling our time); and there is the vice of collecting trinkets and gadgets (the gluttony of filling our space). Each of these faces of gluttony reflects a means of meeting certain needs or filling certain voids. Ultimately, they indicate ways of avoiding an encounter or experience with our most vital cravings, which can only be quenched by "the living water of eternal life" (Jn 4:14).

In the second century, Clement of Alexandria warned against excessive food on both medical and moral grounds.[6] For Clement, gluttons "are shipwrecked on pastries, honeycakes, and desserts!"[7] Yet perhaps the most comprehensive definition of gluttony is offered by John Chrysostom's deacon, Evagrius of Pontus, who maintained a strict ascetic regimen of abstinence in the desert of Egypt:

> Gluttony is the mother of lust, nourishment of evil thoughts, laziness of fasting, obstacle to asceticism, terror to moral purpose, imagination of food, sketcher of seasoning, an unrestrained horse, unbridled frenzy, receptacle of disease, envy of health, obstruction of bodily passages, groaning of bowels, extremity of anger, ally of craving, pollution of the intellect, weakness of the body, difficulty in sleep, and gloom of death.[8]

It comes as no surprise, then, that—in this, as in so many other details of the ascetic life, in the wake of Evagrius—Barsanuphius and John place gluttony at the pinnacle of their list of vices (*Letter* 137b).

One conventional reason for the importance of vigilance and struggle against this vice is the allegation that gluttony generally weakens human morals, paving the way for other, more serious temptations. In some ways, gluttony is more than just a cause of sin; it is, in fact, the "original" sin! It is what led to the "fall of Adam" in the garden of Eden. In the fourteenth century, Geoffrey Chaucer

---

[6]Clement of Alexandria, *Stromateis* II, 2. See https://www.newadvent.org/fathers/02102.htm
[7]Ibid., II, i, 3–4.
[8]Evagrius Ponticus, *The Praktikos & Chapters on Prayer*, trans. John Eudes Bamberger (Kalamazoo, MI: Cistercian Publications, 1981), 17f. See Teresa Shaw, *The Burden of the Flesh: Fasting and Sexuality in Early Christianity* (Minneapolis, MN: Fortress Press, 1998).

summarized this in verse: "Oh gluttony, full of cursedness/Cause of our original ruin/Root of our damnation."[9] However, gluttony is surely incidental, if not accidental, to Adam and Eve's sin. To interpret original sin as the vice of gluttony is plainly to miss the point of the Genesis story; had Adam and Eve truly been gluttons, they would have consumed all the apples!

Plato wrote in the *Timaeus* that gluttony could serve as a distraction—a word that literally implies "hindering" or "hampering" (dis-, δυσ-) our "traction"—from elevated concerns.[10] And Philo, Plato's Jewish admirer in first-century Alexandria, regarded gluttony as the main stumbling block on the way to holiness, a veritable obsession and consequently the principal cause of lasciviousness. For Philo, the ideal ascetic community is both vegetarian and celibate.[11] In the third century, Tertullian even suggested an intimate connection between gluttony and lust, which in the following century Jerome visually promoted for posterity in his ascetic propaganda: "These two are so closely united that, had there been any possibility of separating them at all, the genitals would not have been affixed to the belly."[12]

As we might expect, the connection between gluttony and lust or greed has all but disappeared in the modern psyche, which dismisses it as a remnant of medieval narrow-mindedness. However, Abba Barsanuphius is clear about the connection: "Since I am unable to keep silent, let me make a suggestion. If you do not eat for the sake of pleasure but for the sake of the body's weakness, God will not condemn you. For we monitor food to avoid excessive eating and bodily arousal" (*Letter* 510). In his *Screwtape Letters*, C. S. Lewis describes the "chief use of [excess in food] as a kind of artillery preparation for attacks on chastity."[13] In fact, Dante's *Inferno* consigns gluttons to the third circle of hell, a lower region and more

---

[9]See Geoffrey Chaucer, Prologue to "The Pardoner's Tale," in *The Canterbury Tales*, ed. Helen Cooper (Oxford: Oxford University Press, 1996), sections 210 through 300, 260–77.
[10]Plato, *Timaeus*, 72.
[11]Philo, *On the Contemplative Life*, 34–5.
[12]Tertullian, *De Ieiunio adversus Psychicos* I, 1–2; Jerome, *Letters* 54, 9; see also Augustine, *Confessions* X, 31 (43–4).
[13]C. S. Lewis, *Screwtape Letters* (San Francisco, CA: Harper, 2001 [repr. 1942]); "Letter 17."

hideous fate than that reserved for the lustful, inasmuch as gluttons choose to worship themselves,[14] while the lustful at least fix their adoration on each other.

So it appears that, of all the vices, gluttony arguably enjoys the most intriguing history, regarded as a supreme form of idolatry and the most extreme form of materialism. Indeed, from biblical times, the principal objection to gluttony is that it turns attention from "heavenly things" (where the mind *should be*) to "earthly things" (which the mind *should avoid*), thereby becoming a substitute for God. In the stern warning of Paul to the Christians in Philippi: "Their god is their stomach" (Phil 3:18–19; see also Rom 16:17).

The Power of Choice: Looking at the Menu

The problem, of course, does not normally lie in food itself; it is commonly the inordinate *desire* or *passion* for food—the intense and involved longing that comes between the soul and God, distracting us from love for and devotion to God. The desire and the distraction alike derive from the potency and potential of human choice, from the divine gift of will, created as we are "in the image and likeness of God" (Gn 1:26). For all the vehemence of early monastic debates about free will and its relationship to divine grace, no one doubted that the glutton too had a choice when it came to what, when, and how much to eat:

> Question. "What happens when I am unsure who is actually scandalized by my desire to eat? What should I do?" Response by John. You are able to test and see whether he is scandalized or not. For instance, if you need to eat, do not say: "Give me some food." Rather, say: "I see that I am hungry for one reason or another." When he hears this, he will reveal himself; and in this way, you will learn his disposition, as to whether or not he is scandalized. (*Letter* 377)

---

[14]Dante, *Inferno*, Canto 6, Circle 3.

The issue was not so much the fact that the monk ate; it was that the monk made wrong choices. Indeed, a monk may be obliged to eat when it is a question of "cutting off his own will."[15] Abba John assures us that no food is harmful unless consumed with passion:

> If God sanctified and purified everything so the faithful might partake of everything, then one should receive whatever is offered with thanksgiving and without discrimination. Indeed, holy and pure things do not harm anyone, unless one's conscience or one's suspicion believes that one is being harmed. For such a person is in fact hesitant in faith, which is why passion abounds within. Therefore, if one believes in the one who came to heal every sickness and every weakness among his people, then that same person is able to heal not only bodily illness, but also the inner self. However, if one is in doubt, then one should avoid harmful foods, condemning oneself for not being able to tolerate them and for being overcome in thought, not being found to be with sure faith. This is how one is guarded from consuming food with passion, which is harmful for both soul and body. (*Letter 526*)

Early monastic literature is more concerned about what the monk *chose* than what the monk *chewed*. Indeed, for Abba John, desire is the propulsion of choice and the compulsion of gluttony:

> A brother asked the same Old Man: Father, what is the difference between eating food according to one's desire, and eating it according to one's [natural] condition?
> Response by John. Eating according to one's desire is longing to consume food, not for the body's need but for gluttony's sake. For example, if you see that your condition takes to herbs rather than to pulse, not for the sake of desire but for its lightness, this is where the difference lies. Moreover, certain conditions tolerate sweet things, others tolerate salty things, and others demand bitter things; and this is neither passion nor desire nor gluttony. However, *to long for or crave after something, in spite of its heavy nature, is called desire, which*

---

[15]*Letter 528.*

is the servant of gluttony.[16] So be careful when the passion of gluttony overcomes you and masters your thought. However, if you resist, making *moderate* use of your food for your need, then this is not considered gluttony. (*Letter* 161)

It appears that all the ancient sages frown upon the excesses of gluttony.[17] Many of them describe their relationship with food as a ferocious, lifelong battle for choice and control. Gluttony is not always—or not only—about too much food; it is usually—and ultimately—about wrong choices and placing our choices above the needs of others and the will of God. As a battle for power, then, gluttony can undoubtedly lead to evil; in fact, it is the source of countless evils. Even God foresaw this in contemplating the creation of Adam.

So, for the elders of Gaza, just as for the entire desert tradition, gluttony must be cut off at the very root! Abba Barsanuphius writes:

As far as cutting off the root of the passions ... this occurs by cutting off one's own will as much as possible and by afflicting the senses in order to keep them disciplined, so that they may not be wrongly exercised. This is how you should cut off the root of these things and of everything else. (*Letter* 462)

The Way of Renunciation: Shedding and Surrendering

Abba John reiterates the admonition for vigilance against gluttony: "Great vigilance is required ... If [captivity] leads your intellect to gluttony, you should reign it back to asceticism" (*Letter* 86). Such caution has a long history in monastic literature. It was gluttony's misfortune that the codifying of virtues and vices coincided with the flowering of monasticism, which discerned the treacherous deceit of

---

[16]Emphasis mine.
[17]See Veronika Grimm, *From Feasting to Fasting, the Evolution of a Sin: Attitudes to Food in Late Antiquity* (London: Routledge, 1995). See also R. D. Chatham, *Fasting: A Biblical-Historical Study* (South Plainfield, NJ: Bridge Publishing, 1987). For a fascinating analysis of gluttony, see Francine Prose, *Gluttony* (New York: Oxford University Press, 2003).

this particular temptation.[18] For John Climacus, gluttony and lust occupy the middle—in other words, the very heart and soul—of the ladder of divine ascent.[19] Monastics believed that gluttony had a language of its own, its own peculiar grammar, and vocabulary. Yet it was a discourse frequently heard in complicated and conflicting ways, which require careful unraveling to discern the language of holiness.

And in the syntax of asceticism, the first rule is renunciation. Anyone remotely familiar with the way of the ascetics knows that the first step of the ladder is renunciation. Withdrawal or renunciation—"despising the world and all that is in it"—is the fundamental and essential method employed by Anthony of Egypt for the sake of remembering "always to keep the fear of God before [his] eyes."[20] In the desert, everything is about detachment; everything is about letting go. Silence is surrendering the security or justification provided by words, fasting is renouncing dependence on or attachment to earthly resources, and spiritual direction is about life no longer revolving around oneself but instead including others.

There are of course many stages of renunciation, just as there are multiple steps on the spiritual ladder. Perhaps we should imagine renunciation not so much as the first stage, but as *a series of stages of refinement*. There are a number of successive renunciations and refinements that one undergoes in the desert. One of the more tangible forms of renunciation or refinement is the struggle against gluttony. Renunciation resembles the constant shedding of coats of skin (Gn. 3:21), which sharpens or refines our senses, until "our inner vision becomes keen."[21] When we learn what to let go of, we concomitantly learn what is worth holding on to.

> Abba Zosimas said: "In time, through neglect, we lose even the little fervor that we suppose we have in ascetic renunciation. We become attached to useless, insignificant and entirely worthless

---

[18]For an extreme example, see R. Bell, *Holy Anorexia* (Chicago: University of Chicago Press, 1985).
[19]John Climacus, Steps 14 "On Gluttony" and 15 "On Lust" in the thirty steps of the *Ladder*.
[20]Anthony 33, *Sayings*.
[21]Doulas 1, *Sayings*.

matters, substituting them for the love of God and neighbor, appropriating material things as if they were our own or as if we did not receive them from God. 'What do you have that you did not receive? And if you received it, why do you boast as if it were not a gift?'" (1 Cor 4:7)[22]

The first step or principle of renunciation is progressively learning to relinquish or gradually becoming detached:

> Question. Since every food contains natural sweetness, is this harmful to the person who consumes it?
> Response by John. God our Master created sweetness in every food, and there is no harm in eating of this with thanksgiving (1 Tm 4:4). However, one should always guard against attachment; for this is what harms the soul. (*Letter* 773)

That is precisely how it must be in the spiritual way: We are obliged to surrender what we *think* we want in order to acquire something greater that we *truly* need. It is a painful, albeit crucial process of bidding farewell to certain objects or particular habits in order to learn what could be and what really matters. In order to gain a new perspective, one inevitably has to shed or die to the old ways. "We have ignored the Apostle Paul, who says: 'Put away all anger, wrangling and slander, along with all malice' (Eph 4:31), and I would add gluttony to this list ... in order to become pure from filthy, righteous from sinful, and alive from dead" (*Letter* 604).

The Way of Moderation: Ascetic Refinement

As already noted, gluttony can assume different forms: overeating can be otherwise expressed as overspeaking, overreacting, overjudging, overacting, over-succeeding, overconsuming ... We can "binge" with words and not just food! We can "consume" with our

---

[22]Zosimas, *Reflections* X, c.

emotions and not just sweets! We can "swallow" other people's basic need for survival and not just our fair share of sustenance.

The ascetic response to gluttony is ultimately a way of authentic liberation and communion. Someone who struggles against gluttony is ultimately free, uncontrolled by abusive attitudes, uncompelled by compulsive ways. The ascetic is characterized by self-control, self-restraint, and the ability to say "no" or "enough." The goal of asceticism is moderation, not repression. Asceticism aims at refinement, abstinence, and surrender—not detachment, disengagement, or destruction. Aristotle did not dare to reject indulgence unilaterally; instead, he counseled moderation in everything, including eating and drinking.[23]

Ascetic refinement therefore includes recognizing the positive attributes of food. The Gaza elders are not obsessive either about or against food; indeed, tasty food is a good thing. Food is "a gift from God,"[24] while preparing food should be done competently and carefully.[25] In fact, food is sacred, and eating should be a slow, intentional process. We should sit down to meals with gratitude and grace because we can actually discern and discover God in food. Some Church Fathers even identify food with Christ, the divine manna provided in the desert (Jn 6:31); in the words of John Chrysostom, "the bread of God comes down from heaven and gives life to the world."[26] Jesus performs the miracle of the loaves and fishes that feeds a hungry throng, and clearly states that it is not what goes into the mouth that defiles us, but every word that comes out of it (Mt 15:11):

> Response by the Great Old Man to a brother, when the thought was sown within that not abstaining from food prevented him from reaching what was promised.

---

[23] Aristostle, *Nicomachean Ethics*, trans. D. Ross (New York: Oxford University Press, 1998), 29.
[24] *Letter* 338.
[25] *Letter* 489.
[26] John Chrysostom, *Homilies on the Gospel of John*, echoed in Chrysostom, "Prayer of the Prothesis" in the Divine Liturgy. See Ephrem Lash, (transl.), *The Divine Liturgy of Our Father among the Saints John Chrysostom* (Chipping Norton, Oxfordshire: Greek Orthodox Archdiocese of Thyateira and Great Britain, 2011), 1–15.

It is not because I wish to abolish abstinence and the monastic discipline that I am always telling your love to exercise the needs of your body as necessary—far be it for me! Rather, I am saying that if, after God, the inner work does not assist us, then one is laboring in vain on the outward self.[27] For that is why the Lord said: "It is not what goes into the mouth that defiles a person, but what comes out of the mouth defiles" (Mt 15:11). Indeed, inner work with labor of heart generates purity, which engenders true stillness of heart, which in turn brings humility, rendering a person the dwelling-place of God ... That person becomes a God-bearer, or even a god, according to the one who told us: "I have said, you are gods, all children of the Most High" (Ps 81:6, Jn 10:34). Therefore, *do not let the thought, or rather the evil one, trouble you, that bodily foods supposedly prevent you from attaining to those promises.*[28] No; for they are holy, and evil cannot issue from good, but only from those things that come from the mouth. The things, then, that come from inside the heart (Mt 15:18–19) are the ones that prevent and hinder a person from arriving swiftly at the promises that lie before us. (*Letter* 119)

What matters still more than what goes into the stomach is retaining the focus of the heart on the divine, which is possible only through balanced and disciplined diet. For Barsanuphius and John, the key always lies in moderation:

For a healthy person ... wishing to exercise abstinence, one cup of wine each day is sufficient, and no more. However, if one is frequently ill, then one should take two full cups. The same applies to cooked food: one should eat only one bowl and not worry about anything else. As for how the Fathers adopted a very strict diet, they found that their bodies were obedient. Therefore, those who controlled themselves well and with discernment were able to conform their routine to their body. (*Letter* 159)

---

[27]Cf. Arsenius 9, *Sayings*.
[28]Emphasis mine.

Moderation is especially significant and pertinent in cases of illness.[29] And here the Gaza elders reveal incomparable discernment and compassion:

> The same person was relieved of his illness and asked the Old Man: Father, when I eat, I am heavily weighed down. Then, I am unable to fast; for my body feels weak and I sweat a great deal ...
>
> Response by Barsanuphius. Brother, I greet you in the Lord, praying that he might strengthen you and grant you patience. However, you must learn that this warfare comes from the devil, who weighs you down with food in order to make you relax. For he also tempted me over a long period, weighing down heavily on me, even making me vomit night after night. However, I began to eat just a little food, and then he changed his tactic. Whenever I approached to eat, just as I placed a bite in my mouth, he would make me vomit. So I began to eat every two days, in order that I might grow accustomed to the food, but that too became his tactic. Nonetheless, with the grace of God, through patience and thanksgiving, my temptation has ceased. I had become so weak that I cannot even describe it to you; yet I did not give up but struggled until the Lord gave me strength (2 Tm 4:17). Brother, when I was ill, that is what I did. So pay closer attention to yourself and God will have mercy on you. For there is only one that is envious of you, and "the Lord has annihilated him" (2 Thes 2:8). (*Letter* 512)

For Abba John, there is also a distinction between eating "according to one's natural condition" ("for the body's need") and eating "according to one's personal desire" ("for gluttony's sake"). In all things, John advises temperance: "Be careful when the passion of gluttony overcomes you and masters your thought ... However, if you make moderate use of your food for the sake of your need, then this is not considered gluttony" (*Letter* 161).

---

[29]On the nature and meaning of illness, particularly as this plays out in the process of spiritual direction, see Andrew Crisp, *Thorns in the Flesh: Illness and Sanctity in Late Ancient Christianity* (Philadelphia, PA: University of Pennsylvania Press, 2013), esp. 138–65.

This means that the criterion of moderation lies in consuming "a little less," always stopping relatively short of satiety, which in itself is ultimately an indicator of craving a little more. Abba Barsanuphius says: "Abstinence means getting up from the table with *a little less* (hunger and thirst), as the elders ordained for those who have not yet achieved progress" (*Letter* 154).[30] Abba John concurs, adding remarks that echo the precision of a "weight-loss" or "12-step" plan and allowing for seasonal or climatic variations:

> The Fathers say about the measure of abstinence that it means always consuming a little less, whether in regard to food or drink; namely, one should not fill the stomach with one or the other. Furthermore, one ought to calculate the food cooked and the wine consumed. In winter, one does not drink as much; and so the "*little less*" should be calculated accordingly. The same applies to food. (*Letter* 155)

> One should avoid only harmful foods. If a certain food happens to be neither harmful nor beneficial, then *one should not eat to the point of satiation* but only a little.[31] For if one eats even beneficial food to the point of satiation, then one is harmed. (*Letter* 530)

Extending the Table
It's Not about You

It sometimes appears that gluttony is a private matter, entailing personal or private sin. In fact, however, it is a broader or social sin—against others and against God. It is the diametrical opposite of sharing with others and dependence on God. Indeed, we may consider gluttony a substitute for intimacy and love.[32] So the cure for gluttony involves refining one's own senses and becoming

---

[30]See also Abba Isaiah, *Ascetic Discourse* 4.
[31]Emphases mine.
[32]For a contemporary psychological discussion of this, see G. Roth, *When Food Is Love: Exploring the Relationship between Eating and Intimacy* (New York: Plume, 1991).

more sensitive to others. Hence the copious rules in the *Letters* of Barsanuphius and John about how to approach a table or sit down at a meal:

> Question to Abba John. Father, What happens when the passion is not there beforehand but is suggested at mealtime? What should I do? Should I abstain from food or not?
> Response. Do not abstain altogether, but struggle against your thought, remembering that food is eventually reduced to a foul smell and is of no profit, as well as that *we are condemned when we eat while others entirely abstain.* If the thought ... masters you, so that you are unable to *eat in orderly manner,* then cut off the food. But if others are seated beside you, in order to prevent them from noticing anything, eat a little at a time. Of course, if you should happen to be hungry, fill your need with bread or some other food that does not tempt you. (*Letter* 162)[33]

This introduces a firm social argument against gluttony—namely the fact that, for most people, gluttony involves eating more than we need in the full knowledge that millions of others with whom we share the earth's resources are starving. It also demonstrates how gluttony is the result of much deeper—often far less "visible"— vices, such as greed and pride, which hardly seem to trouble most of those preoccupied with consumption or distribution of food. This, too, may be a direct consequence of gluttony; it may be that other senses are numbed by the focus on oneself and one's own needs. Responding to the needs of others by means of food and drink is a cardinal and critical monastic virtue.[34]

Abba John practically foreshadows "Tiffany's Table Manners"[35] when he addresses the extraordinary effect of an ordinary etiquette for eating:

> When you see your thought taking pleasure in a particular food and driving you to anticipate others, or else taking pleasure in

---

[33] For more dietary rules, see also *Letters* 132, 151–2, 157–9, and 166. My emphasis.
[34] See *Letter* 459.
[35] See Walter Hoving, *Tiffany's Table Manners for Teenagers*, Fiftieth Anniversary Edition (New York: Random House Books, 1989).

attracting this food before you, remember that this is gluttony. So pay attention to yourself in order not to perform its will, and do your best to refrain from partaking eagerly,[36] albeit in orderly manner. Try instead to push the food before those seated beside you. It is not necessary, as I have told you, to refuse altogether to partake of food on the grounds of gluttony, but be very careful not to eat in disorderly fashion.

Even apart from gluttony, the Fathers write that we should not stretch our hands before others at the table;[37] for this is inappropriate and alien to common manners. However, when the food set before us is such that it is unclear what the portion of each happens to be, but instead everyone is supposed to share it with others, then it is not improper to do so, although again we should do so in orderly fashion in order not to fall into gluttony and condemnation. Another sign of gluttony is when one desires food before the appropriate time, which must not be done without good reason. In all things, rather, we should invoke the help of God, and he will come to our assistance. (*Letter* 163)

This other dimension or dimension of the "other" in gluttony—the factor of being sensitive to others and to God—ultimately inaugurates the perspective of the kingdom, an eschatological element personified by monastics as prophets of the age to come. The "great old man" observes:

As for the ages spoken of in Ecclesiastes, you should know that one's entire life is called an age ... If you want to learn how ignorant and superficial people distort Scripture by allegorizing according to the devil's teaching, the Apostle says: "Food is meant for the stomach, and the stomach for food, but God will destroy both the one and the other."[38] He is speaking here of

---

[36]For Thomas Aquinas, other ways of committing gluttony include *praepropere* (eating too soon) and *ardente* (eating too eagerly), as well as *laute* (eating too expensively), *nimis* (eating too much), and *studiose* (eating too daintily).
[37]Abba Isaiah, *Ascetic Discourse*, 3.
[38]1 Cor 6:13.

gluttony, indifference, and prodigality; so God did not abolish food and the stomach from the saints. For the Apostle who said this knew well that he was speaking about the passions, which the Lord abolished from himself and from those like him. Thus he began by saying: "We are no worse off if we do not eat, and no better off if we do."[39] Nevertheless, the meaning of these words is as follows. *It is in the future age that God said that human beings would be equal to angels,*[40] *neither eating nor drinking, nor again desiring anything else.*[41] And, of course, nothing is impossible with God.[42] For he demonstrated this through Moses, who lived this way for forty days and nights.[43] The one who did this for Moses is also able to do the same for anyone else, for all the years of eternity. And if someone should rave, saying that Moses nevertheless ate afterward, we were also given a partial example of what will happen in the future, as well as of the resurrection, through our Savior, who resurrected other dead people through the Apostles as well. All of this demonstrates that there will be a resurrection. Even if the Apostles died afterward, we should still not doubt the resurrection. Furthermore, it is said: "One does not live by bread alone, but by every word that comes from the mouth of God."[44] How can you object to this, unless you distort it, too, like the rest of the Scriptures? (*Letter* 607)

In all, then, the spiritual struggle against material gluttony is positive and creative, not negative: it looks to service and compassion, not selfishness; to detachment and sacrifice, not denial; to renunciation and reconciliation, not escape. "Without asceticism, none of us is authentically human."[45]

---

[39] 1 Cor 8:8.
[40] Cf. Lk 20:36.
[41] Cf. Mt 22:30.
[42] Lk 1:37.
[43] Cf. Ex 24:18. Emphasis mine.
[44] Mt 4:4.
[45] See K. Ware, "The Way of the Ascetics: Negative or Affirmative," in *Asceticism*, ed. Vincent Wimbush and Richard Valantasis (New York, NY: Oxford University Press, 1995), 13. Also Panagiotis Nellas, *Deification in Christ: Orthodox Perspectives on the Nature of the Human Person* (Crestwood, NY: St. Vladimir's Seminary Press, 1987), 180f.

Sharing the Feast

Centuries of misunderstanding and abuse have regrettably tainted the concept of asceticism, identifying it either with individualism and escapism or else equally toward idealism and angelism. All of these detrimental tendencies verge on the point of disincarnation, promulgating scorn, and contempt for the material world. However, at least in its more authentic expression, asceticism is genuinely a way of intimacy and tenderness, a way of integrating the senses, soul, and society. In this respect, asceticism is essentially a social discipline. No person should ever practice in a way that insults the Creator. It is no wonder that after years of harsh labor and sparse living, the early desert fathers and mothers emerged in their relationships as charming and compassionate, accessible, and tranquil.

One example of such asceticism endures in the discipline of fasting. To this day, Orthodox Christians fast from all dairy and meat products for almost half the year, as if in an effort to reconcile one half of the year with the other, to integrate secular time into the time of the kingdom. To fast is not to deny the world, but in fact to affirm the world, together with the body and all creation. It is to recall that humanity cannot "live by bread alone" (Mt 4:4) and to acknowledge that "the earth, and all the fullness thereof, is the Lord's" (Ps 23:1). Fasting is what connects and consolidates the individual with the rest of society and the world. It is the bond of community.

Like every other ascetic discipline, to fast is to learn to give, and not simply to give up. As another act of "letting go," it is not an act of deprecation, but an offering of gratitude. It is a way of breaking down barriers between myself and my neighbor as well as between myself and my world. In a word, to fast is to love. It is leaving something for others and moving away from what I want to what the world needs. It is liberation from greed, control, and compulsion. Fasting is valuing everything for itself, and not simply for myself.

Thus the aim of asceticism is to regain a sense of wonder, to be filled with an overflowing feast of goodness and of godliness. It is seeing all things in God and God in all things. And here *ascesis* encounters and engages *theosis* as the vision and taste of God. The most divine experience is to discover the wonder of God in the beauty of the world and to discern the boundlessness of grace in the limitations of the whole of creation.

The biblical image of this struggle is the scene of Jacob wrestling with the angel of God in Genesis 32:24–30. The image is much more than a fight that results in a wound or "hollow" caused by the angel's blows. It also results in blessing: a new name (from Jacob to Israel) and ultimately the vision of God "face to face." It is in fact a model of "the struggle with God,"[46] a symbol of intense embrace and impassioned love. The hollow is not a symbol of defeat. It represents the empty space—a puncture or hole—that only God can fill or fulfill. Everything we do is a reflection of this love, whether its fulfillment or its failure. The struggle is definitely daunting, but the reward is undeniably fulfilling: "If we love one another, God abides in us and His love is perfected in us" (1 Jn 4:12).

By contrast, gluttony numbs the senses. If we want to see and taste and hear and smell and touch, then we require abstinence. Asceticism demands that we pay attention to the strings of the heart and the stirrings of the body. It requires being silent in order to listen, moving slowly and gently, recognizing the needs of the body and respecting the hunger of the soul. Gluttony dulls and deadens the body. If we want to have a life, if we want to learn why we are alive, if we want to love and be truly alive, if we want any sense of meaning and purpose in life, then we must let go of all that we depend on and cling to, all that weighs and holds us down. We have to put down the fork, say no to food, and stop eating aimlessly. Precisely because the answer does not lie in food.

Paradoxically, gluttony provokes hunger. Maybe we have to starve before we can reach deep inside to discover the resources we had all along. This will lead to a life abounding with grace—a life full of "holy hunger"[47] and holy desire, far stronger than any craving for food; a life where we are no longer constantly kidnapped by lower desires, by a hunger for lesser gods; a life where our passions are neither eliminated nor extinguished, but transformed from glory

---

[46]Title of a book by Evdokimov, *The Struggle with God*. The French original literally translates as: *Stages of the Spiritual Life*.

[47]See Margaret Bullitt-Jonas, *Holy Hunger: A Woman's Journey from Food Addiction to Spiritual Fulfilment* (New York, NY: Knopf, 1998).

to glory (2 Cor 3:18) until we share in the feast of the kingdom. Abba Barsanuphius urges: "Fill your stove-pot with spiritual foods, such as humility, obedience, faith, hope, and love" (*Letter* 227). And the "great old man" also assures us that "divine food ... lasts a long time" (*Letter* 17). Ultimately, as Abba John explains, hunger that reflects humility is the only method whereby we can reach "the degree ... of requiring little food":

> You oblige me to speak about things beyond my limits, but I fear that I may be condemned in speaking about the achievements of others. For it is written: "My bones cling to my skin" (Ps 101:5–6), namely that all of a person's bones become one; this refers to all human thoughts that become one according to God. Afterward the bones cleave to the flesh; that is to say, the flesh becomes spiritual and follows godly thoughts. Then the joy of the Spirit comes to the heart, feeding the soul and fattening the body, while strengthening both alike.[48] So the body is neither weak nor despondent. For Jesus becomes the mediator, presenting that person before the entrance gates, where "grief and sorrow and sighing are no more" (Is 51:11) ... What brings a person to this degree is perfect humility. (*Letter* 153)

---

[48] For the connection between heart and body, cf. *Macarian Homilies* XV, 20.

6

Mourning and Tears

The Way of Brokenness and Imperfection

Springs of Living Water

Of all the classical texts of Christian spirituality without exception, Step Seven "On Mourning" in the seventh-century *Ladder of Divine Ascent* of John Climacus extolls tears as one of the more tangible and visible ways of repentance. In tenth-century Constantinople, Symeon the New Theologian would press this doctrine to the point of dogma, claiming that tears are indispensable in the spiritual and sacramental life.[1]

The phenomenon of tears might be described as "native" to Christianity and clearly played a dominant role in the ascetical and mystical experience. The early monastic tradition in fact served as a cradle for this treasure bequeathed to Christianity by Jesus, who "blessed those who mourn" (Mt 5:4) in his Sermon on the Mount.[2]

---

[1] *Discourses* IV, 10. See *Symeon the New Theologian: The Discourses*, transl. C. J. De Catanzaro (New York: Paulist Press, 1980), 80–1.
[2] The fullest treatment of the subject of tears is by I. Hausherr, *Penthos: The Doctrine of Compunction in the Christian East* (Kalamazoo MI: Cistercian Publications, 1982). On tears in ascetic spirituality, see Kallistos Ware, "Introduction," in *John Climacus: Ladder of Divine Ascent*, Classics of Western Spirituality, trans. C. Luibheid and N. Russell (Mahwah, NJ: Paulist Press, 1982), 20–7. See also Kimberley Christine Patton and John Stratton Hawley, eds., *Holy Tears: Weeping in the Religious Imagination* (Princeton and Oxford: Princeton University Press, 2005).

The development of tears proceeds from the New Testament through the Egyptian desert tradition to the Palestinian elders and the Sinaite school, with John Climacus and Symeon the New Theologian standing out as the greatest witnesses in later centuries.

While not unknown in the Western tradition, especially in writers like John Cassian—who undoubtedly learned about the "deep waters of the heart" while living among the early desert fathers of Egypt—the East accorded tears special priority, perhaps on account of the emphasis there on the heart as a vessel of the Spirit. Once more, a seemingly everyday experience of grieving and shedding tears becomes charged with extraordinary insight and intensity in the spiritual life.

Tears and mourning are in fact so intertwined with and integral to one another that both are a living spring that feeds spiritual growth. We read that the "other old man," John, never took holy communion without shedding tears (*Letter* 570)—echoing earlier desert fathers, such as Arsenius of Scetis in the preceding century, but also foreshadowing later monastic writers, such as Abba Isaac the Syrian in the following century and notably Symeon the New Theologian in the tenth century.[3]

Both Old Men share the emphasis on tears, but Barsanuphius is careful to distinguish the manifestation of tears from any negative expression of guilt that looks backward. The "great old man" describes tears as a positive expression of longing and desire for a grace that was lost, yet which still lies ahead:

> One who is conscious of what was lost will weep for it. Moreover, one who sincerely desires something will endure many travels and trials, in the hope of achieving what is desired. (*Letter* 400)

> Question. If one acquires these gifts through mourning, as you have said, then how can I safeguard this mourning when I move in and out among people, attending to chores and serving others? And does mourning of the heart exist without tears?
>
> Response by John. It is not tears that cause mourning, but rather mourning that causes tears. Someone who is among people can acquire mourning if that person cuts off one's own will and does not pay attention to the faults of others. For it is

---

[3]*Discourses* IV, 1. See *Symeon the New Theologian*, 70–1.

from mourning that the thoughts are gathered; and when they are gathered, they too give birth to godly sorrow (λύπη), and sorrow gives rise to tears. (*Letter* 285)

The process of gathering one's thoughts requires discernment in mourning and tears:

> Question. A brother asked the Great Old Man: Tell me, father, whether the compunction (κατάνυξις) that I think that I possess is genuine and whether I should live here on my own. Also, pray for me because I am troubled by bodily warfare.
> Response by Barsanuphius. Brother, your weeping and compunction are not genuine now, but they come and go. For genuine weeping, which comes with compunction, becomes like a servant submitted to us without separation; and the person who possesses this does not experience any spiritual warfare. It even wipes away one's former faults and washes away all blemishes. Moreover, in the name of God, it continually protects the person who acquires it. Indeed, it also expels laughter and distraction, while maintaining mourning unceasingly. For it resembles a large shield that deters all the fiery arrows of the devil. A person who possesses this receives absolutely no combat, whether that person is with others or with prostitutes; that gift always stays with us and fights for us.
> Therefore, I have demonstrated for you the sign of weakness and of courage. Do not think that God could not relieve you from battle; he could have done so, especially for the saints praying for you. Nevertheless, because he loves you, God wants you to be tested through many battles and trials in order to arrive at the degree of good repute. You cannot reach this point unless you keep all that I have decreed in my letters—teacher of vainglory such as I am. Apply yourself now, child, as I said, and I believe that you will make progress in Christ. Do not be afraid. May the Lord be with you. (*Letter* 461)

Tears are a useful platform for gaining insight into the spiritual world and worldview of the Palestinian elders. They are the clearest signs of the uncontainable divine grace contained in the fragile human body.

In this respect, mourning and tears are prized virtues in the letters, described as "accompanying" every aspect of ascetic life

(*Letter* 165). They are so closely identified and integrated with the monastic life that Abba John refers to monks as "those who mourn" (*Letter* 618). Weeping is a course of renunciation and surrender, which further implies that it is closely associated with the very first steps of monastic life and incorporated into every stage of the ascetic life. Tears therefore are regenerative and restorative, while weeping adumbrates a silent albeit painful method of healing the wounds of the heart:

> As for the wounds, wash them away … with tears. For tears wash away every stain. (*Letter* 148)

> Weeping cleanses a person from sins, but it comes with toil, along with great effort and patience, as well as by remembering the fearful judgement and the eternal shame, as well as by renouncing oneself. (*Letter* 257)

Such words may resound negatively or harshly to contemporary ears. The suggestion is that, by initially surrendering life, we can eventually rediscover ourselves. In struggling against what we are *not*, we are striving to know what we truly *are*. Because we frequently tend to forget who and what we are. The tragedy is not that we imagine we are *more* than we actually are, but that we tolerate being *less* than God calls us to be. Pride is not the ultimate error; forgetfulness of our origin and destiny is the ultimate sin. That is what leads to hardness of heart and pride, which are the polar opposite and utter banishment of mournfulness: "Hardheartedness and pride drive tears away from you. Remove these and tears will swell" (*Letter* 512). Indeed, the more "hardened the heart," the "greater also the mourning" (*Letter* 552), though in the end, as we shall see, only grace can "purify the fountain of tears for the flowing of spiritual water … if the fountain of your heart's tears has dried up" (*Letter* 18).

No wonder, then, that the two Old Men emphasize remembrance of death and judgement; these are, after all, another dimension to remembrance of God. Feeling comfortable with death is a way of embracing mortality. So often, however, we endeavor to cheat death, instinctively seeking to avoid or escape mortality. We refuse to face change and pain. Instead we search for ways to sidestep them—financially, technologically, medically, or emotionally. By contrast, Barsanuphius and John are convinced that this life is a time of mourning and weeping. We are to shut the door of the cell, even as—indeed, *especially* when—we experience moments of panic or powerlessness.

> Our time is given us to examine our passions, as well as to weep and mourn for them. (*Letter* 603. See also *Letter* 260)

> So be humble before God, weeping for your sins and mourning over your passions. (*Letter* 607)

> One who regards oneself as sinful should mourn over one's sins, and do nothing else. (*Letter* 699)

And there, in the cell, we are to wait and weep. Otherwise, if we do not first shut the door of the cell, then the door of the kingdom will also be closed to us, just as it was for the foolish virgins in the gospel parable (*Letter* 37).

> To sit in one's cell means to remember one's sins and to weep and mourn for them, as well as to remain vigilant so that the intellect is not taken captive, but rather to struggle—even when it is taken captive—to return it to its proper place. (*Letter* 172)

> Let us not waste our little time in distractions, brother, but let us acquire mourning filled with tears, so that we may be blessed with those who mourn. (*Letter* 125)

Just as mourning is continual, so too tears are literal—visible and tangible, not imaginary or figurative. Barsanuphius speaks of "drowning the soul many times and with much sorrow" (*Letter* 48).
There is a clear and intricate method to this technique: "We know the results of tears; for the experience of Peter's mourning has taught us" (*Letter* 532). Unless "one pays close attention" and remains vigilant, then "one may completely deviate from the way of mourning" (*Letter* 459). Describing tears as a "way" is of course directly reminiscent of the desert tradition in Egypt:

> Abba Poemen said: "Weeping is the way that the Scriptures and the Fathers give us, when they say: 'Weep!' Truly, there is no

other way than this." He also said: "It is impossible not to weep, whether voluntarily or when compelled through suffering."[4]

But alas, it seems that we lose sight of this "way" early on and misplace our innate ability to grieve. So we must gradually relearn and painfully reacquire this time-honored phenomenon.

Variations on a Theme
Godly Sorrow: An Overture to Joy

Beyond the abovementioned grounds for emphasizing the way of tears, there is a deeper reason why tears are primary, even primal in the spiritual life. For Barsanuphius and John, there is no stage beyond the knowledge of imperfection. Perfection is reserved for God, not for us; imperfection is ours to acknowledge and know, never to forego or forget. Abba John writes:

> It is written: "The righteous fall seven times a day, and rise up again" (Prv. 24.16). Rising up again means the righteous person is struggling. And anyone struggling acts exactly like this: falling and rising again, until one sees what will happen later. (*Letter* 454)

Why, then, do the Gaza elders describe life as perpetual weeping? In the Palestinian desert, the gospel injunction to "be perfect, as your heavenly Father is perfect" (Mt 5:48) is a genuine vision of realism. It does not remain a vague fantasy of romanticism. But the source and object of tears is the light of the resurrection that shines beyond the cross, transforming sorrow into joy. The bitterness of tears is sweetened through repentance; tears of fear blossom into tears of love.[5] There is a link between the shedding of human tears and the shining of divine grace. Tears are at once sweet and sad, the foretaste of crucifixion and the anticipation of resurrection.

---

[4]Poemen 119, *Sayings*. See also Arsenius 41, *Sayings*.
[5]See Alexis Torrance, *Repentance in Late Antiquity: Eastern Asceticism and the Framing of the Christian Life, c. 400–650 CE* (Oxford, UK: Oxford University Press, 2013), esp. chapter 5.

In this perspective, light and dark complement one another; gain and loss coincide; grace and grief coexist. It is here that the positive or "joyful" dimension of mourning unfolds. The concept of cheerful mourning is dialectical: repentance is a balance of perdition and resurrection, of despair and hope, of death and life. Sadly we appear to have lost the capacity to balance joy and sorrow. But Barsanuphius is deeply conscious of this overture of joy. In *Letter* 196, the "great old man" responds to a question about how to secure the "inviolable treasure" and "impregnable tower" of the heavenly kingdom: "Let us weep in order to laugh (Lk 6:21)," he responds, adding: "Let us be sorrowful in order to rejoice. Let us mourn in order to be comforted" (Mt 5:5). The "other old man" offers a definition of "godly sorrow" intimately connected to "modest joyfulness" and foreshadowing the concept of "joyful sorrow"[6] coined in the next generation by John Climacus:

> Mourning is godly sorrow (2 Cor 7:10), which is produced by repentance. The characteristics of repentance are fasting, psalmody, prayer, and the study of God's words. Cheerfulness is joyfulness, which appears in the words and on the faces of those who possess it with modesty. Therefore, let the heart have mourning, while the face and the words should have modest joyfulness. In this way, both can be held together. (*Letter* 730)

The concept of sorrow mingled with joy reflects the simultaneous experience of Gethsemane and Tabor, of Holy Friday and Easter Sunday condensed: "dying, and behold living ... sorrowful, yet always rejoicing" (2 Cor 6:9–10). The Palestinian elders epitomize the entire evangelical and patristic teaching, where joy (*chara*) and grace (*charis*) share a common root and reason—etymologically, theologically, and spiritually. Ordinary, everyday life becomes an overture to the extraordinary experience of the kingdom.

Silent Tears: Progress through Imperfection

At first glance, the emphasis on brokenness and tears, or on mourning and repentance, may leave a negative impression. After all, so many letters deal with vices to be avoided and passions to

---

[6]Title of Step 7 of the *Ladder of Divine Ascent*.

be conquered. Yet the initial impression is somewhat misleading because the balance between the negative and the positive goes far deeper than any superficial calculation or observation. This is because Barsanuphius and John are not afraid of the darker aspects of human nature. They do not regard them merely as temporary stages, but instead recognize in them the transcendence of human finality and mortality. Like their predecessors in the Egyptian desert, they welcome sin and failure as the ultimate opportunity for divine grace and strength "perfected in weakness" (2 Cor 1:9). Their grounded communication with those who approach them each day provides the elders with a realistic experience of and appreciation for the sacredness of the very ordinary. While geographically detached from broader society and literally invisible to daily pilgrims, the two Old Men demonstrate a delicate responsiveness and discerning respect for the challenges that their visitors encounter in their personal and social circumstances.

In this way, the silence of tears issues in an eloquent reflection of the "unseen" lifestyle of our Palestinian elders, whom no one sees and with whom no one speaks. Perhaps it is more important to shed tears than to define them. So few comprehend that tears of brokenness, as symbols of imperfection, are in fact the *sole* way of spiritual progress. Our two elders have little to say about deification; they prefer to record the obstacles along the way to holiness, the gradual stages, and painful steps of the spiritual journey. They know that this alone is what lies within our reach and reality. They are convinced that a single, silent tear can advance us further in the spiritual way than numerous, "loud" ascetic achievements.

At the same time, however, while the concept or theology of deification may not be explicit in Barsanuphius and John, the tradition and teaching of transformation lies at the very core of their logic and letters. The "great old man" writes: "The Son of God became human for you; you, too, should become a god for him" (*Letter* 199). In this regard, the Gaza elders echo the maxim of Athanasius that "God became human in order that we may become divine."[7] The emphasis is always on searching the depths of the soul (*Letter* 603), rather than researching the intricacies of the mind (*Letter* 604).

---

[7]Athanasius of Alexandria, *On the Divine Incarnation*, chapter 54 (Crestwood, NY: St. Vladimir's Seminary Press, 1982). See PG25.192.

The silence of tears is precisely such a way of interiority, a radical way of exploring the inaccessible cellars of the heart. Through sorrow, we learn by undergoing, not just by understanding. The connection between tears and silence is all-important because even words can be a way of affirming our existence or justifying our emotions and actions. The more compelled we feel to assert ourselves, the less peaceful we actually are with ourselves and others. Silence is a way of relinquishing self-justification. Through tears, we abandon infantile images of God and give in to the living image of God. We confess personal powerlessness and profess divine powerfulness. Tears confirm our readiness to surrender—to allow our life to fall apart in the dark night of the soul, to renounce our old ways in expectation of new life.

When we admit hopelessness and desperation, recognizing that we have "hit rock bottom" in our relationships, whether with people or with God, we also discover the compassion of a God who voluntarily assumed the vulnerability of the cross. One would not seek divine healing unless one had to in order to survive, until one were prepared to admit there was no other way out the impasse. Our hearts are the dwelling place of God, but they are made of glass and are ever so fragile. And tears manifest this brokenness and woundedness.

God enters the open wound—the broken window or tender teardrop—of our heart, bringing healing to the soul and the world, not to comfort but to identify with us out of infinite and healing compassion. God understands, having undergone the fragility and vulnerability of assuming child-likeness and death on a cross. Such sensitivity or susceptibility is the only professed way to holiness. The more profound our personal misery, the more abundant God's eternal mercy; the deeper the abyss of human corruption, the greater the grace of heavenly compassion; the more involved our exposure to the suffering of the cross, the more intense our experience of the light of resurrection.

Barsanuphius and John reveal remarkably subtle insight into "the mysterious land of tears."[8] Their teaching on tears is a theology of depth, revealing the fragility of life and reflecting a spirituality of imperfection. For them, as for the inhabitants of the early Egyptian

---

[8] From Antoine de Saint Exupéry, *The Little Prince* VII (San Diego, CA: Harvest Books, 2000), 34–5.

desert, life is a continual balance of tensions. To wait is to weep, and to weep is to be humble. But such waiting is the surest way of achieving grace. By waiting, one learns to accept oneself and to embrace one's life. And patience is critical because the onset of tears is gradual, drop by drop. Deprivation, too, is a token of restitution. God gives and God takes: but the giving and taking—as well as the period itself of withholding—are all part of the way of tears. Tears signal the fullness of life, with all its sorrows and joys. And tears of joy come at the end, not the beginning, of a long struggle.

Compunction: Touched by an Angel

Genuine weeping is not initiated or pursued by human effort; it is a spontaneous reaction, a gratuitous response. Marking the tension and transition between being and becoming, spiritual tears flow without physical contraction of facial muscles; instead, they are a consequence of divine grace. Abba John instructs a monk that "guarding the compunction of the heart" requires hard work (*Letter* 278), while Abba Barsanuphius informs another monk that it derives from "constant vigilance" (*Letter* 428). Both of them are convinced that compunction is a gift from above, whereby a monk is "touched" by God (*Letter* 128). The phenomenon is delightfully illustrated by the thirteenth-century French tale about "Le chevalier au Barizel," once ordered to fill a barrel with water. The knight enthusiastically travels all over the world to fulfill this task, yet the water always passes through the barrel. Seeing that his efforts achieve nothing, he weeps, and one teardrop is sufficient to fill the barrel.

As a gift, tears testify to a divine visitation; John Climacus explains that "the Lord has arrived as an uninvited guest,"[9] and Symeon the New Theologian speaks of "the anticipated divine guest."[10] For Barsanuphius, this visitation may even occur while simply reading, alone or in church:

> When you happen to be reading, and you see compunction in your heart, read as much as you can. Do the same whenever you recite the Psalms. (*Letter* 87)

---

[9] Step 7 "On Mourning," in *Ladder,* 139.
[10] Symeon, *Catechetical Orations* 2, 211–12, see C.J. de Catanzaro ed., *Symeon the New Theologian: Discourses* (Mahwah, NJ: Paulist Press, 1980), 47–59.

> When your thought is at peace, and you observe that you are receiving compunction from a brother's recital of the Psalms, take advantage of this. (*Letter* 445)

Or else, it may result from advice offered by someone, as in the case of "a brother that was moved to compunction on hearing these words and therefore left edified" (*Letter* 762).

The notion of "compunction" is clearly distinguished from the concepts of "weeping" (*Letter* 343) and "mourning" (*Letter* 461). Compunction may be "genuine" (*Letter* 394) or "godly" (*Letter* 393); but it may also "occur through the action of the devil unto greater condemnation" (*Letter* 394). Abba John notes:

> As for the coming and going of your present mourning, which is not genuine, this happens because we become relaxed and then again add fervor to the thought. When the warmth remains, compunction becomes great and permanent, while genuine mourning also follows suit. About this, you must certainly be sure to press yourself so that it may come to you. (*Letter* 462)

The two elders struggle to articulate what is essentially an inexpressible reality, an ecstatic experience. How can anyone describe with accuracy the effect of grace, of being "touched" by God (*Letter* 394)? How can anyone communicate with adequacy the impact of a divine wound, of the soul smitten by God's love? Barsanuphius and John speak in terms of the heart (*kardia*, *Letter* 444)—or the intellect (*nous*, *Letter* 445)—as being pierced by grace. "Compunction will truly come to you, and God will protect you from all evil" (*Letter* 237). "When you feel this kind of compunction" (*Letter* 486), you are never "overcome by excessive sorrow ... [but] assume humility and gratitude instead of ingratitude" (*Letter* 490). "Genuine compunction of heart should accompany every thought" (*Letter* 136). It should accompany every action, whether standing or sitting (*Letter* 509). And it should accompany every moment of prayer (*Letter* 411), day and night (*Letter* 442).

"Touched" or "pricked" in this way, the heart is flooded with tears, which emerge when words become insufficient or exhausted. They leave behind conventional human language that seems gratuitous or superfluous. More pertinently, tears transform and consecrate all words, creating a new language, another way of communication.

They provide a sense of faithfulness in relationships. They reveal a dimension of interiority and intensity. They represent the way of spontaneity and authenticity. They become our true voice, our mother tongue.

Nourished by the Spirit

In the end, as already noted, tears are less about "doing" and more about "being." They result from a process of "travailing in childbirth until Christ is formed inside us" (Gal 4:19). Where human tears abound, divine grace flourishes. Such divine visitation through compunction, where new light breaks into the heart, implies genuine transformation. Through tears, we receive the light of Christ; we are illumined. Through tears, we receive the life of the Spirit; we are inspired.

Tears enable the heart to discern and distinguish between the presence and the absence of God. We can weep only for someone or something that we actually know, and not merely imagine. Knowledge through tears is the sole criterion for spiritual progress. The degree of this knowledge is what measures virtue and sin, not any accumulated merits or faults. When the knowledge of God—whether his presence or his absence—assumes greater significance than any particular virtue or vice, then the outer person becomes attuned to the inner person. Then the bitter and murky roots of the heart are embraced as part and parcel of the sweet and fragrant flowers on the surface. Then one knows that "the kingdom of God lies within" (Lk 17:21) and tears flow like the surprise of new life, marking the dawn of new light.

Nothing external can ever measure, predict, or exhaust us. We are always a work in progress, forever the same and yet ever developing and changing. This is why we can gain—or lose—paradise in any given detail, at any fleeting moment. Like their predecessors in the desert of Egypt, Barsanuphius and John are well aware that the lost can be found, the sick healed, the dead brought to life. That is their pledge to those who approach for comfort and counsel. Changes are real; in the history of spirituality, they are called conversions. A loss can become a triumph in seed, a curse can be a blessing in disguise, a "people in darkness can see the great light" (Mt 4:16).

Such vulnerability and transparency, the result of being crushed so lightly and delightfully by God—or so profoundly and painfully by life—inevitably render the heart more spontaneous and responsive. It also seals the heart with the distinctive mark of holiness. If the two Old Men do not intellectually develop the *concept* itself, nonetheless they do actually flesh out the *course* of deification (*theosis*); in their eyes, deification is no less, and no more, than falling down and getting back up, starting anew. If our eyes enjoy the vision of God (as the mystery of becoming divine), then it is because our tears can express the beauty of humanity (as the mystery of being truly human). And tears are the ultimate and most intimate companions along the way toward deification.

In this perspective, the silence of tears reflects a surrender to new patterns of learning and living, a softening of the soul and clarity of the mind. As with so much else in the letters of Barsanuphius and John, their emphasis on the gift of tears is a testimony, not a teaching. Their letters reveal extraordinarily subtle insights into the complexity of tears and their significance for spiritual life. Mourning should accompany everything we do and say. Barsanuphius counsels: "Embrace mourning with all your heart; for it is an associate of every good work" (*Letter* 256). Life means continually balancing tensions, perpetually standing beneath the cross. This was the conviction passed down over generations from Egypt to Palestine: that tears bring us to rebirth and the whole world to healing.

In the words of Abba John: "Tears become like bread, so that one begins to be fed by the Spirit" (*Letter* 152). They signify true homecoming. Through tears, we can enter the treasury of the heart. And when we allow our heart to be broken, when we allow life as we know it to fall apart, we are free to be reborn and—quite simply—to be more and more. The ultimate form of renunciation in the ascetic life is letting go of life. What is far more important than learning to live is learning to die.

7

Discernment and Compassion

The Way of Awareness and Authenticity

A Preliminary Caveat

If there is a specific and distinct quality for which Barsanuphius and John acquired unique and unequivocal reputation among their contemporaries and successors, it is undoubtedly discernment. For the two Old Men, the essence of the spiritual life "is all about ... discernment" (*Letter* 713). The two elders do not simply emphasize or elaborate on discernment in their communications as in their correspondence; they actually exemplify and epitomize this gift in their experiences and exchanges. In fact, the principle and practice of discernment are in all likelihood the very reason why sixth-century Palestinian spirituality was originally discovered and for a long time became more popular in the West than in the East; it was without question what captivated the Jesuits when they came across the spiritual discourses of Dorotheus of Gaza.[1] The way in which the two extraordinary elders approach and apply the notion of discernment provides exceptional intuition into the perception and

---

[1] See Chitty, *The Desert a City*, 140.

practice of what is frequently—both faithfully and fraudulently—promulgated as the function of spiritual direction.

People have conventionally identified discernment with specific people and specific places. One of the questions posed to Abba John pertains to the action one should take in the case where "there are no elders in a particular region in order for one to seek the advice of those who are truly capable of discernment. Should one perhaps … depart to another region where there are people more qualified in discernment?" In response, John quips: "Yes, one should do precisely that, but then make sure you comply with whatever they say" (*Letter* 539). Clearly one's spiritual life is perceived as being in jeopardy without some discerning oversight. But how can one be sure that someone possesses this rare gift in the first place?

In one letter, Barsanuphius admits—and is aware that others, too, acknowledge—that he is personally endowed with this unusual capacity: "If you hold me to be a discerning person, as someone who knows according to God that which occurs, then you would trust that no one should dare to deviate from my word without my knowledge" (*Letter* 226). This is a bold assertion and one often claimed by ordained clergy of all levels and lay monastics through

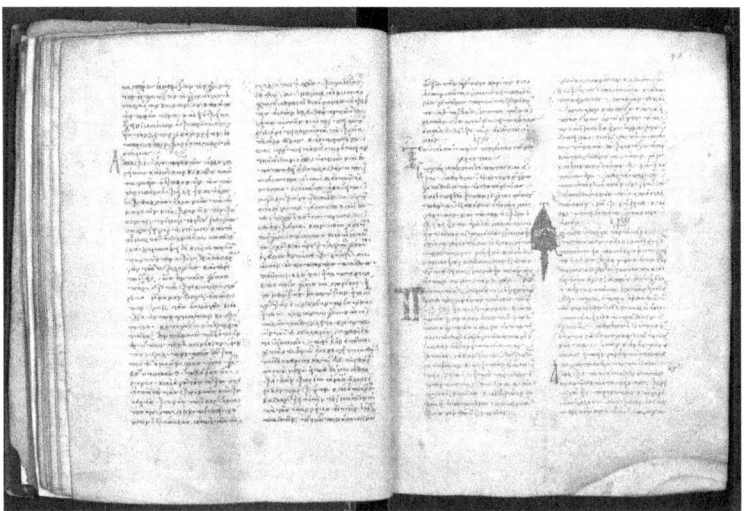

FIGURE 4 *Vatopedi manuscript*, Letters *241–243*.

the centuries. The truth is that we increasingly and desperately need the gift of discernment in a world that grows progressively dark. Spiritual discernment can provide protection and direction at a time when everyone seemingly has a "viral" or "virtual" opinion about everything—often without discretion, consideration, or verification. What is frequently missing from churches and confessionals is a genuine sense of discernment understood not as a moralistic or prognostic instrument, but as a spiritual means of penetration or method of interpretation—as a way, that is, of leading people out of a lack of spiritual perception or impasse, enabling them to perceive the world with a different lens, ultimately through the eyes of God.

But how easily they talk about discernment, they who have never in fact known discernment! We live in an age where too many professing to be spiritual authorities and directors rarely consider their own integrity, but primarily their institutional ordination or charismatic reputation. Yet a religious leader should never speak from a position of prerogative or privilege; a spiritual director should always speak from a position of parity—better still, of humility. Metropolitan Anthony Bloom (1914–2003) once said in a sermon: "The church ought to be as powerless as God." There is no telling the damage one can do in the church when one mistakes one's will to discern or intention to do good with the authority to distinguish and do what one judges to be right.[2] To paraphrase Pliny the Younger: "Everyone is prejudiced in favor of one's own powers of discernment."[3]

Lineage of Discernment

So where did the gift of discernment originate and how did it develop? What are the criteria by which one authoritatively exercises and authentically expresses it? And how should we discern discernment itself?

---

[2]See Hannah Hunt, "Uses and Abuses of Spiritual Authority in the Writings of St. Symeon the New Theologian," in *The Philokalia: A Classic Text of Orthodox Spirituality*, ed. Brock Bingaman and Bradley Nassif (Oxford: Oxford University Press, 2012), 203–15.
[3]Pliny, "Panegyric in Praise of Trajan," in *Masterpieces of Eloquence*, ed. M. W. Hazeltine and others (New York: Collier, 1905).

Whether conceived as *discernment of spirits* in the conscience of the church through the conscience of an individual and the conscience of a community (which is, in fact, the most common interpretation in the apostolic and post-apostolic period), or comprehended as *discrimination between courses of action*, whether elaborated as *insight* into personal thoughts, or *foresight* into prospective actions (which is the most prominent application in the rise and reform of monasticism across the ages), discernment is arguably the most vital and valuable spiritual capacity in Eastern and Western traditions alike.

The apostolic period perceived discernment as a gift offered to the community, not a skill enjoyed by an isolated individual. Paul's 1 Corinthians is a letter addressed to the entire church. This is especially evident among the Antiochene exegetes, including John Chrysostom and Theodoret of Cyrus.[4] Indeed, whereas Latin authors of the first Christian millennium—following the examples of Pelagius and Ambrosiaster in the late-fourth and early-fifth centuries—focus their attention on discernment among particular clergy rather than within the whole church, Christian commentators in the East repeat or reflect Chrysostom and Theodoret until at least the eleventh century.

It was Origen of Alexandria who introduced the theology of discernment as an integral part of spiritual methodology in general.[5] Monastic writers then systematically articulated this as an intrinsic part of ascetic discipline, beginning with Athanasius in his *Life of Antony*: "Everyone marveled at the gift, which the Lord had given to Anthony for the discerning the spirits."[6] Athanasius's biography of the legendary "father of monasticism" arguably treats discernment of spirits more thoroughly than any other example of

---

[4] See John Chrysostom, *Homiliae in epistolam primam ad Corinthios* 29 (PG61.240) and Theodoret of Cyrus, *Interpretationes in Pauli epistolas* at 1 Cor. 12:10 (PG82.325). On discernment in Scripture and late antiquity, see Antony Rich, *Discernment in the Desert Fathers: Diakrisis in the Life and Thought of Early Egyptian Monasticism* (Eugene, OR: Wipf and Stock, 2007), esp. 1–38.

[5] M. Viller and K. Rahner, *Aszese und Mystik in der Väterzeit: Ein Abriss* (Freiburg: Herder, 1939), 75.

[6] Athanasius' term in the *Life* for "gift" is *charis*, chap. 44; elsewhere (chaps. 22, 38, 88), it is *charisma diakriseos pneumatön*. See the Greek text on discernment in *Life of Anthony*, in PG26.837–976.

patristic literature, while the enormous influence of the *Life* makes the impact of discernment all the more significant in the tradition. In line with subsequent Eastern exegesis, the *Life of Anthony* always refers to discernment of spirits as gift or grace. Needless to say, it was after thirty-five years of ascetic rigor that Anthony assumed the audacity to speak of discernment.[7]

A shift transpires with regard to the interpretation of discernment in the *Historia monachorum in Aegypto (History of the Monks of Egypt)*, composed by an anonymous author around the year 400. Discernment becomes the fruit of monastic discipline. For instance, in the chapter on Pityrion, a third-generation beneficiary of Anthony, the author directly associates discernment with the struggle against demons and victory over passions: "Pityrion especially spoke about discernment of spirits, teaching his disciples about certain demons accompanying our passions ... and adding that, whoever wishes to drive out the demons, must first conquer the passions."[8] Like Anthony, Pityrion assumes that the term "spirits" refers to evil spirits, although these are no longer the external demons of the desert; they are now the internal passions of the heart. Drawing on desert wisdom, Evagrius of Pontus philosophically weaves the biblical and ascetic traditions into a primarily theoretical or philosophical proposition, while John Cassian systematically expounds the predominantly practical and anecdotal aspects of discernment.

This pragmatic or realistic language is nowhere more evident than in the *Sayings of the Desert Fathers*, where the phrase "discernment of spirits" is entirely absent, while the term "discernment" (*diakrisis* and its cognates) prevails in conventional lists of virtues and qualities.[9] The *Sayings* describe discernment as a virtue or weapon, but also as an experience or insight—the capacity to see beyond rigid prescriptions and rigorous practices. Discernment is the power to comprehend the spirit of the rule rather than the letter of the law; in this sense, it always functions in connection with compassion and charity.

---

[7] Athanasius, *Life*, chaps. 22, 38, and 44.
[8] Pityrion (15), 2–3, in A.-J. Festugière, *Historia monachorum in Aegypto: Edition critique du texte grec et traduction annoté*e, Subsidia Hagiographica 53 (Brussels: Société des Bollandistes, 1971), 110. Translation mine.
[9] Fr. Dingjan, "La discrétion dans les apophtegmes des Pères," *Angelicum* 39 (1962), 406 n. 13.

Diadochus of Photice, a disciple of Evagrius, perhaps comes closest to composing a formal treatise on discernment in the middle of the fifth century. His most renowned work is entitled *One Hundred Gnostic Chapters* or *A Hundred Chapters on Spiritual Perfection*, but in some manuscripts, the treatise bears the title *Practical Chapters on Knowledge and Spiritual Discernment*. Instead of presenting discernment as a fundamental or stereotypical monastic virtue or ascetic achievement,[10] Diadochus offers a perceptive analysis of discernment as a mystical faculty or spiritual sense.

In the seventh century, John Climacus devotes one of the longest "steps" (Step 26) in his *Ladder of Divine Ascent* to discernment, which he regards as intimately related to the human discipline of asceticism, albeit inseparably connected to the divine gift of grace.[11] The Sinaite abbot even constructs an elementary sequence or hierarchy—a sort of ladder within the ladder—for his diverse definitions of discernment; in so doing, he provides a unique perspective and unprecedented premise for this quality: "From humility comes discernment ... from discernment comes insight, and from insight comes foresight."[12]

Discerning Ways
Safeguarding the Gift

Echoing their scriptural roots and adhering to their monastic predecessors, Barsanuphius and John advocate and advance the dual nature of discernment as both given and gained, as accepted and acquired. On the one hand, they perceive discernment as a rare gift *for some*; on the other, they promote it as a mandatory virtue *for all* (*Letters* 518, 621–2, 647, and 681).

The "great old man" believes that a person can reach discernment only "with God's assistance" (*Letter* 646). It may take concentrated

---

[10]Monastic virtue or ascetic achievement is how the *Conferences* of John Cassian and the *Rule* of Benedict of Nursia describe discernment (*discretio*) during roughly the same period. See Joseph Lienhard, "On 'Discernment of Spirits' in the Early Church," *Theological Studies* 41, 3 (1980), 505–29.
[11]See also Anthony of Egypt 8, in *Sayings*, and John Cassian, *Conferences* 1.23 and 2.4.
[12]John Climacus, Step 4 "On Obedience," in *Ladder*, 114.

effort and prolonged prayer—"sometimes one may spend ... entire days" in the process (*Letter* 522)—to determine whether one's actions align with godly discernment. Abba Poemen "sat quietly alone, discerning his thoughts for hours."[13] And on receiving the gift of discernment, Barsanuphius advises: "Let us guard this grace with gratitude; and let us not become like swine, unable to discern precious pearls" (*Letter* 647). He believes that "those who have spent a long time in the monastic life ... ought to be able to discern the deeper thoughts of others" (*Letter* 98). Thus he prayed to God to heal Abbot Seridos, whom "he regarded as a genuine son" from childhood illness, while praying that the abbot himself might be granted the gift of discernment:

> So he entreated God to grant [Seridos] the gift of discernment; once this was acquired, he was able to direct souls to life with the grace from above, as well as to heal the afflicted, bring the healing medicine of the word of the Spirit, and reward those who struggle with peace. (*Letter* 570c)

Barsanuphius advises Theodore that a mature monk can distinguish between two or even three thoughts at the same time—between "proper" and "crooked" thoughts (*Letter* 265), as well as between instinctive, irregular, and aberrant thoughts—in order to "detach the thorns and prickles, thereby seizing the grapes that strengthen and gladden the heart" (*Letter* 124). He describes discernment as an intuitive antenna or invisible receiver, capable of recognizing and reflecting "warmth and cold" in one's inward thoughts and outward actions (*Letter* 154). As a result, one learns to distinguish "whether things are right or wrong" (*Letter* 17), good or bad (*Letters* 7 and 546), calm or turbulent (*Letter* 474), ultimately "discovering with certainty that in the alleged good that comes from the devil, there may no trace of good at all, but only vainglory or turmoil or something similar" (*Letter* 405).

The "other old man" again adopts a more practical approach, persistently underlining that "we [actually] *require* discernment" (*Letter* 518). In fact, "*everyone* requires discernment" (*Letter* 22), he writes, while for any wrongdoing, "one should always blame

---

[13]Poemen 32, *Sayings*.

oneself for lack of discernment" (*Letter* 624): "One should *always* do *everything* with discernment. Knowing one's limits is genuine discernment. Doing *anything* beyond one's measure, whether almsgiving or anything else, is absence of discernment" (*Letter* 621).[14] His advice is simple and sensible: "If it is something good, do it; if it is not, then do not do it. However, in order that the good may not be done with turmoil, examine the governing thought and discern how this is arising" (*Letter* 478).

Where the two elders clearly and categorically concur is on the inseparable link between discernment and humility, two virtues often cited together in a single breath. Indeed, discernment they expressly define as the absolute antithesis of conceit of trust in oneself.[15] Whether discernment is a gift or feat, humility—the virtue of deferring to and lowering oneself before everyone and everything—is what ultimately enables us to rise above trivial circumstance and petty conduct in order to behold the divine mystery in all people and all things.

In this context, the elders again underline the importance of moderation and discretion, recommending the middle or royal way: "This is the way of the Fathers" (*Letter* 212), they say: "If you endeavor to exceed your measures, then learn this: that you shall lose even what you have. Travel neither too far in one direction, nor too far in the other, but always keep to the middle way" (*Letter* 314).[16] Furthermore, the two Old Men highlight the importance of integrity and prudence for the proper exercise of discernment: "'Every rotten tree produces rotten fruits.' By contrast, prudence leads to discernment. As I have told you previously, retain the integrity of a dove with prudence; for all of its thoughts are good and beneficial. 'Every good tree produces good fruits'" (*Letter* 238).

As an expression of stability and maturity, however, a person should not take discernment for granted (*Letters* 288, 318, and 570c). Abba John cautions a monk: "For the time being, you are unable to discern these things, because your heart is still easily transformed" (*Letter* 644). Not everyone is "capable of discerning

---

[14]Emphases mine.
[15]See Abba John, *Letters* 333 and 503, and Abba Barsanuphius, *Letters* 416 and 604.
[16]On the middle way as moderation, see *Letters* 79, 158–9, and 621.

matters in godly manner" (*Letter* 714). If integrity and prudence reflect the *way* that leads to discernment (*Letter* 238), discernment resembles the *door* that opens up to further gifts, such as wisdom and knowledge, strength and support.[17] Above all, discernment informs the advice that monastics offer to others, acting as an assurance about "whether the teachings of their elders are mingled with their own teachings ... or whether they need to be assured by God through supplication and prayer about their truth" (*Letter* 604). Simply put, there is no other mechanism for testing the authenticity of our actions or the authority of our elders.

Situational Ethics

Discernment is always positive and constructive, serving as "an emollient of the soul, an authentic balm."[18] However, for this to transpire, discernment must involve extraordinary awareness of intention (πρόθεσις)[19] and disposition (προαίρεσις).[20] Barsanuphius and John transcend any rigid code of scripted or prescriptive ethics (with sometimes inhumane consequences) and teach a more compassionate situational or occasional ethos (with no established formulas and few binding directives, where the individual assumes responsibility for his or her actions). Spiritual discernment signifies that spiritual direction is never abstract but always specific, never general or generalized but always particular and personal. Simply put, each of us is different; we cannot tar everyone with the same brush:

> There are sacks of a certain kind, and there are sacks of another. One sack might hold a single measure of corn, while another might hold three. If someone tries to force the sack that holds a single measure to hold up to three measures, it will not be able to contain the corn. The same applies here. We cannot put all people on an equal footing; for one person may speak without bringing any harm, while another is unable to do this. (*Letter* 469)

---

[17]See *Letter* 360.
[18]Stelios Ramfos, *Like a Pelican in the Wilderness: Reflections on the Sayings of the Desert Fathers* (Brookline, MA: Holy Cross Orthodox Press, 2000), 218.
[19]See *Letters* 1, 60, 239, 453–5, 472, 493, 611–13, 648, and 720.
[20]See *Letters* 17, 70, 462, and 646.

This is precisely why there can never be any hard rule of discipline or penance. The letters are replete with examples of rigorous as well as relaxed approaches to shortcomings and failures. Different people require different responses and remedies—healing actions measured by astute discernment—in order to soothe or mitigate a particular condition in context. No spiritual advisor should apply any intervention arbitrarily or impose one indiscriminately. Ascetic discipline offers creativity, value, and meaning to life; it is a framework of living that permits flexibility, a school of learning that life is more than just a sterilized technique of universal healing and salvation but involves the messy business of reconciliation with oneself, one's neighbor, and God.

Therefore, discernment is inherently liberating; it is never legalistic. In fact, it dispels any notion of abstract morality or sanctioned cure. It is often easier, albeit always riskier, to prescribe simplistic formulas; it is often convenient, but always precarious, to follow superficial slogans, such as moralism or puritanism, traditionalism or nationalism. Discernment dictates that answers provided at any given moment and for any given individual may differ drastically from answers in alternative situations and for different persons. Hence the author of the "Prologue" (possibly Dorotheus of Gaza) reminds the reader that:

> [The two Old Men] responded to questions bearing in mind the weakness in the thoughts of those inquiring, discreetly condescending to their level that they might not fall into despair, just as we see in the *Lives of the Old Men*. So we must not receive as a general rule the words spoken in a loving way to specific individuals for their particular need; instead, we should immediately discern that the saints addressed their response in a sure and concrete way to those who approached them.

It also behooves us, however, to recall that longing for personal healing does not revolve around what today we might consider an awareness of or attention to individuality—the modern fascination with free choice or individual rights. The early desert tradition was overall dismissive of any concept of self-will or self-help; it consistently promoted dependence on God and deference to others. For Barsanuphius and John, the exercise of choice in the conventional, contemporary sense has less to do with what is personal and relates more to what is egotistical. Abba John recognizes that:

> we should ask such freedom of people that are not in fact scandalized by it; for not everyone is edified in the same way. Someone who possesses discernment will be edified and rejoice; another who lacks discernment may be scandalized. (*Letter* 376)

Attentiveness to Detail

Determining that people are on disparate levels mandates adopting different standards in spiritual relationships. Not only do people differ from one another (*Letter* 157), but the circumstances within one and the same person will vary from time to time (*Letter* 842). This is where conscience, coupled with humility, plays an important role in the correspondence:

> So long as the deed does not match the conscience, then it is not genuine but ironically just a demonic illusion. (*Letter* 275)

> You are beginning to walk the right and truthful way, when God leads you to consider yourself as beneath all creatures. (*Letter* 276)

The etymology of the term "con-science" (συν-είδησις) implies a concurrence of multiple aspects and a coincidence of manifold factors, each of them intricately interconnected and yet inseparably interdependent. It is a knowledge far more intuitive than analytical, a knowledge that invites and involves the subconscious, conscious, and supraconscious levels.

Discernment may of course pertain to things "yet to come" (*Letter* 459), enabling one to perceive the reason or rationale behind an occurrence (*Letter* 459), or else to prepare one about what to say in a given situation (*Letter* 690). However, it is not always a charisma related to foresight; it frequently finds confirmation in hindsight (*Letter* 475). Moreover, it sometimes gets reduced to a procedure of diagnosis—the detection of spiritual disease or the determination of psychological dysfunction. The Gaza elders are less interested in what *leads to* or legitimizes specific circumstances or actions. They are more concerned about what *limits or liberates* us in our relationship with God and others. In this respect, they suggest that one of the most apparent ways by which access to holiness and wholeness occurs is through awareness and attentiveness. The technique entails intense and vigilant watchfulness—a process of self-awareness and self-examination. Failure to notice or observe what is going inside or around us transpires when our vision is clouded by self-absorption.

So discernment is the first step of clarity in vision. Nevertheless, it is insufficient, even inappropriate, if it comes at the expense of love. I must learn to distinguish between what is good or bad for me, but what is right or wrong for me cannot be measured regardless of its consequences for others. The aim is always to discover wholeness, but at no cost to others; put differently, the aim is to experience *healing as communion*, where my relationship with "our Father in heaven" (Mt 6:9) reflects my love for all others "on earth as in heaven" (Mt 6:10)

Ultimately, discernment interacts at every moment and every turn of life as we search for the will of God with every challenge, every change, and every context. Discernment endows value and validity to the most intimate details of life and the most intricate subtleties of the spiritual life in the effort to relate the inner heart to the outer world.

The Discerning Disciple

Discernment is a foundational intuition of spiritual formation, a fundamental instrument of spiritual direction. So the spiritual guide must penetrate the depths and secrets of the disciple's heart—beneath superficial compromises and beyond artificial conventions that mask deeper intentions and difficult emotions—to reveal his or her authentic personality without disguise or disgust. And along this journey, insight and oversight dovetail where the discernment of the director encounters the discernment of the disciple. It is there that the fruit of unconditional supervision comes face-to-face with the fruit of unremitting surrender, where the relationship between elder and disciple becomes the mystery that generates conversation and communication in community.

By encouraging their disciples to search beyond apparent solutions lurking within the comfort of rules and complacency of regulations,

Barsanuphius and John sustain the dimension of community and communion in the practice of discernment as well as an unprecedented collaborative ministry in the exercise of direction.[21] The aim is to promote community, not to surrender to authority:

> Leave aside human rules and listen to him, who says: "The one who endures to the end will be saved" (Mt 10:22 and 24:13; Mk 13:13). Therefore, if one does not endure, one will not enter into eternal life. So do not look for a command. I do not want you to be "under law, but under grace" (Mt 10:22 and Mk 13:13). For it is said: "The law is not laid down for the righteous" (Rom 6:14). (*Letter* 23)

By urging their disciples to search more deeply and more diligently for meaningful answers—within themselves and despite any "first response" therapy (*Letter* 504)—the two Old Men cultivate the soil of the soul in a more wholesome manner that gives depth to every detail and every deed, every encounter and every experience. In the sacrament of spiritual discernment and spiritual direction, their letters bring to life the words of modern Greek poet Yannis Ritsos: "Every word is a doorway/to a meeting, one often cancelled,/but that's when a word is true:/when it insists on the meeting."[22]

Thus discernment becomes both a way of guarding oneself and of guiding others. The ascetic pays close attention to the meditations of the heart and movements of the body in order to mature in charity and compassion. Such discernment implies vigilance over intentions and actions by sitting in one's cell without distraction or delusion. When the eye of the soul is illumined and transformed, discernment becomes a light[23] that guides[24] and enables others to perceive the way and will of God.[25] But lack of discernment implies "blindness,"[26] whereby not only are we unable to distinguish

---

[21] See Hevelone-Harper, *Disciples of the Desert*, 384.
[22] Yannis Ritsos, "The Meaning of Simplicity," in *Parentheses, 1946–47* in *Repetitions, Testimonies, Parentheses*, trans. Edmund Keeley (Princeton, NJ: Princeton University Press, 1991), 125.
[23] Diadochus, *Century*, 6.
[24] Barsanuphius, *Letter* 173.
[25] *Macarian Homilies* 4.1 and 6.3.
[26] John Climacus, Step 26, *Ladder*, 230.

between good and evil, but—more importantly—we also fail to differentiate between sinner and sin.[27]

Discernment further implies recognition of the proper time and proper place to act with resolve or abstain with restraint. Echoing Ecclesiastes 3:1, Abba John speaks of "a time and a place" for the opportunity to determine the origin of one's thoughts: "You should determine an appropriate time for this, whether morning or evening, to discern your thoughts about what happened during that night or day" (*Letter* 395). Presuming too much or assuming too little—putting one's foot in one's mouth!—is part and parcel of lack of discernment. To adopt an image suggested by Barsanuphius in *Letter* 160 and subsequently stressed by John Climacus, moving too quickly is like trying to climb the entire ladder in a single stride: "We cannot place one foot on the first rung of the ladder and immediately expect to set the other foot on the top rung."[28] Discernment is thereby linked to *kairos*[29]—an awareness of the appointed or appropriate moment of action or inaction, counsel or silence, intervention or interference—where discernment becomes the priority to cultivate and nurture the freedom of the other.

"One who possesses discernment understands how and whence this occurs. We are required to do our best and no more" (*Letter* 503). The relationship with a spiritual elder is therefore a model, not an idol, and this relationship is a starting-point, never an end in itself. It is a microcosm of our relationship with God and the world, neither reducing nor replacing, but instead governing and guiding all relationships.

Advice and Judgment

As we have already seen, Barsanuphius and John often parallel discernment with prudence (*Letter* 158), with being soft as a dove (*Letter* 238). But in the *Sayings*, Abba Poemen also likens

---

[27]Syncletica 13, in *Sayings*; and Barsanuphius, *Letter* 453.
[28]John Climacus, Step 14 On Gluttony, in *Ladder*, 166.
[29]See Isidore of Pelusium, *Letter* 1.258; Basil of Caesarea, *Shorter Rules* 261; and Evagrius of Pontus, *Praktikos* 15.

discernment to the sharpness of an axe.[30] More than mere judgment (κρίσις), discernment involves slicing through (διά-κρισις) to the heart of the matter and piercing with precision (*Letter* 476) to what really matters. A person of judgment places things in their *proper* perspective, whereas a person of discernment perceives things in their *broader* perspective, placing God at the center of reality. The prefix διά in discernment (*dia-krisis*)—a preposition that signifies "through" but also signals "penetration through and through"— adds a third, a different, and divine dimension to discernment that penetrates the heart and rises above the very superficial or purely moral dilemma between good and evil.

Discernment as διά-κρισις denotes perception, precision, and penetration. Discernment as διά-κρισις entails a forthrightness (*Letter* 40) that cuts through the chaff and breaks through the façade of evil. Discernment as διά-κρισις abolishes a false and mechanical adherence to religious rules and rigid regulations. Discernment as διά-κρισις eliminates political idle-talk and nonsense, especially in religious circles. Discernment as διά-κρισις exceeds the cosmetic and fraudulent: by repudiating the darkness of deceit and radiating the light of truth, discernment discloses a deeper yearning for authenticity (*Letter* 288)—beyond the superficial and duplicitous.

Transparency and authenticity, however, do not imply arrogance or audacity. In fact, for the two Old Men, authentic discernment is a quintessential aspect of silence and solitude[31]—the ultimate confirmation of being and living in accordance with the image and likeness of God. This means that discernment may sometimes have more to do with what one actually does *not* say or does *not* do. It articulates what Ritsos describes above as "the silence [that] remains on its knees." If John Climacus is right to claim that "discernment is—and is recognized to be—a solid understanding of the will of God in all times, in all places, in all things; and occurs only among those who are pure in heart, in body, and in speech,"[32] then we should respect others more often with our silence and resignation, rather than by rushing to educate or legislate—the perennial temptation of every Christian believer and arguably every spiritual director.

---

[30]Poemen 52, *Sayings*.
[31]See J. Guillet, G. Bardy, et al., *Discernment of Spirits* (Collegeville, MN: Liturgical Press, 1970).
[32]John Climacus, Step 26 "On Discernment," *Ladder*, 229.

What becomes problematic is when there is too much of *us* and too little of *God* in spiritual discernment and spiritual direction. Henri Nouwen writes of "a ministry of absence,"[33] where the suspension of words is sometimes more effective and supportive than any presumed information or instruction. Spiritual directors are often impatient to school, itching to correct, swift to impugn. They forget how the discipline of silence is a vital part of discernment for everyone. Authentic discernment recognizes the cause of error and source of wrongdoing within—rather than outside—oneself.

This explains the transparent dimension of asceticism, whereby we learn to become what we are called *to be* instead of manifesting what we want others *to see*. That is why one should always refrain from judgment. An example highlighted in the correspondence is whether one should eat more when another eats less (*Letter* 546). It is not up to us to criticize or condemn, say the elders; "if one eats only once a day but does so with lack of discernment, then of what benefit is this?" (*Letter* 503). A spiritual guide recognizes how to discern between action and accident, between something that occurs out of negligence or out of necessity, between an act that arises from ignorance or provides occasion for instruction (*Letter* 521).

In this context, discernment becomes on the one hand a way of integrating the spiritual life, while on the other hand a way of penetrating the mysteries of divine compassion. Darkness is not always the absence of light; sometimes it may indicate a stage of growth. If we are honest with ourselves and with God, then we will admit that the spiritual life is by and large a series of movements between shadows, learning to "see in a mirror dimly" (1 Cor 13:12). Sometimes it may be imperative to walk in uncertainty, to tread an uncomfortable or inconvenient path, in order to reclaim the freedom with which God has endowed us. Sometimes we discern and discover the goal in the midst of struggle and suffering, rather than in the serenity or satisfaction of success. Sometimes we may not experience the grace of resurrection unless or until we endure the disgrace of the cross. Sometimes discernment means recognizing the spiritual way in the desolate interlude between Good Friday and Easter Sunday.

---

[33]See Henri Nouwen, *The Living Reminder: Service in Prayer in Memory of Jesus Christ* (San Francisco, CA: HarperOne, 2009).

In this perspective, discernment stands on the border between the mind and the heart, while at the same time serving as a bridge that connects our lives to others. When our interior life is at odds with our external conduct, the spiritual and emotional consequences are devastating, both for ourselves and others, as well as for our social and natural environment. This raises the importance of compassion in the practice of discernment; that is what lies behind the quintessential precept of the Gaza elders inferred from Paul's exhortation to "bear one another's burdens" (Gal 6:2). The spiritual guide is capable of discerning and distinguishing the particular needs of a disciple without comparison or competition.

Equipped with such discernment, the spiritual elder may not always wait for a person to open up, but will occasionally assume the initiative of revealing many thoughts of which the disciple may still be unaware. As people visit Barsanuphius and John at Thawatha, the two Old Men frequently address their challenges before they even arrive or record them in writing! There are other times when the response of the elders is not immediately conspicuous and sometimes sounds or seems irrelevant to the pilgrims. Yet because their response relies on and reveals the spirit of discernment, it is the appropriate answer at the appropriate time, acknowledging the intention and motivation of the visitor.

Thus discernment functions as a kind of spiritual plumb line, preserving a critical balance and distinguishing between far more than simply good and bad (*Letters* 17, 37, 478, and 546); there may be times when what is apparently right actually proves wrong (*Letter* 411). At the same time, discernment recognizes the difference between truth and untruth (*Letters* 469 and 604), natural and unnatural (*Letter* 154), undeviating and devious (*Letter* 265), self-sufficiency and security (*Letter* 621), or freedom and humility in obedience (*Letters* 258, 333, 376, 416, and 503). Discernment of truth is the proof of authenticity and transparency:

> If you want to discern matters, you will attract afflictions. Confide everything to your abbot and do whatever he discerns as best. For he knows what to do and how to care for your soul ... Someone who wants to do one thing and be relieved of another is either trying to reveal oneself as more discerning than the one giving the order, or else being ridiculed by demons ... If those

giving an order are brothers, and you think that this is harmful or beyond your ability, just ask your abbot and do whatever he tells you. (*Letter* 288)

Always balancing one's body, heart, and mind in moderation and judiciousness, discernment serves as the antidote to duplicity, where directness is always superior to deceit.[34]

Treading Lightly

Discernment implies discipline, but first and foremost it involves self-discipline (*Letter* 159). For the two Old Men, it is a tool for monks to "govern *themselves*" (*Letter* 318), to "control their *own* body" (*Letter* 524). In the case of Abbot Seridos, it is a gift that enables him to "carry out his spiritual ministry and endure the administration" of the community (*Letter* 570c).

There can be no self-righteousness in discernment, no entitlement in authority, and no complacency in power. This is why Barsanuphius emphasizes that we have no individual rights (τό δικαίωμα), no dispensation or authorization (τό ἀψήφιστον) to control or constrain others. No one deservingly holds any position of power; we are all ordained by God's grace to serve by God's mercy. None can claim to be qualified for what we are or do—even, and especially, through the gift of ordination. We have all achieved what we are and have with the help of others—above all, with the grace of God. We are all in positions by election or selection, by coincidence or inheritance—even if we claim or condone some authority over others. And that is precisely where damage occurs—for without discernment, we will only hurt rather than help.

There is ultimately a sense of sacred surrender and spiritual subtlety to the way of discernment—a humble deference and holy sensitivity to the movements and motivations of others (*Letters* 395, 493, 503, and 646). Behind every expression of sin lies discomfort and pain; even the most extreme example of sin conceals and

---

[34]Barsanuphius is clear about this: "Speaking in riddles is self-serving and lacking in discernment" (*Letter* 40).

represses a lack of security, affection, and acceptance. We should not reduce sin to moral transgression; it conceals insecurity, alienation, and isolation.

It is vital, then, to look beneath the superficial or ordinary. The spiritual director can see beyond any surface distorted or perverted to the beauty that is forgivable and lovable. And along the way, nothing is meaningless or lost; everything is a vital stage along a broken road. If we do not tread lightly and carefully, we risk trampling people's desires and dreams. Stepping gently and softly is at the heart of the gift of discernment. There can be no room for arbitrary imposition, no justification for assertive control, and no excuse for abrupt rejoinder (*Letter* 258). In the words of Aldous Huxley in "Island":

> Learn to do everything lightly …
> Just lightly let things happen …
> Lightly, lightly –
>   it's the best advice ever given me …
> Nothing ponderous or portentous …
> And … no theology, no metaphysics …
> You must walk ever so lightly.

8

Solitude, Silence, and Stillness

Subtle Variances of the Soul

Introduction
Echoes from the Desert

A privileged historical status and strategic geographical setting primordially set apart the Gaza region for a distinctive heritage combining continuity and creativity in its monastic practice and development. Its remoteness and accessibility would render it a unique haven for remarkable and intense expressions of the subtle variances of the soul, as well as refreshing and influential examples of solitude, silence, and stillness.

These inner workings of the heart and external methods of prayer converge and culminate in the practice of "prayer of the heart" and "prayer of the intellect" compiled in the eighteenth-century anthology of the *Philokalia*,[1] edited by the same Nikodemus who produced the correspondence of Barsanuphius and John. Yet they neither emerge nor exist in a vacuum; in fact, they disclose an

---

[1] *Philokalia: The Complete Text*. English translation by Kallistos Ware, G. E. H. Palmer, and Philip Sherrard (London: Faber and Faber, 1979–95). First four volumes available; fifth and final volume forthcoming (2022). Translated from the 3rd Greek edition (Athens: Astir Editions, 1957–63).

extensive development over many centuries of monastic formation and theological formulation. Thus fourteenth-century hesychasm[2] is not simply the result of a few exceptional ambassadors, such as Gregory of Sinai (*c.* 1260–346) or Gregory Palamas (1296–359); hesychasm is an organic extension and succession of countless unknown hermits and writers, many of whose lives and lines are not even recorded in the *Philokalia*.[3]

A Monastic Lifestyle

As we have repeatedly noted, Barsanuphius and John themselves are a continuation and, in many ways, an incarnation of principles treasured in the early Egyptian desert. The "great old man" is expressly shaped by the Evagrian notion—so central and vital to the spiritual worldview of the *Philokalia*—that the monk was "apart-from all and yet a part-of all."[4] By not opening his door to the elderly Egyptian monk requesting to see him (in *Letter* 55), Barsanuphius is in fact leaving the door open to everyone!

So it is hardly surprising that the two Old Men experience and encourage a life combining a balance of solitude, silence, and stillness:

> You should live in stillness for five days of the week and be in the company of your brothers for the other two days. And if your sitting in solitude is indeed according to God—that is to say if you come to know what you want from sitting in your cell—then you will not fall into the hands of the demon of vainglory. For a person who knows what he has come to do in a particular city, desires that alone and will not divert his heart elsewhere, otherwise he will fail in his objective. (*Letter* 211)

---

[2]Hesychasm signifies the tradition of mystical silence or contemplative prayer in Eastern Orthodox Christianity. See J. Meyendorff, *Byzantine Hesychasm: Historical, Theological, and Social Problems* (London: Variorum Reprints, 1974).

[3]The editors of the English translation of the *Philokalia* recognize this in their introduction to Volume 1: "Hesychasm ... is far more than a local historical movement dating to the later Byzantine centuries. On the contrary, it denotes the whole spiritual tradition going back to the earliest times and delineated in the *Philokalia*." "Introduction," in *Philokalia*, vol. 1, 14–15.

[4]Evagrius, "On Prayer," 124, in *Philokalia*, vol. 1, 69.

What, then, is the objective of the soul in solitude, silence, and stillness? What are the subtle spiritual variations of the soul in monastic seclusion and community?

The Way of the Soul
Knowing Oneself

The mystical classics acknowledge that there is a blurred line of differentiation between the virtues of solitude, silence, and stillness:

> Some of the fathers have called this practice stillness of the heart, others attentiveness, others the guarding of the heart, others watchfulness and rebuttal, others again the investigation of thoughts and the guarding of the intellect. But all of them alike worked the soil of their own heart, and in this way fed on the divine manna.[5]

And while Barsanuphius and John draw subtle distinctions between solitude,[6] silence,[7] and stillness,[8] underlying all three is the singular importance of taking time to examine the various aspects of the soul. What holds them together is the understanding that comes from self-awareness. In fact, self-knowledge is the heart of solitude, the basis of silence, and the center of stillness. Through self-knowledge we reach the heart of communion—an intimate relationship with others and ultimately with God.

In our age of instant communication and immediate gratification, we seem to know far less about ourselves and the motives behind our actions than any other subject. Somewhere on the long trail between childhood and adulthood, many of us lose touch with the vital skills that permit us to know ourselves. Part of the problem

---

[5] See Symeon the New Theologian, "The Three Methods of Prayer," in *Philokalia*, vol. 4, 71.
[6] Here translating the terms *kata monas* (κατά μόνας), *kat' idian* (κατ' ἰδίαν), *kathisma* (κάθισμα), and *kellion* (κελλίον).
[7] Here translating the terms *sige* (σιγή) or *sigan* (σιγᾶν), *siope* (σιωπή) or *siopan* (σιωπᾶν).
[8] Here translating the terms *hesychia* (ἡσυχία) or *hesychazein* (ἡσυχάζειν).

may be that we set impossible goals for ourselves, which only the angels can meet. The spirituality of the desert taught the Gaza elders that perfection is for God alone; we mortals are called neither to forego nor to forget our imperfection. Liberated from any tyranny of perfection, the disciples of the desert are free to be and live as children of a loving God. The fragility and vulnerability of life itself is what ultimately reveals the priority of confronting and embracing our inner desires and personal weaknesses.

Barsanuphius and John can certainly fathom the way of the soul as it struggles to know itself and understand the wiles of temptation that detract or distract from prayer. At the same time, the two Old Men are aware that, while there are as many ways of knowing ourselves as there are human beings, the differences among us are in fact very slight. Moreover, they recognize that specific rules and spiritual regulations will determine the depth of solitude, silence, and stillness. Often our lives are complicated by countless rules or copious regulations, which lead only to stress and anxiety. As a result, we are burned out and afraid to be alone, unwilling to love; we are unable to listen to a voice that is deep within ourselves yet larger than ourselves.

Barsanuphius and John therefore propose simple and practical ways of grasping these truths by "sitting in the cell" (*Letter* 172), practicing silence during conversation (*Letters* 470 and 481), and "beginning to practice stillness" (*Letter* 211). The spiritual life is a radical and revolutionary technique that helps us to break bad habits and establish new ones in their place: "To cut off one's own will while sitting in the cell is to despise fleshly comfort in all things" (*Letter* 173).

Barsanuphius adopts the image of constructing a house to describe this formidable struggle (*Letters* 52, 71, 207, and 535) and considerable effort (*Letter* 41) for transformation through the practice of solitude, silence, and stillness:

> If you wish to construct your home, first prepare the material and all other necessary things. Then, it is up to the professional builder to come and build the house. The necessary building materials for such a construction include firm faith for the building of walls, luminous wooden windows that allow in the sunlight to brighten the house, so that there is no darkness inside. These wooden windows are the five senses ... Furthermore,

you need a roof to cover the house ... The roof is symbolical of divine love, "which never ends" (1 Cor 13:8) ... Finally, the house requires a door, which allows the homeowner to enter and to be protected. When I speak of a door, brother, you should understand the spiritual door, namely the Son of God[9] who says: "I am the door" (Jn 10:9). (*Letter* 208)

In the house of the soul, the elementary quality of solitude is undistracted self-knowledge, awareness of one's passions, and practice of vigilance. The ensuing quality of silence is self-control and self-denial by listening to others and obeying the will of God. And the essential quality of stillness comes when the soul—unencumbered with passions, distractions, and attachments—reaches the goal of true intimacy with and love for God and others. Solitude, silence, and stillness are the shadows that accentuate the ultimate illumination. When these three qualities coexist, the ascetic journey enables us to discover the depth of the soul and to take it with us wherever we go: "When you arrive at the point of stillness, then you shall find rest with grace, *wherever* you may happen to withdraw" (*Letter* 789).

Solitude: The Door to the Soul

Solitude—or, as Niketas Stethatos calls it, "taking up one's abode in the desert"—is what allows us the time and the space to become alert to others and ourselves.[10] The entire spectrum of writers in the *Philokalia* is in agreement. For Peter of Damascus, solitude is the quintessential form of discipline, "consisting ... of living a life without distraction, far from all worldly care ... removing ourselves from human society and instead having only one concern."[11] For

---

[9]While Barsanuphius and John do not explicitly refer to the invocation of "the name of Jesus" (cf. Niketas Stethatos, "On the Inner Nature of Things," 97, in *Philokalia*, vol. 4, 136; Gregory of Sinai, "On Stillness," in *Philokalia*, vol. 4, 263–74; and Kallistos/Ignatios Xanthopouloi, "Century 22 and 49," in *Philokalia*, vol. 5, [forthcoming]), they do refer to "invoking" (*Letter* 427) and "saying" (*Letter* 430) "the name of God" (*Letters* 103, 417, and 424). See the section on the Jesus Prayer in Chapter 3 (above).
[10]Stethatos, "On the Practice of the Virtues," 75, in *Philokalia*, vol. 4, 98.
[11]Peter of Damascus, "The Seven Forms of Bodily Discipline," in *Philokalia*, vol. 3, 89.

Gregory Palamas, lack of solitude "shatters that single-pointed concentration of the intellect, which constitutes the inward and true monk."[12] This is why Nilus the Ascetic commends solitude "[as] the mother of wisdom."[13]

For Barsanuphius and John, solitude is a fundamental prerequisite for spiritual progress (see *Letter* 616). This is why, to a monk inquiring whether he should accept money in order to feed the poor, Abba John is revolutionary, virtually uncharitable: you are to avoid this "even if you see someone dying in front of your very cell" (*Letter* 619)! This is because both elders appreciate how easily love and service can serve as excuses to avoid the inner enterprise of transformation. They recognize that even prayer can be a pretext to circumvent the difficult work of solitude and silence (see *Letter* 739). The "other old man" explains: "As far as almsgiving goes, not everyone can bear the application of this virtue, but only those who have reached stillness through mourning for their own sins" (*Letter* 618).

Unfortunately, we tend to confuse self-knowledge with self-absorption. However in reality, self-knowledge leads away from self-absorption toward a sense of "forgetting oneself."

> Show complete hatred to acquire complete love; show complete estrangement to acquire complete intimacy; abhor adoption to receive adoption; surrender your will to perform your will; cut yourself away and bind yourself; put yourself to death in order to give yourself life; forget yourself and know yourself. Then, behold, you will have the works of a solitary. (*Letter* 112)

Whereas we routinely encourage the need for knowing and loving others, we rarely reward knowing ourselves in solitude. Barsanuphius reiterates the stark conviction of Abba Alonius: "I and God are alone in this world" (*Letter* 346).[14] And he adds: "Being alone and laboring a little is of more benefit to you than being with others" (*Letter* 359).

The truth is we are never less alone than when we are alone: "You are not alone in your struggle ... For many others are struggling

---

[12]Gregory Palamas, "To the Most Reverend Nun Xenia," 1, in *Philokalia*, vol. 4, 293.
[13]Nilus the Ascetic, "Ascetic Discourse," in *Philokalia*, vol. 1, 231.
[14]Alonius 1, *Sayings*, 30.

with you in prayer" (Col 4:12) (*Letter* 832).[15] Knowing why we do what we do facilitates the awareness of why other people also do what they do, and in the end the acceptance of other people as they are (see *Letter* 316). In the end, narcissism is not too much self but insufficient true self. Self-absorbed people suffer from too little rather than too much self. The antidote to self-centeredness is self-awareness. This is why Gregory of Sinai believes that "nothing so fills the heart with compunction and humbles the soul as solitude embraced with self-awareness."[16]

The trouble is that we seek intimacy by facing in the wrong direction. Instead of looking inward for consolation, we turn outward toward others. In this regard, the isolation of solitude serves as a necessary preliminary step to intimacy and communion. "When you are alone in your cell, examine your heart, and you will discover whence this hardness [toward your brother] came to you" (*Letter* 614). Intimacy begins from within; it reflects the inner landscape of the soul. It is the solid ground from which we can reach out to others, even God. According to an apocryphal saying attributed to Jesus in the *Gospel of Thomas*: "When you make the two one, and make the inside like the outside, and the outside like the inside, and the upper side like the underneath ... then the kingdom is at hand."[17]

Solitude, then, is the great stabilizer—it is like a secret compass in our relationship with God, others, and ourselves. For Barsanuphius and John, it helps us distinguish between genuine concern and "people-pleasing" (*anthropareskeia*, ἀνθρωπαρέσκεια); the latter one strictly avoids (see, e.g., *Letters* 260–1 and 824–5). Solitude leads to silence, which is equivalent to "restraining of one's heart from giving and taking (Phil 4:14), from people-pleasing and other such things" (*Letter* 314). Solitude is about being, and not simply doing. It renders the soul attentive: receptive and susceptive to grace. "Do not despair at the labor [of being alone], and you shall

---

[15]*Letter* 141 adds that the grace of God is always present; *Letter* 248 notes that the prayer of our spiritual director accompanies us; and *Letter* 832 observes that we also have the communion of saints with us!

[16]Gregory of Sinai, "On Commandments and Doctrines," 104, in *Philokalia*, vol. 4, 235.

[17]Saying 22. See Thomas O. Lambdin, trans., *The Gospel of Thomas* (Amazon Digital Services, 2010). See also the translation by Marvin W. Meyer, *The Nag Hammadi Scriptures: Revised and Updated Translation* (San Francisco, CA: HarperOne, 2009).

find humility … If you are humbled, you will receive grace; and if you receive grace, it will assist you" (*Letter* 359).

Solitude also smashes the graven image of prayer as "not working" when we do not receive what we want. Prayer does not want; it simply wonders and humbly waits. The two Old Men are adamant that when God answers prayer, it is almost always in ways that we least expect. "God will arrange the matter in a way that you do not know" (*Letter* 359). In fact, answered prayer provides ways that deflate—perhaps even destroy—self-reliance that seeks immediate attainment of pre-meditated goals. In this regard, solitude is hardly reducible to selfishness; it actually dissolves any hint of self-centeredness—it is what Barsanuphius and John call "not reckoning oneself as anything" (τό ἀψήφιστον): "Be carefree from all things; then you will have time for God. Die to all people; this is true exile. Moreover, retain the virtue of not reckoning yourself as anything; then you will find your thought undisturbed" (*Letter* 259).

So the two Old Men constantly maintain a delicate balance between the gloomy devil of instant vainglory (see *Letter* 204) and the blue sea of prolonged despair:

> When a person descends to humility, that person discovers progress. Remaining in your cell only renders you useless if you remain without affliction. When we are carefree prematurely, the enemy prepares turmoil instead of tranquility in order to bring us to the point of saying: "I wish I had never been born!" (*Letter* 692)

This is why they recommend retaining a sense of balance, "not moving to one or another extreme, but instead journeying in the middle way" (*Letter* 314).

Needless to say, progress in solitude takes toil and time. The transformation is not sudden; we do not magically become new people, our old faults forgotten. We can never run from who we are. We can never escape our temptations and passions: temper, vanity, fear, envy, delusion, or arrogance. The "great old man" advises "never to enter the cell on the pretext of cowardice, but only at the proper time" (*Letter* 434). And the "other old man" adds: "When you come to silence through ascetic struggle, then it is good. But when this is not the way that you come to it, but rather keep silent from fear of turmoil, then it is harmful" (*Letter* 481). This level of personal integrity comes from intense self-knowledge that comes through silence. Ultimately, the degree to which we acknowledge and accept others will be checked by the degree that we understand and tolerate ourselves.

In the solitude of the cell, through temptation and tension, the ascetic becomes painfully aware of what is lacking. It is in the cell that the ascetic is haunted by absence of love and yearns for depth of communion. The cell symbolizes the safe haven of the soul, which one never leaves and where one can always willingly return to discover and acknowledge more and more of the authentic self, irrespective of how painful or agonizing an ordeal this may be. Such a discovery eventually becomes a fountain of healing. Embracing solitude in the loneliness of the cell—and, by extension, in the solitude of the soul—means knowing what one thinks, understanding how one behaves, and finally accepting what others do without the need to defend oneself. It is assuming responsibility without the least trace of self-justification. It is the source of authentic vulnerability and openness.

In such vulnerability or openness, solitude connects with the Cross of Christ (see *Letter* 185). Abba John writes: "That is when one reaches silence, [precisely] when one bears the Cross" (*Letters* 314 and 320).[18] People who have been pushed—whether by personal suffering, difficult circumstance, or misplaced choice—to breaking point frequently possess a richness of vision less apparent in those without any experience of conflict. The reality of conflict as a constant and crucial part of life may be difficult to accept, but how we experience tension and ambivalence deeply affects how we accept ourselves and others. The truth is that we discern God in the very midst of tensions and trials.

Solitude reminds us that the soul is not a conflict-free zone where we can evade or ignore the perils of the world and temptations of the soul: "In the cell, we feel pain and compunction. What prevents compunction from coming to you is your own will. If a person does not cut off one's own will, then the heart does not feel pain" (*Letter* 237). Solitude inaugurates the practice of ignoring one's own will—of listening to the will of God and of others. No wonder

---

[18]See also Abba Isaiah of Scetis, *Ascetic Discourse* 13, in J. Chryssavgis and R. P. Penkett, *Abba Isaiah of Scetis: Ascetic Discourses* (Kalamazoo MI: Cistercian Publications, 2002), 105–9.

that the Gaza elders underline the need to "rejoice in the Lord, rejoice in the Lord, rejoice in the Lord" (*Letter* 10) in and despite all circumstances. For while "we cannot be without affliction ... we have been commanded to 'give thanks in all circumstances' (1 Thes 5:18)" (*Letter* 96). It is here that solitude converges with service, and the cell opens up to the world

Silence: The Way to the Soul

If solitude endows us with the quality of attention and sensitivity to our motives, self-awareness imparts the art of attentiveness and listening to others—it is knowing who we are in relation to others. That is the power of silence. And it is why the *Philokalia* underlines the importance of always using few words. St. Theodore the Ascetic is clear on this:

> Expel from yourself the spirit of talkativeness. For in it lurk the most dreadful passions: lying, loose speech, absurd chatter, buffoonery, obscenity. To put the matter succinctly, "through talkativeness, you will not escape sin" (Prv 10:19), whereas a silent person "is a throne of perceptiveness" (Prv 12:33). Moreover, the Lord said that we must give account for every idle word (Mt 12:36). So silence is most necessary and very profitable.[19]

Physical contact and verbal communication are as connected with intimacy and love as silence is. In solitude, the space between ourselves is important; in silence, the space between our words becomes equally important. Solitude marks the connection between cell and community, as well as the correlation between loneliness and liturgy. This is why "when you pray, go inside your room, shut the door, and pray to your Father in secret; and your Father who sees in secret will reward you" (Mt 6:6).

Silent space is always necessary; "silence is always more admirable" (*Letter* 36), "always better" (*Letter* 697), "glorious above all else" (*Letter* 469), "good in every case" (*Letter* 283), and "more necessary and more beneficial than everything" (*Letter* 314). In response to someone asking for prayers, Barsanuphius writes: "Do not compel

---

[19] Theodore the Ascetic, "A Century of Spiritual Texts," in *Philokalia*, vol. 2, 31.

me to speak when I desire to venerate stillness and silence" (*Letter* 69). The same truth resonates in the *Philokalia*: "Silence is more valuable than speech."[20] Because silence is capable of conveying and communicating far more than any written or spoken word, Jane Brox, a modern student of the social history of silence, eloquently articulates the same wisdom as Barsanuphius and John:

> Silence can seem like a luxury. Or the fraught world has labeled it that way. But from what I know of it, I would argue that silence is as necessary as the constitutionally guaranteed freedom of speech that we so carefully guard and endlessly ponder, for it affirms the meaning of speech even as it provides a path to inner life, to beauty and observation and appreciation. It presents the opportunity for a true reckoning with the self, with external obligation, and with power.[21]

The "great old man" claims that silence is actually a divine command, a quality demanded by God (*Letter* 603). He would never say the same of inward stillness, which he considers a gift, an attribute received from above (*Letter* 94). Silence provides the latitude and capacity to listen to and soak up what another person is trying to say. Far more than merely an acoustic absence, it is retaining a sense of wonder before another person—like the draw of breath as we gasp in wonder. This is because we bring to relationships the same self that we are (or perhaps are not) in touch with who we are when we are alone. So the two Old Men harshly rebuke those who complain about losing the spiritual gifts attained in solitude—including the gift of silence—when they happen to be with other people (*Letter* 268).

Silence, moreover, is a skill whereby we acknowledge that what is going on in someone else's world matters. Otherwise, the river of connection between "me" and "you" renders the force of my own desires and prejudices more "conscious" in my mind and in my heart. As a result, I create my own version of you, with little if any chance of real contact or palpable connection. However

---

[20] See Elias the Presbyter, "A Gnomic Anthology I," in *Philokalia*, vol. 3, 34.
[21] Jane Brox, *Silence: A Social History of One of the Least Understood Elements of Our Lives* (Boston, MA: Houghton Mifflin Harcourt, 2019), 254.

through silence we discover that—to invert the rumination of naturalist John Muir—"going in ... is really going out."²²

> Another Christ-loving layperson asked the same Old Man (John): Sometimes, I am in conversation with someone, and suddenly my thought is distracted, so that I feel alone and ultimately forget what that person has just said. Not because my intellect is transferred somewhere else, but because it is simply beside [My note: full of?] itself ...
> Response. This is a diabolical temptation ... However, if one candidly reveals this to the other person in conversation, saying: "Forgive me; for I was distracted by the devil," then the devil is put to shame and the temptation ceases. After that, you may continue the conversation with vigilance. (*Letter* 692)

These elders recognize that, where there is an impoverished self, there is invariably an endangered relationship. Silence is the criterion of truthfulness, integrity, and balance. For Elias the Presbyter in the *Philokalia*, "a sense of the right moment and a sense of proportion go hand-in-hand with intelligent silence. Truth is the banquet of all the three together."²³ Similarly for the two Old Men, "neither being bold in silence nor despising silence in times of distraction: this is truly the middle way" (*Letter* 315).

There is, however, a fundamental paradox here. Barsanuphius and John are well aware that to achieve self-knowledge, we need to trust at least one other person:

> From this you may learn whether you are living like the others in the monastic community; by not doing anything of your own will, eating neither alone nor with the brothers, but doing whatever you have been ordered without any discussion. (*Letter* 250)

> Doing something through the abbot is always a lesser wrong ... However, doing something alone brings double warfare, not only from the heart but also from other people. (*Letter* 324, also *Letter* 173)

---

²²See Linnie Marsh Wolfe, *John of the Mountains: The Unpublished Journals of John Muir* (Madison, WI: University of Wisconsin Press, 1938 [repr. 1979]), 439.
²³Elias the Presbyter, "A Gnomic Anthology," I, in *Philokalia*, vol. 3, 37.

Obedience is essentially an act of listening carefully; it is the art of paying close (*hyp-akoe*) attention.[24] Mark the Ascetic alludes to the dangers of extreme isolation when one "relies on one's own judgement with no one else as witness."[25] Barsanuphius concurs that "when you hasten to do something on your own, the results is from the devil" (*Letter* 93). In brief, the basic advice is almost reminiscent of good "prep school" education: "It is never good to speak before being asked" (*Letter* 698). But the goal is never to restrain or repress the will; it is always to strengthen and stabilize it: "Feel neither arrogant if your words are accepted, nor grieved if your words are rejected" (*Letters* 698 and 738). Obedience is the measure of authentic solitude and silence: "If you wish to learn whether you are harmed or benefit by staying on your own, then take this as a sign. If you are staying there as a result of obedience, you can be certain that you are benefiting" (*Letter* 248).

What is more, the fine balance between isolation and intimacy is extremely difficult to sustain without a spiritual director. Through someone else's belief in ourselves, we begin confidently—by the act of confiding and confessing—to rediscover the solid ground within us. Sharing our thoughts and temptations openly with at least one other person enables us to become familiar with the desires or conflicts that drive our behavior. Being prepared to listen to and accept the reality of our nature and ourselves renders us more aware of—and eventually more caring toward—other people.

Barsanuphius and John frequently cite Galatians 6:2 precisely because bearing—or sharing—responsibility for "the burdens of others" is critical to maturing spiritually. Assuming and acknowledging responsibility for the consequences of one's thoughts and actions never imply blaming others, whom therefore we perceive as less threatening: "To come to perfect silence, one must first endure insults from other people, as well as despise, dishonor and hurt ... so that our labor may not be in vain" (cf. 1 Thes 3:5) (*Letter* 185). Silence is the alphabet in the language of tolerance and love. Because under the steamroller of words, intimacy sometimes gets crushed. However, silence allows us to broaden and deepen our relationship with others.

---

[24] On the close link between obedience (*hypakoe*) and silence or stillness (*hesychia*), see Peter of Damascus, in *Philokalia*, vol. 3, 103–8.

[25] Mark the Ascetic, "Letter to Nicholas the Solitary," in *Philokalia*, vol. 1, 158.

While the "great old man" always prefers silence, the "other old man" loves conversation: "My babbling does not allow me to keep silent without replying; for I have an uncontrolled tongue" (*Letter* 211). Indeed, Abba John claims: "Since we have not yet reached the point of treading the way of the perfect, on account of our weakness, we should in fact speak" (*Letter* 469). And elsewhere he observes:

> As for the silence, of which the Fathers speak, you have no clue what this is about. In fact, not many people know at all. For this kind of silence is not a matter of shutting one's mouth. There may be someone who speaks tens of thousands of words that are useful; and this is reckoned as silence. There may be another who speaks just a single idle word, and this is reckoned as trampling the Savior's teachings. (*Letter* 554)[26]

The balance between solitude and society is a distinctive feature of the neighboring monastery, where Barsanuphius's scribe, Seridos, served as abbot. There, as we have seen, cells opened up to windows allowing for didactic conversation and instruction; monks were encouraged to support visitors, including lay persons and family relatives—"not in order to please people or to seek praise, but out of purity of heart" (*Letter* 595).

Finally, it would be an oversight not to mention that Abba John is the first to coin the phrase "non-silence" (*to asiopeton* or *to me siopan*), where one may be silent but fails to manifest one's thoughts honestly and thus remains unhealed (*Letter* 320). This implies that both silence and speaking can be counterfeit. Although not discussed in the letters, the silence of shutting out another person can inflict deep pain. To adopt the contemporary vernacular, giving someone the "silent treatment" is hard-hearted and insensitive. When we disconnect our theology from others or else do not relate to the wider community, then it is a false language, miscommunication. And Barsanuphius and John have little tolerance for spiritual chatter (cf. *Letter* 36) that renders God small and manageable. They do not offer a manual of reproofs or recipes, with homilies for healing or formulas for salvation. Seductive as the "quick-fix" may be, the

---

[26]See also Poemen 27, *Sayings*.

two Old Men know that human beings are unpredictable, far too complex for such an approach to bear long-term benefits. Beware the person who always has the answer!

The fine balance between isolation and intimacy is ultimately impossible to attain without divine grace. Authentic silence is ultimately a reflection of the fellowship of the Holy Trinity: "If you prepare your house [of silence] in this way ... [the Son of God] will come with the blessed Father and the Holy Spirit, and they will make a home within you [Jn 14:23], teaching you what stillness is and illuminating your heart with ineffable joy" (*Letter* 208). It is not coincidental that the word for Spirit—in both Hebrew and Greek—implies silent breath, like the wind we neither see nor hear (Jn 3:8), though we know it refreshes and restores us. In the end, prayer is not about diffuseness of expression or amplification of sound. Sometimes, prayer can be futile or ineffective when we fail to reach out softly or silently enough.

Stillness: Where God Dwells

Solitude and silence finally issue in the mystery of stillness; indeed, they are "the foundation of stillness."[27] For Gregory of Sinai, stillness is so "eloquent"[28] that anyone who wishes to plumb the mysteries should "cleave to stillness."[29] For Abba Philemon, "the only path leading to heaven is complete stillness."[30] And for Niketas Stethatos, it is "the upper room,"[31] "the knowledge of divine mysteries ... the abyss of divine intellections, the rapture of the intellect, intercourse with God, unsleeping watchfulness, spiritual prayer ... solidarity and union with God."[32]

---

[27]See Gregory of Sinai, "On Commandments and Doctrines 99," in *Philokalia*, vol. 4, 233.
[28]Gregory of Sinai, "On Stillness," 15, in *Philokalia*, vol. 4, 274.
[29]Gregory of Sinai, "On Commandments and Doctrines," 127, in *Philokalia*, vol. 4, 246.
[30]See "A Discourse on Abba Philemon," in *Philokalia*, vol. 2, 349. It is in this "Discourse" that the phrase "Lord Jesus Christ, Son of God, have mercy on me" first appears.
[31]Niketas Stethatos, "On the Inner Nature of Things," 66, in *Philokalia*, vol. 4, 126.
[32]Stethatos, "On the Inner Nature of Things," 64, in *Philokalia*, vol. 4, 125. See also Gregory of Sinai, "On Stillness," in *Philokalia*, vol. 4, 266, where Gregory explicitly quotes Barsanuphius.

Stillness is the moment when we realize that God is the ground of our being (see Jer 10:10), "the solid rock of our foundation" (*Letter* 345), before whom we are no longer afraid of "being frail" or "being nothing"—what our two Old Men call *to apsepheston* (*Letters* 227, 259, 271, and 604). Abba John says: "Wherever there is stillness ... there also God dwells" (*Letter* 454). Abba Barsanuphius claims that stillness is a spiritual gift bestowed by God "in its proper time" (*Letter* 208). It is a gift conferred when the self completely surrenders to God.

Stillness points to the source and center of authentic living, of living in the present. There is no need to dwell on the past or obsess about the future. All attention converges on the immediate present, which allows us to appreciate the ordinary moment every day. It enables us to be more focused or engaged, less distracted or scattered. Diving inside this inner core we discover a calming, transforming experience, which can be tapped whenever we are overcome by helplessness or barrenness. Again, the externals do not change, but the filter or lens through which we see and respond to the world changes. We still observe the ordinary, but everything appears extraordinary—undistorted by our disposition or predisposition, in a color and perspective that reflect the dimension of another world.

From this angle, stillness is closely related to death. It reflects an expectation of the age to come. Be vigilant, Barsanuphius advises: "Pay attention to yourself and expect your impending death" (*Letter* 256). "The cell is a cemetery ... It is a place of rest ... a sanctuary that contains the dwelling-place of God" (*Letter* 142)! Stillness can almost feel like death, death to oneself (*Letter* 55), but it can also resemble the slow, silent growth of living roots sprawling deep beneath the earth. Barsanuphius likens "perfect stillness" (*Letter* 6) to "the arrival of a ship in a harbor, where it no longer fears dangers, distress, or the onset of winds" (*Letters* 8–9).

There is nothing simplistic or sluggish about the cultivation of stillness. Living life to the full comes only when we face the ultimate questions, including meaninglessness and death.[33] How we address or avoid these concerns has profound consequences on our experience of solitude, silence, and stillness. Which is why

---

[33] On the connection between prayer and death, see Symeon the New Theologian, "Practical and Theological Texts," 87, in *Philokalia*, vol. 4, 43.

remembrance of death is a crucial monastic virtue, a daily and tangible reminder of weakness and imperfection. If we want to come out of life seasoned and polished, we need only think of death; there is hardly an outward sense of perfection in nursing homes and hospices. Remembrance of death allows brokenness to be revealed in truth so that the lie of illusory flawlessness may split wide open and healing can begin.

Nevertheless, stillness is hardly scary; it is profoundly sacred. It closely teams with a desire for "life in abundance" (Jn 10:10), beyond "mere survival." Most of us tend to deny the connection between death and stillness by entering a whirl of activity that renders death inconceivable, even improbable. Stillness is like waiting respectfully and reverently. It is a renewing sense of anticipation, an overture to heavenly resurrection. In the state of sacred stillness, we know we are fully alive, not dead; we are aware of having needs and temptations, as well as of being able to face and embrace these without turning elsewhere. In stillness we are not empty; we are not alone; we are not afraid. "In stillness, [we] know that God is" (Ps 46:11).

Finally, stillness introduces an apophatic element to the nature of intimacy and love. In the *Ladder of Divine Ascent*, John Climacus reveals that, upon reaching the top rung, one rests in the presence of God's love. Thalassius the Libyan also closely associates "stillness and intense longing for God."[34] In fact, for Niketas Stethatos, silence and stillness are even greater than love.[35]

Through stillness, then, comes the refreshing suggestion of loving God and others by "*not*" knowing" them. Because if we are fixed to our preconceptions about God or fears of people, we may never enjoy perfect stillness (see *Letters* 6 and 496). When we think that we "know" someone, we have already shut our eyes to that person's constant process of change and growth. The fact is that we limit ourselves when we root others in their past instead of rejoicing in their potential.

In the isolation of solitude, we can risk being who we genuinely are; in the echo of silence, we begin facing other people as they are; and in the intimacy of stillness, we embrace the other person in their entirety, in their eternal dimension—beyond what we could ever

---

[34]See Thalassius, "Second Century," in *Philokalia*, vol. 2, 314.
[35]See Stethatos, "On the Inner Nature of Things," 75–7, in *Philokalia*, vol. 4, 128–9.

comprehend, beyond what we would tolerate, or beyond what we might expect to profit. "Solitude," writes Sherry Turkle,

> reinforces a secure sense of self, and with that, the capacity for empathy. Then, conversation with others provides rich material for self-reflection. Just as alone we prepare to talk together, together we learn how to engage in more productive solitude.[36]

An Extraordinary Legacy

Solitude, silence, and stillness are qualities that present us with subtle, yet significant variances of the wonders of the soul and the wounds of the heart. Barsanuphius and John offer us an alternative perspective of this world, not an occasion to escape the reality of this world. And this fresh perspective we may experience in the simple pastime of reading a book or completing a crossword, as in the standard pleasure of daily exercise or walking a dog, and especially in an intentional moment of retreat or regeneration. The most ardent expression of mystical union might be embedded in the busiest of daily lives and blandest of unassuming routines. We can elevate the very ordinary to the extraordinary, while the very personal can converge with the social:

> Whether you are sitting down or walking about, whether you are working or eating, or whatever else you are doing ... do not hesitate to pray. (*Letter* 441)

In defining the three stages of the solitary life, the two Old Men underline that solitude, silence, and stillness relate to every detail, to "every aspect and conduct and concern" of life (*Letter* 52). This is why they advise that "we should be with others as if not being with them" (*Letter* 173). This is also the inspiration behind a poem entitled "Sitting on the Fence" by Michael Leunig: "'Come sit down beside me'/I said to myself/And, although it doesn't make sense/I

---

[36] Sherry Turkle, *Reclaiming Conversation: The Power of Talk in a Digital Age* (New York: Penguin Press, 2015), 10.

held my own hand/As a small sign of trust/And together I sat [alone] on the fence."[37]

After the death of Abba John, Barsanuphius moved back into his friend's—originally his own—cell and remained there in total seclusion until his death. According to a legend preserved in the *Historia Ecclesiastica* of Evagrius Scholasticus, at the time of Evagrius's writing (c. 593), some fifty years after Barsanuphius's presumed death, the "great old man" was believed to be still alive. When the Patriarch of Jerusalem ordered the cell door opened, a consuming fire flashed from the cell.[38] It appears that the silence of Barsanuphius was stronger than death itself. It certainly proved influential for generations of subsequent monastics and laity interested to this day in the way of prayer and silence.

---

[37]Permission courtesy of poet: "Sitting on the Fence" copyright Michael Leunig, 1972.
[38]See Evagrius, *Historia Ecclesiastica* IV, 33, in PG 87,ii.2764.

Conclusion

From my initial introduction to the world of Barsanuphius and John during studies in Oxford, through my intensive research into their letters that I translated on sabbatical in Princeton, to the inspirational motivation that I have drawn from their wisdom for my scholarship and ministry, the two Old Men of sixth-century Gaza have been a source of captivation, conversation, and consolation over the course of many years. The distinct aroma of their sincerity and maturity, along with the refreshing grace of openness and freedom in the stifling institutionalism of academic and religious circles alike, constantly recalls me to the deeper aspiration of both education and ordination.

Above and beyond any scholarly eminence or spiritual consequence, Barsanuphius and John advance a palpable concept of the heavenly, while acknowledging the fragile sacredness of the human. The profound compassion and gentle refinement that emerge from their letters are surprising, even breathtaking. At the same time, their insightful judgment and gracious tenderness reflect a personal and profound experience of divine charity as well as a unique and unparalleled exposure to human experience.

So when they write of ultimate truths and essential values, the reader recognizes that they speak with authority and authenticity about "what they have heard with their ears, what they have seen with their eyes, what they have looked upon and touched with their hands concerning the word of life" (1 Jn 1:1). Clarity and originality resonate in the letters of these elders from Gaza, beyond and despite historical remoteness or cultural isolation. In addressing perennial challenges of the soul with precision and perception, the generosity of their Christian instruction and spiritual direction transcends time and space, cutting directly across centuries and civilizations. The result kindles a process of growth both in the recipient of their time and reader of today (see *Letter* 449).

In their letters, the grace of God is always with us (cf. Mt. 28:20) and the saints of old continue to be relevant. Their wisdom, as historian Peter Brown has noted, is "searching yet infinitely flexible, unfolding with quiet generosity, letter by letter, situation by situation, to embrace an entire world of troubled persons—monks, clergy and laity—throwing its fine net also over us moderns."[1] Their words resonate with the deepest recesses of the heart; their responses radiate a calming effect on the soul. By respecting the precariousness and vulnerability of human nature, they reveal the magnitude and magnificence of divine grace.

It should come as no surprise, then, that Barsanuphius and John avoid "taking sides" in theological controversies of their time. For them, creed and confession are more than just concise and formal tenets, authorized and authoritative teachings; orthodoxy and heresy were not simply matters to be balanced or extremes to be reconciled. At the same time, however, it would be a mistake to dismiss these hermits as something less than theologians, as inferior to more impressive or intellectual thinkers of the past.[2] For Barsanuphius and John, doctrine and dogma are perennial stories of salvation, not merely lists of beliefs or articles of faith. Religious convictions and principles translate into moral standards and disciplines. Theology and ethics are two sides of one and the same coin. Orthodoxy is not so much a profession of correct ideology, but the practice of a living tradition where "the Word assumes flesh" (Jn 1:14). It is, moreover, discerned less in the precision of the letter than in the imprecision of life.

In this perspective, acceptance or rejection of the Council of Chalcedon is not really a matter of political dissent or division.[3]

---

[1]Peter Brown, endorsement of John Chryssavgis, *Letters from the Desert: Barsanuphius and John*, Popular Patristics Series (Crestwood, NY: St. Vladimir's Seminary Press, 2003).

[2]For example, Fr. Georges Florovsky infers this when he distinguishes between "Eastern Fathers" or "Byzantine Fathers" (implying theologians) and "Ascetic and Spiritual Fathers" (inferring monastics). See Richard Haugh, ed., *The Collected Works of Georges Florovsky* (Belmont, MA: Nordland, 1974–89), esp. volumes 7–9 vis-à-vis volume 10.

[3]See John Meyendorff, *Imperial Unity and Christian Divisions: The Church 450–680 AD*, The Church in History, vol. 2 (Crestwood, NY: St. Vladimir's Seminary, 1989).

Indeed, acknowledging the conciliar definition about two natures in Christ—united "without confusion and without change, without division and without separation"[4]—is not primarily a question of doctrinal confession or personal conviction. It is first and foremost an accurate formulation in theological vocabulary of an empirical acquaintance with a mystical experience conveyed through spiritual direction to those inquiring about how doctrine issues into life and practice.

And within this process, every mundane detail and every ordinary facet matter to the two Old Men, who pay careful attention to trivial, even tangential aspects contained in the hundreds of letters that they receive. They omit nothing whatsoever from their responses to these letters, even if this means a lengthy, digressive communication by the scribe. This is why people open their hearts to them.

What is at stake is far more than "sweating the small stuff."[5] It is a reminder that, while details should not overwhelm or consume us, they are frequently indicators of our spiritual predicament. This is why Barsanuphius and John take the time to respond to minor, seemingly mundane details of questions that they receive. After all, it is difficult to rush a reply dictated verbatim to a scribe. There will inevitably be repetition and correction, attention to particulars and cognizance of predicaments. Dictation the old-fashioned style is a comprehensive and effective way of letting your correspondents know that the person dictating notices and acknowledges them. It is an elementary, albeit palpable way of learning and loving.

This is why the letters of Barsanuphius and John are always carefully constructed, never hastily conveyed. A single person garners the undivided attention of the elders as they respond to questions. And a single issue or set of issues is the exclusive objective of their written responses. The most unique individual in the world and the most vital question of the moment gets recorded in an unremarkable document scratched out directly from the two Old Men by their trusted scribes. The ordinary candor of their communications accounts for their extraordinary influence. It also explains their far-reaching consequence for the highest echelons of church and society, as well as for readers through the centuries to our day.

---

[4]T. Herbert Bindley, ed., *The Oecumenical Documents of the Faith* (London: Methuen and Co., 1899), 225.
[5]Title of a book by Richard Carlson (New York: Hyperion, 1997).

But there is another iconoclastic aspect of these letters. In a world precariously enchanted by exceptional charisma, Barsanuphius and John speak straightforward, forthright truths—unpretentious in their style and unembellished in their substance. Illusion and delusion have no place in their spiritual counsel. Their aim is not to impress; it is to inspire and instruct, to encourage and educate.

There are certain characteristics that belong to universal spiritual teachers—wherever and whenever they live. Barsanuphius and John are exceptional examples of holiness and openness because they pay attention to specific human beings in specific contexts—not to institutions, structures, or positions. In their relationships, they are not hopeless sentimentalists but utter realists. They never justify or rationalize evil; yet, they also never despair or surrender in the face of sin. Their spiritual paradigm is always rooted in love and respect, in the recognition that to be perfectly human is to be imperfect and that to become a saint is to embrace everyone as repentant sinners.

Ultimately these remarkable elders maintain a spiritual balance—never pretending that the path to holiness is easy but ever pursuing the extraordinary in the very ordinary of reality and frailty in life, while at the same time promoting connections between the individual and the community. Their matter-of-fact wit and down-to-earth wisdom demonstrate an uncompromising application of the Gospel precepts, endowing their advice with eternal value and universal validity. In this sense, their experience becomes the experience of the whole world—the vocation to follow the way of Christ "without wounding one's neighbor" (*Letter* 26) but by "bearing one another's burden's" (Gal 6:2, *Letter* 96).

SELECT BIBLIOGRAPHY

Barsanuphius and John

Choi, Hyung-Guen, *Between Ideals and Reality: Charity and the Letters of Barsanuphius and John of Gaza*, Macquarie Center, NSW: Sydney College of Divinity Press, 2020.

Chryssavgis, John, *The Correspondence of Barsanuphius and John, with Translation, Introduction, Notes and Complete Indices*, Washington, DC: Catholic University Press, 2006–7 [2 volumes].

Hevelone Harper, Jennifer, *Disciples of the Desert: Monks, Laity, and Spiritual Authority in Sixth-Century Gaza*, Baltimore, MD: Johns Hopkins University Press, 2005.

Perrone, Loroenzo, *La Necessità del Consiglio: Studi sul Monachesimo di Gaza*, Abbazia del Praglia: Edizioni Scritti Monastici, 2021.

The Desert Fathers and Mothers

Brown, Peter, *The Body and Society: Men, Women and Sexual Renunciation in Early Christianity*, New York: Columbia University Press, 1988.

Harmless, William, *Desert Christians: An Introduction to the Literature of Early Monasticism*, New York: Oxford University Press, 2004.

Swan, Laura, *The Forgotten Desert Mothers: Sayings, Lives and Stories of Early Christian Women*, New York: Paulist Press, 2001.

Vivian, Tim, *The Sayings and Stories of the Desert Fathers and Mothers*, vol. 1, Collegeville, MN: Liturgical Press, 2021.

Ward, Benedicta, ed., *The Sayings of the Desert Fathers: The Alphabetical Collection*, London: Mowbrays, 1975.

Wortley, John, *Give Me a Word: The Alphabetical Sayings of the Desert Fathers*, Yonkers, NY: St. Vladimir's Seminary Press, 2014.

ACKNOWLEDGMENTS

This book has been brewing for almost two decades ever since I translated the 850 extraordinary letters of Barsanuphius and John while on sabbatical at Princeton. Numerous interruptions in my life and work—some painful, others joyful—as well as a gnawing suspicion that I could never do justice to these exceptional elders, delayed the completion of a manuscript with any semblance of integrity.

Along the way, however, I owe a debt of gratitude to all those who made this publication possible, including:

- my teacher and mentor, Metropolitan Kallistos (Ware), who introduced me to the letters and provided the foreword to this book;
- friends who contributed comments on the manuscript, including Professors Peter Brown, Columba Stewart, John Behr, and especially Tim Vivian, whose extensive knowledge and insightful grasp of the early monastic tradition provided unequivocal inspiration and improvement;
- Abbot Ephraim of the Vatopedi Patriarchal Monastery on Mt. Athos for permission to publish from their *original manuscript* of Barsanuphius and John, Sister Eugeniki of the Annunciation of the Theotokos Monastery at Oinousses for the *handpainted icon* of Sts Barsanuphius and John, and Metropolitan Savas of Pittsburgh for the cover of the *Venice edition* of Barsanuphius and John;
- academic circles and religious communities in the United States, the UK, and Australia, who invited me to address conferences and retreats on the two Old Men;

- my faithful editor, Marilyn Rouvelas, who has persistently demonstrated more confidence in my work than I ever would, tirelessly and selflessly pouring over editorial and other details;
- and my publisher, Anna Turton, who eventually tipped the balance by encouraging me to submit the manuscript to T&T Clark.

INDEX

advice x–xii, 3–5, 16–17, 20, 24, 28–30, 33, 35, 37–40, 43, 45–7, 52, 65, 80, 88–90, 93–4, 96–7, 102, 106–7, 109, 124, 144–5, 148, 154–5, 160, 165, 178, 188
Aelianos 27–59, 34, 45, 55–7, 87
angel 69, 99, 130–2, 143–5, 169
ascesis 17–18, 52, 66, 70–6, 84, 90, 102–5, 110–17, 122–34, 138, 151–3, 162, 169–73
attentiveness 70, 93, 157–8, 168, 172, 175
authenticity 5, 37, 52, 89, 107, 124, 130–1, 145, 147–63, 174, 178–81, 185
authority xi, 6, 21, 25, 35–6, 43–5, 50–3, 56, 60–2, 89–90, 95–7, 103, 107, 149, 155, 159, 164, 185
awareness (self-awareness) 94, 98, 155–60, 168–75

Barsanuphius the Great (and John the Prophet) 4–9
bearing (one another's burdens) xii, 47, 77–8, 90, 94, 99–100, 110–11, 163, 178
Bible 15, 58–62, 68, 77–8, 82, 129–30, 138, 150

Chalcedon (Council of) 4, 20–1, 186
community 2, 11, 16, 26–33, 39–41, 44–5, 50–8, 67–8, 88, 90–2, 103, 107, 110, 118, 131, 150, 158–9, 164, 168, 175–9, 188
compassion xi, 1, 5–8, 24, 33, 36, 39, 43, 46–7, 62–4, 68–9, 88, 98–9, 106–7, 111–14, 126, 130–1, 142, 151, 155, 159, 162–3, 185
compunction 73, 136, 143–5, 172–4
crucifixion (and cross) 11, 36, 42, 46, 62, 66, 91, 104–5, 139, 142, 146, 162, 174

desert (and wilderness) x, 1–4, 6–7, 14–16, 30, 49, 63, 66, 80, 94, 105, 122–4, 143, 151, 169–70
desert fathers (and mothers) x, 2–7, 15–21, 25, 30, 44, 71, 74–5, 80–2, 89, 94, 121, 131, 135, 138, 141, 145, 151, 156, 167–9, 189
discernment 4–5, 8, 20, 39, 42–5, 50, 57, 60, 84, 96, 125–6, 136, 147–65
doctrine xi, 46, 64–6, 134, 141–2, 150, 165, 179, 186–7
Dorotheus of Gaza 10, 17–18, 20–1, 26–7, 31, 35, 42, 49, 52–5, 74, 88–9, 147, 156

evil (spirits) 22, 70, 75, 77, 83–4, 96, 99, 112, 114, 117, 121, 125–6, 129, 136, 144, 151, 153, 160–1, 173, 177–8, 188

fast xi, 8, 35, 46, 98, 116–17, 122, 126, 131, 140
food 8, 35, 48, 62, 113–33
forgiveness 5–7, 38, 42, 63, 71, 84, 97, 107, 111

gluttony 114–30, 160
gratitude 69, 71–2, 84, 124, 131, 144, 153

humility 5, 17, 36, 42, 55–7, 64–5, 69–70, 73–5, 83–4, 87, 93, 102, 112–16, 125, 133, 144, 149, 152–4, 157, 163, 173

imperfection 139–42, 169, 182

Jesus Prayer 80–1, 170
John of Beersheba 25, 27, 42, 49–55
John Climacus 63, 80, 122, 134–5, 14–43, 152, 159–61, 182
John the Prophet (and Barsanuphius the Great) 4–9
joy xii, 22, 47, 69, 72–3, 93–5, 98–9, 111–12, 133, 139–40, 143, 180
judgment 4, 7, 62, 72, 96, 101, 160–2, 185

knowledge (self-knowledge) xii, 2, 98, 111, 139, 145, 148, 155–7, 168, 170–1, 174, 177, 180

love 18, 30, 38, 42, 64, 69, 74–7, 87, 92–101, 105–7, 111, 114–16, 119, 123, 125, 127, 131–3, 136, 139, 144, 158, 169–71, 174–9, 182, 188

moderation xi, 46, 123–7, 154, 164
mourning 22, 134–40, 144–6

Origen 10, 27, 48, 60, 62, 66, 71, 150

Paul 3, 23, 47, 57, 59, 72, 77, 90, 100, 114, 119, 123, 150, 163
prayer x, xii, 5, 8, 15, 20–4, 32, 38, 40–7, 59, 63–5, 69, 77–84, 93–8, 106, 140, 144, 153–5, 166–75, 180–1, 184

reckoning (not reckoning oneself) 73–5, 173, 176
renunciation 29, 46, 105, 121–3, 130, 137, 146
resurrection 130, 139–42, 162, 182

sacraments 58, 63–4, 94, 134, 159
Seridos (Abbot) 25–30, 39–41, 45, 48–57, 67, 92, 97, 153, 164, 179
silence 2, 31, 41, 45, 48, 50, 54–9, 63–5, 98, 122, 141–3, 146, 160–2, 166–84
solitude 1, 28, 41, 45, 50–4, 161, 166–83
sorrow xii, 47, 91–4, 133, 136–44
spiritual direction x, 3, 6–7, 24, 26, 32–5, 44, 51–2, 56, 62, 87–112, 122, 126, 148–9, 154–5, 158–9, 162, 172, 185–7
stillness 26, 50, 125, 166–71, 173, 176–8, 180–3

tears 45, 63, 69, 106, 134–46, 169, 173
temptation 5, 35–6, 42, 68–72, 75, 82–126, 161–78
thanksgiving 23, 68, 71–2, 111, 120, 123, 126
Thawatha 11–12, 16, 25–7, 39, 52–8, 96, 163

vigilance xi, 46, 69–70, 79, 84, 102, 117, 121, 143, 159, 170, 177

women 27–8, 30, 94

www.ingramcontent.com/pod-product-compliance
Lightning Source LLC
Chambersburg PA
CBHW051644230426
43669CB00013B/2433